The College History Series

Fightin' Gators

A History of University of Florida Football

The College History Series

Fightin' Gators

A History of University of Florida Football

Kevin M. McCarthy

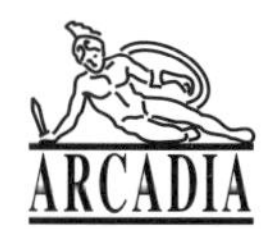

ISBN 0-7385-0559-5

Published by Arcadia Publishing,
an imprint of Tempus Publishing, Inc.
2 Cumberland Street
Charleston, SC 29401

Printed in Great Britain.

Library of Congress Catalog Card Number: 00-100385

For all general information contact Arcadia Publishing at:
Telephone 843-853-2070
Fax 843-853-0044
E-Mail sales@arcadiapublishing.com

For customer service and orders:
Toll-Free 1-888-313-2665

Visit us on the internet at http://www.arcadiaimages.com

Thanks go to the following individuals: Neil Burger, Norm Carlson, Walter Coker, Bruce Fink, Jeff Gage, Buddy Long, Joan Morris, Harriette Peebles, Herb Press, Marshall Prine, Chris Runk, and John Woodhead.

CONTENTS

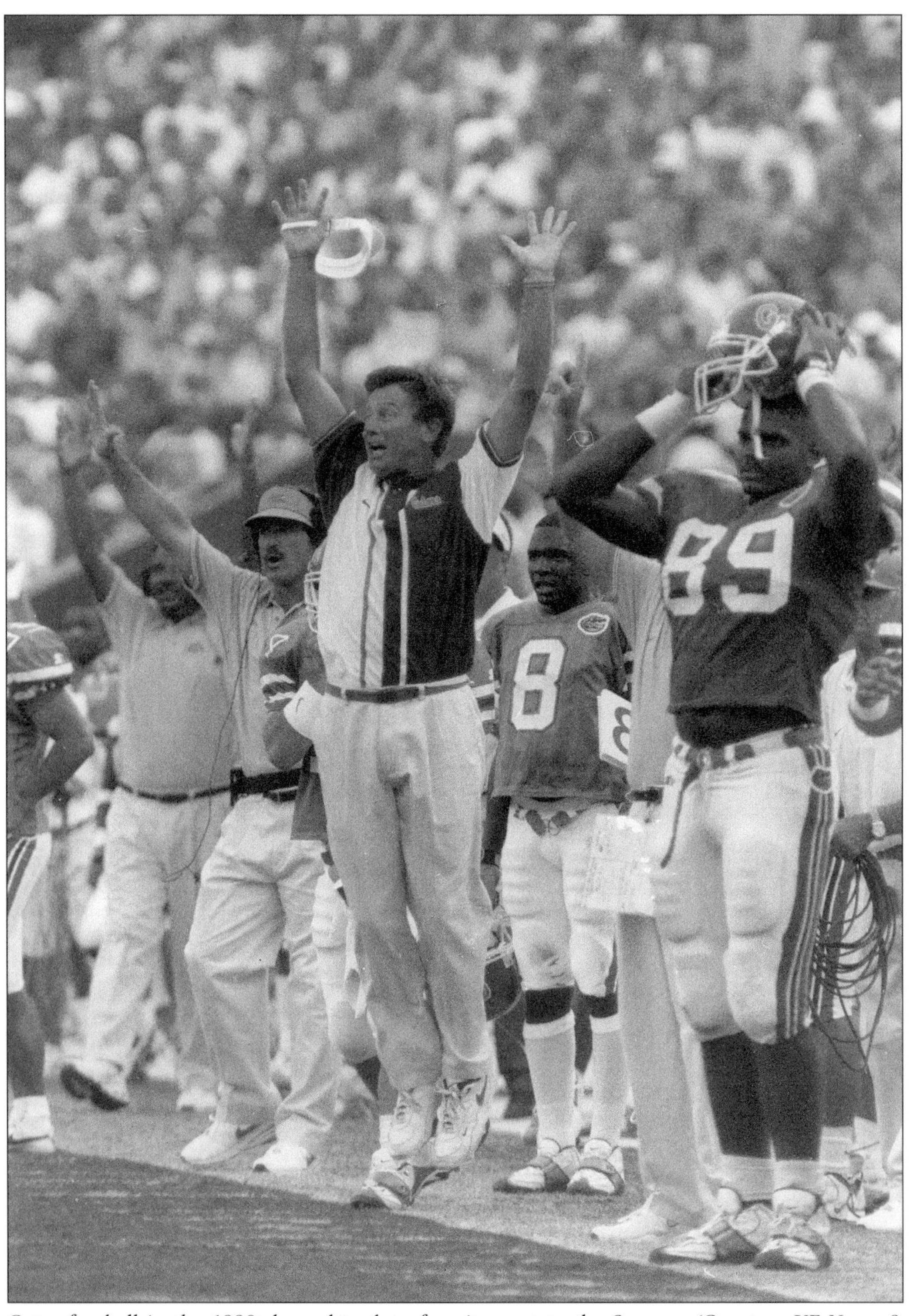

Gator football in the 1990s brought a lot of excitement to the Swamp. (Courtesy UF News & Public Affairs: Jeff Gage.)

INTRODUCTION

When the Fightin' Gator football team won the national collegiate championship in 1996, no one would have predicted such an accomplishment 90 years before that. In the early part of the 20th century, in fact, the school was struggling to survive and even to find the particular town it would thrive in. National recognition, for whatever reason, seemed a distant dream. But as the school developed into a first-rate university, its athletic teams in general, and its football team in particular, grew in excellence.

The University of Florida (UF), the state's oldest and largest university with about 45,000 students, is recognized today as one of the country's most academically diverse public institutions. Tracing its history back to 1853 as the state-funded East Florida Seminary in Ocala, UF would later consolidate with the state's land-grant Florida Agricultural College in Lake City and then make its final move from Lake City to Gainesville in 1906, where it has been ever since, although its agricultural extension branches are all over the state.

In 1906 the school had 16 professors and 102 young, male students, 39 of whom were classified "sub-freshmen" because they were not yet qualified for university study. The students, who wore uniforms, had to pay nothing for tuition if they were Florida residents and only $20 if they were out-of-staters. Its first president was Andrew Sledd, after whom Sledd Hall is named.

For a logo, officials chose the alligator. For a time, they had a live reptile on campus near the bell tower, but they finally released him into a nearby lake when rowdy intruders from opposing teams would sneak onto campus the night before a big game and paint the gator in the other school's colors. The campus newspaper was also called *the Alligator*. The toothy reptile has inspired both the "Gator Chomp," meant to intimidate opposing teams, and the renaming of Florida Field as "the Swamp," where opponents are meant to be devoured.

After World War II, many more students enrolled at UF, including many ex-soldiers, some with families, who took advantage of the G.I. Bill to further their education. The university allowed women in on a full-time basis in 1947, but it was not integrated racially until 1958.

The building trend has continued on campus, but planners have wisely integrated the new buildings with the same type of architectural style as the older buildings. Nineteen of those older buildings, built between 1906 and 1939, were listed as part of a historic district on the National Register of Historic Places in 1989. That part of campus was also named a Florida Heritage Landmark.

Academically, the school is part of the prestigious Association of American Universities, which comprises the top 63 public and private higher-education schools in North America. Only two

U.S. universities offer more programs on a single campus than UF does, a fact that continues to attract students from this country and abroad. Professional degrees are offered in dentistry, law, medicine, pharmacy, and veterinary medicine, which few other institutions can match in terms of breadth and quality. Students can choose from among over 100 undergraduate majors and some 200 graduate programs, and its Honors program offers intensive study to over 1,500 freshmen and sophomores. The school has long been able to attract the very best faculty and students to its 23 colleges and schools. The fact that one of its students won the very prestigious Rhodes Scholarship in 1999 was a fitting way to end one century and begin another.

UF's enrollment of almost 45,000 students in 2000 made it the seventh largest university in the nation. Its faculty, consisting of over 4,000 members, 97% of whom hold Ph.D.'s, continues to win honors and grants in all fields. For example, UF ranked eighth among all universities in the number of U.S. patents awarded in 1998.

Here, then, is a photographic history of an important part of the University of Florida: the Fightin' Gator football team, a part of the school that has brought pride (and a few tears of desperation) over the years, as well as much recognition to the university and much funding to its libraries and academic programs.

One

1906–1919: Coaches Forsythe, Pyle, McCoy, and Busser

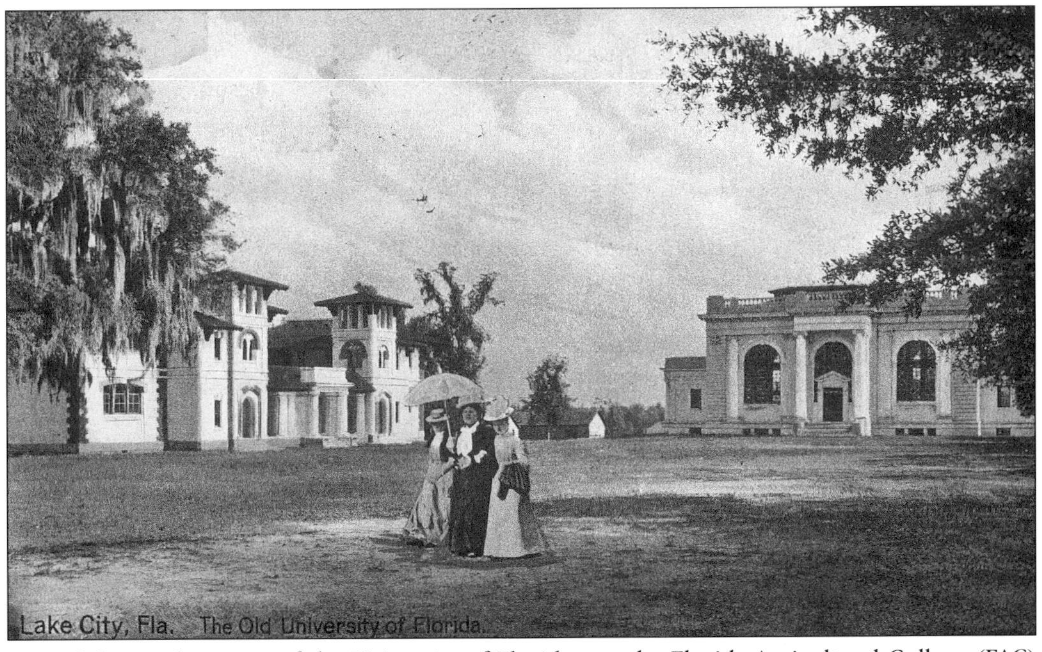

One of the predecessors of the University of Florida was the Florida Agricultural College (FAC) in Lake City, shown here in 1908. The school moved to Gainesville in 1906 and expanded over the years, until its student body numbered close to 45,000 in 2000. (Courtesy Florida State Archives.)

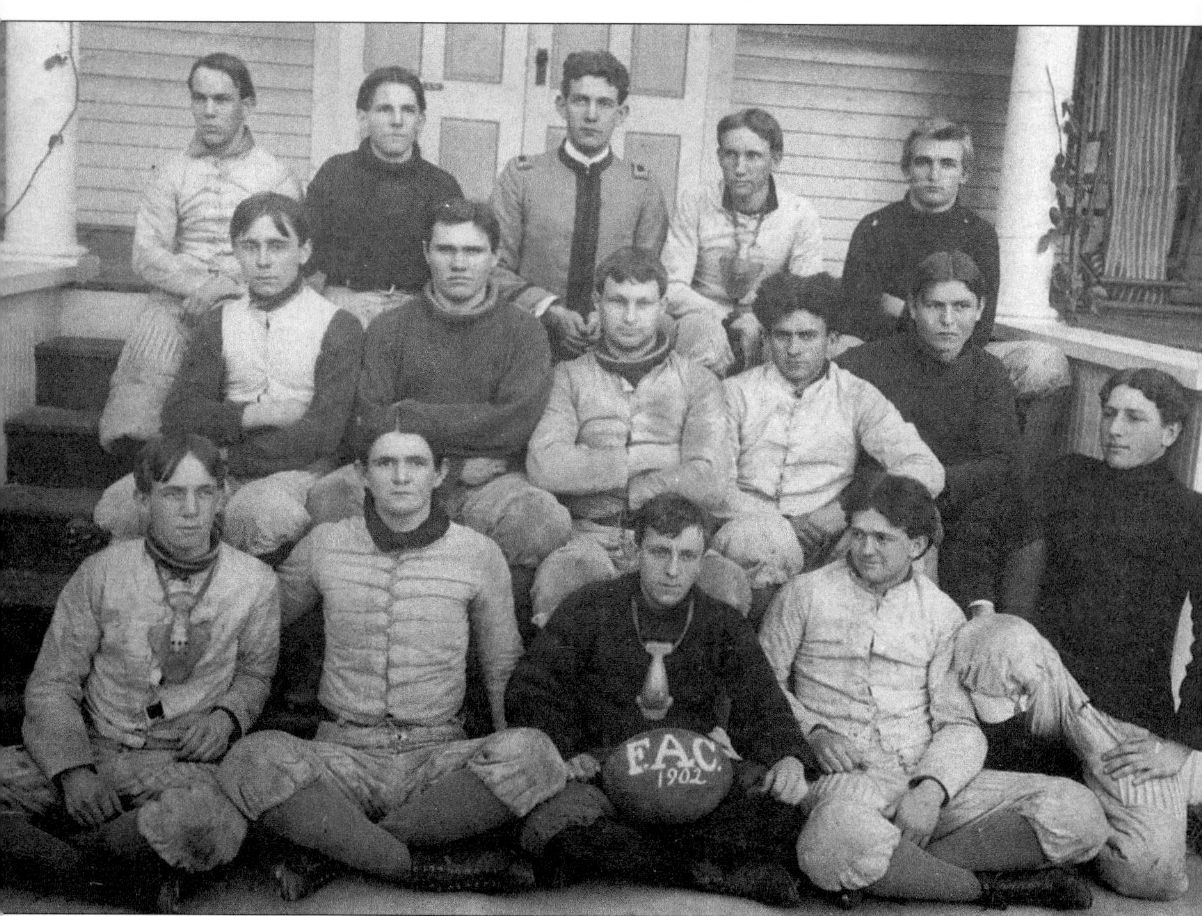

The Florida Agricultural College had a football team in the 1901–1902 season. What may have been the first "unofficial" game of the UF football team occurred on November 22, 1901, when it played Stetson University in Jacksonville. UF lost, 6-0, partly because a stump in the middle of the field prevented a drive that might have led to a UF touchdown. (Courtesy Florida State Archives.)

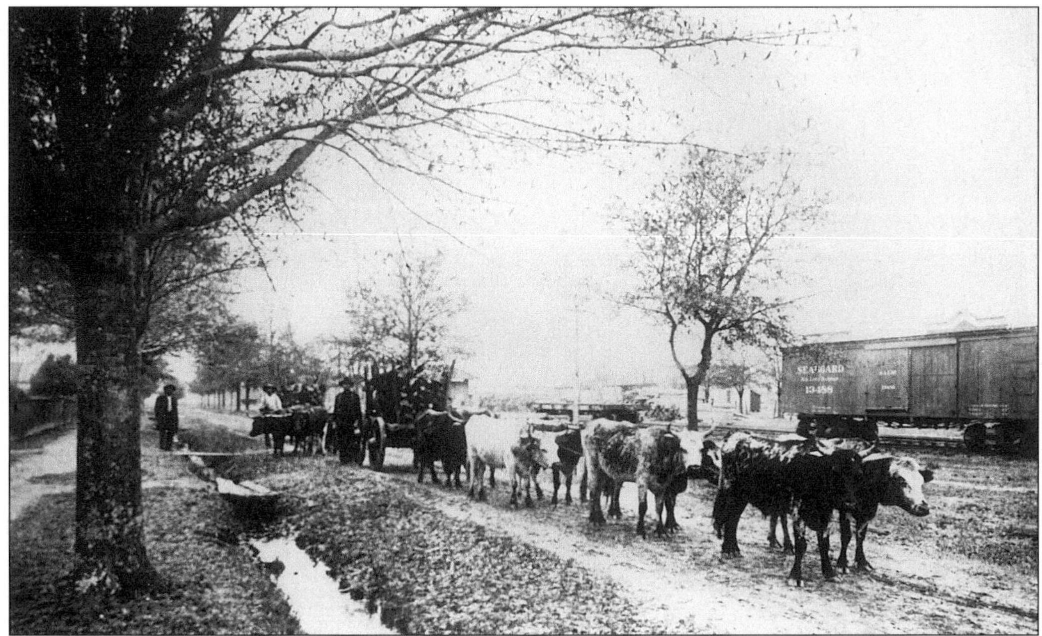

This 1890s image of cows meandering on North Main Street in Gainesville documents how rural the town was. Named after General Edmund Pendleton Gaines (1777–1849), who had fought in the War of 1812 and the Second Seminole War, the town had just several thousand inhabitants in the 1890s. (Courtesy Florida State Archives.)

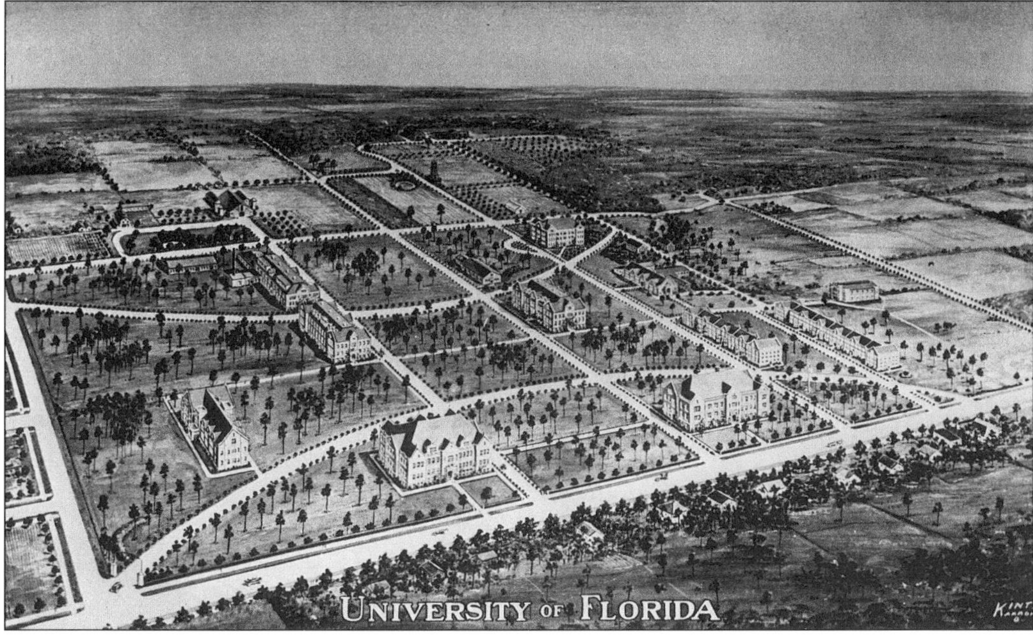

An early drawing pictured a well-organized UF campus. The arrival of UF in Gainesville in 1906 ensured a steady growth for the town and for the surrounding Alachua County. Because the area did not offer the attractions of the ocean or gulf and because it did not have many industries, it did not experience the explosive population growth of other Florida cities. (Courtesy Florida State Archives.)

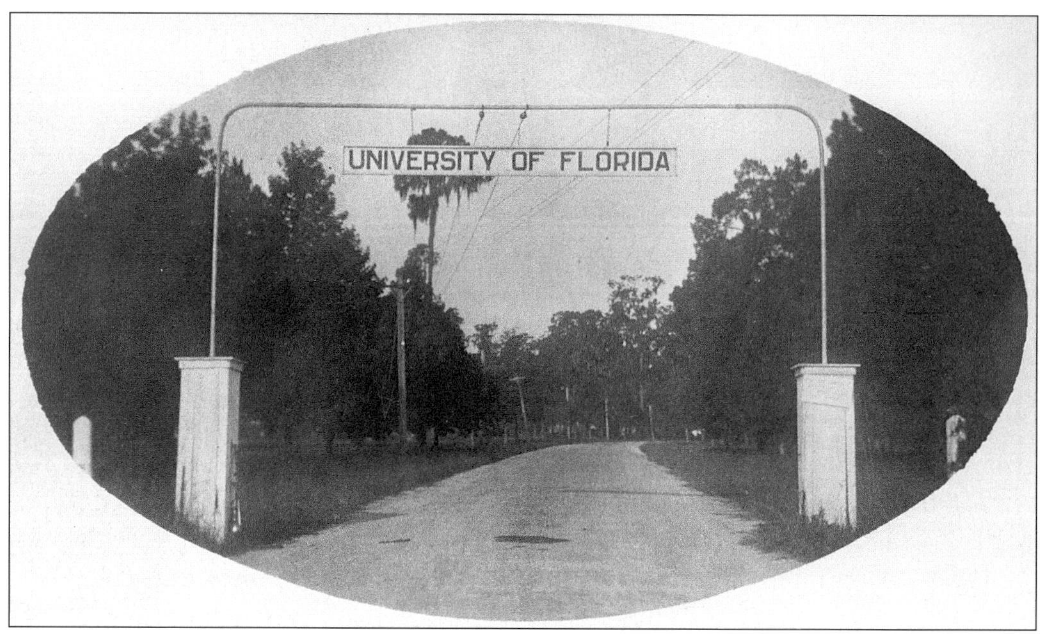

The gate at University Avenue and 13th Street was at first far to the west of the center of Gainesville, but it eventually became one of the busiest sites in the town, especially on football Saturdays after 1990, when over 85,000 fans would show up to cheer the Gators and drown out the opposition. (Courtesy Florida State Archives.)

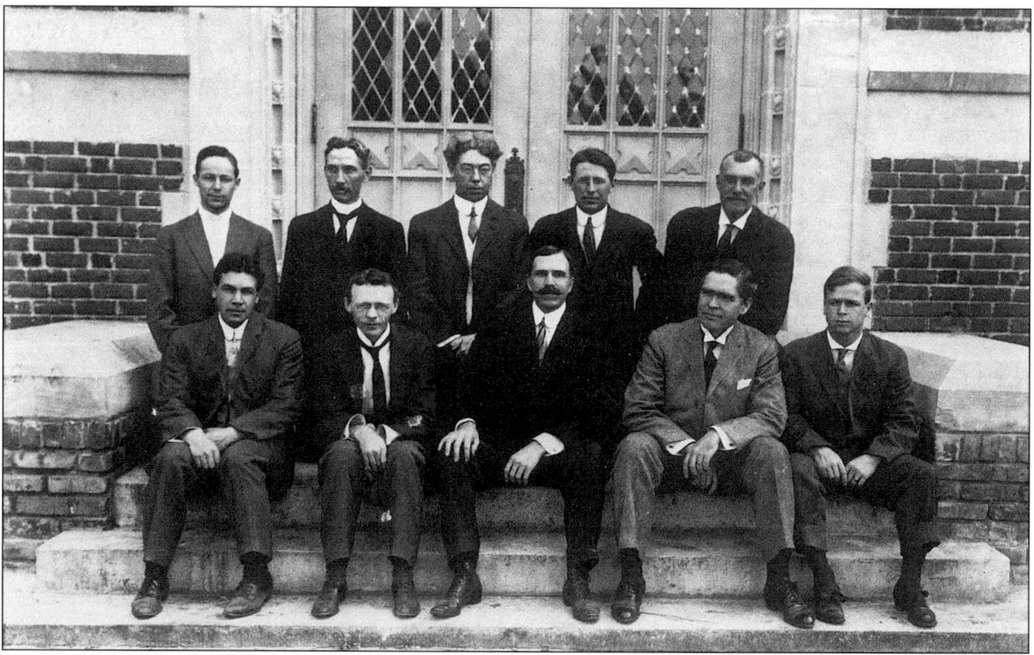

UF faculty included James Farr, second from the left on the bottom row, the head of the English department and the unofficial head coach of the football team. Gator football officially began in 1906, when the team beat Rollins, 6-0. They played the game on a baseball field located just north of where Florida Field is today. The first head coach, Jack Forsythe, managed a 14-6-2 record in his three seasons (1906–1908). (Courtesy Florida State Archives.)

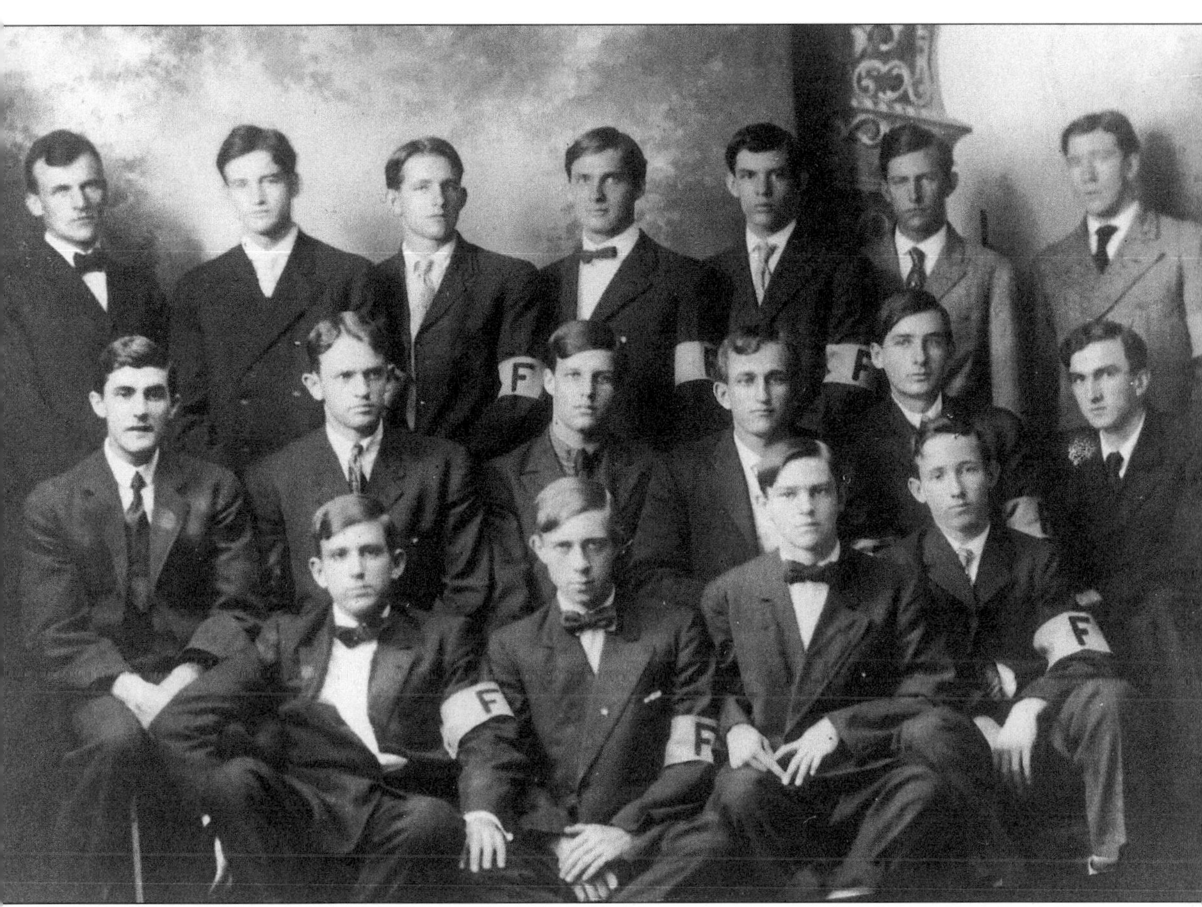

The 1907 Gator team had a 4-0-1 mark, primarily because of the excellent playing of William "Willie" Shands (bottom row, far right), who became a state senator and was the man honored in the naming of Shands Hospital and Clinic. He helped establish the state's medical school at UF in 1958. (Courtesy University Archives, Dept. of Special Collections, George A. Smathers Libraries, Univ. of Florida.)

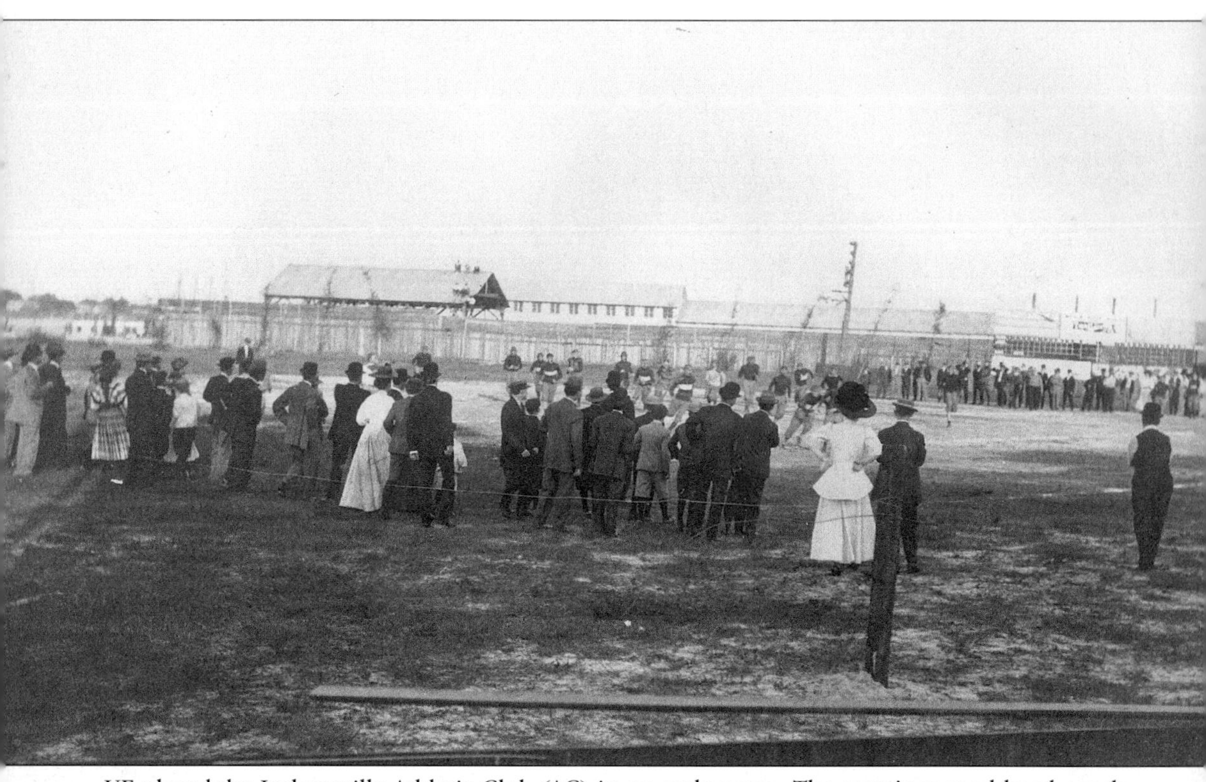

UF played the Jacksonville Athletic Club (AC) in an early game. The team's second head coach, G.E. Pyle, had a 26-7-3 record in his five years (1909–1913), which included games against powerhouses like Auburn, Clemson, Georgia Tech, and South Carolina. (Courtesy University Archives, Dept. of Special Collections, George A. Smathers Libraries, Univ. of Florida.)

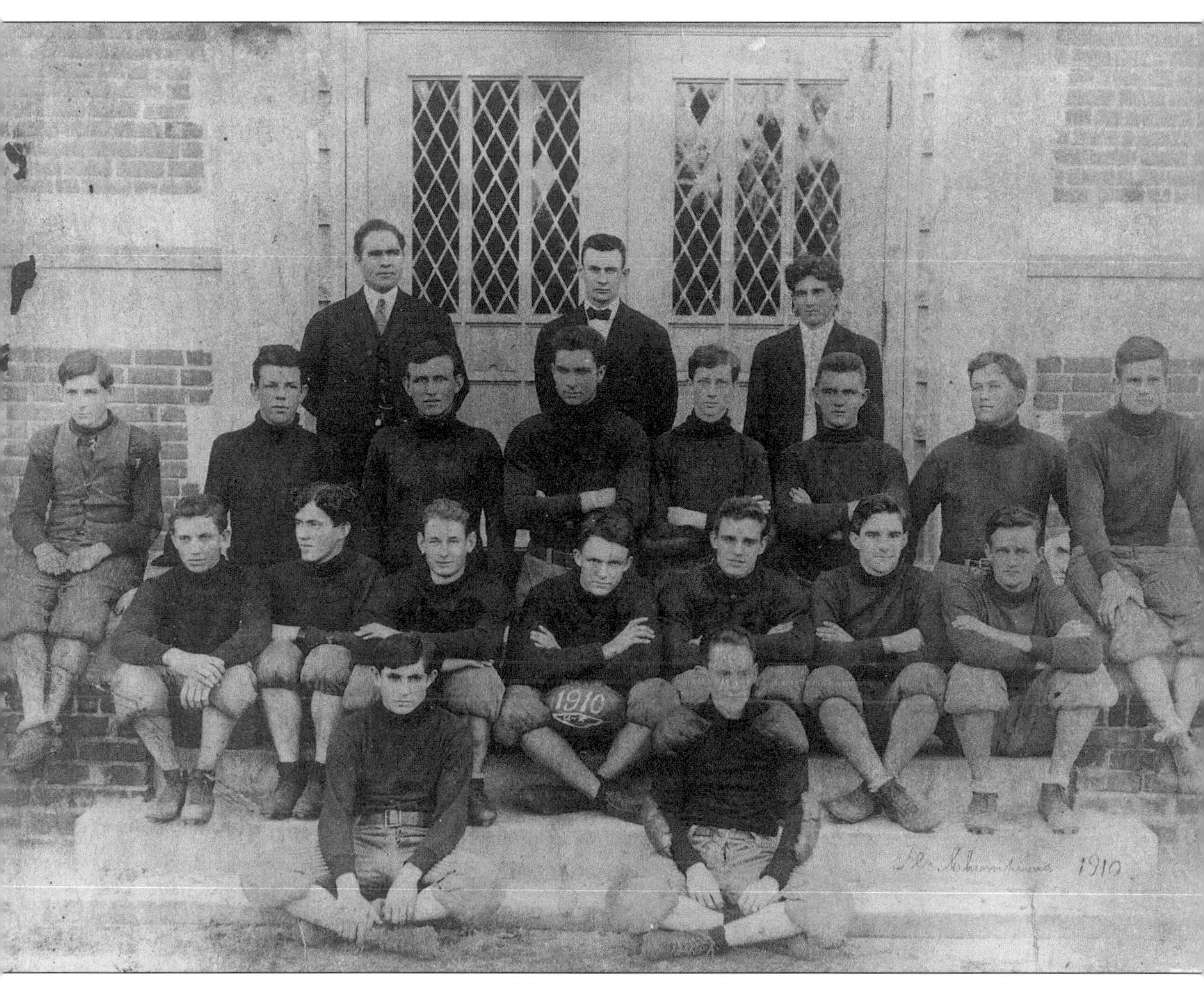

Coach Pyle's 1910 Gators had a record of 6-1 and scored 186 points, while allowing only 15. The team had come a long way from 1904, when that year's team was outscored 224-0. In Pyle's final year, the Gators beat Florida Southern 144-0, which included 22 touchdowns. (Courtesy University Archives, Dept. of Special Collections, George A. Smathers Libraries, Univ. of Florida.)

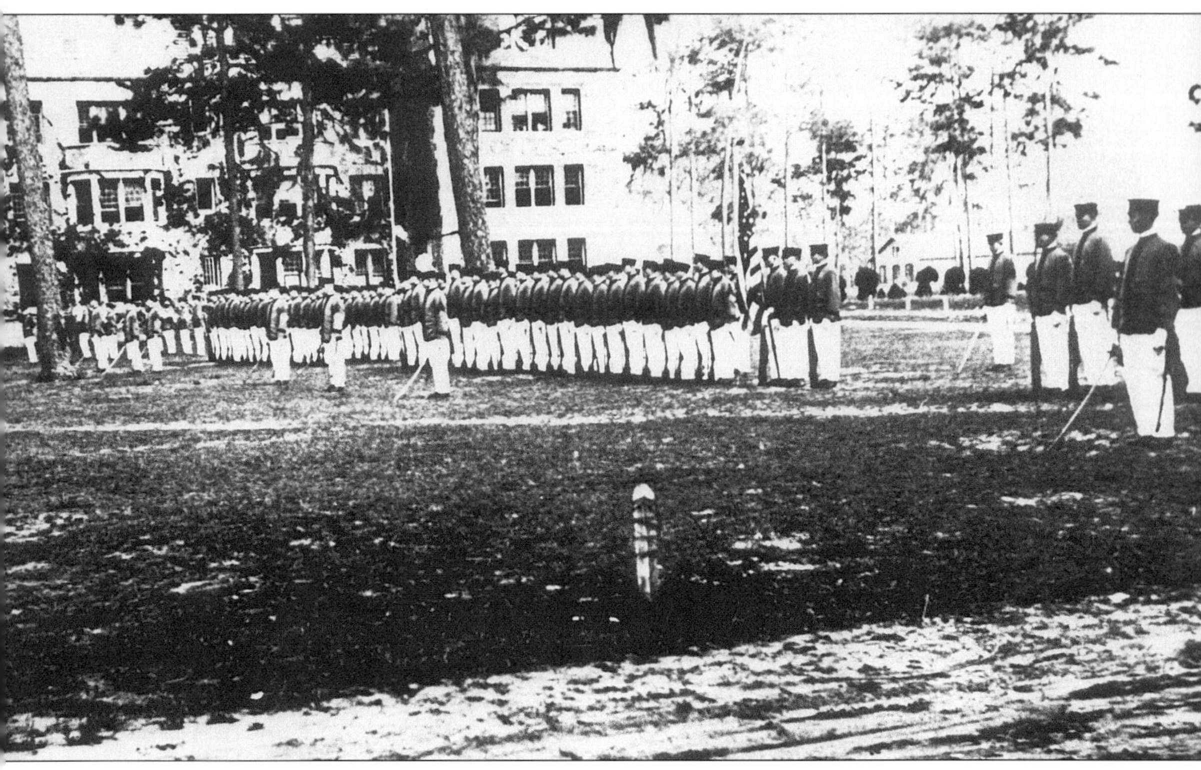

When cadets drilled at UF in Gainesville in 1916, the team's third head coach, Charles McCoy from Sewanee Military Academy, was finishing a 9-10-0 record in his three seasons (1914–1916). When McCoy's 1916 team did not win a game, his contract was not renewed. Such a shutout in wins would not occur again until 1946. The early predecessors of UF, e.g. East Florida Seminary, functioned as military schools for their male students, who wore uniforms, marched to and from class in formation, and woke each morning to the sounds of a bugle call. (Courtesy Florida State Archives.)

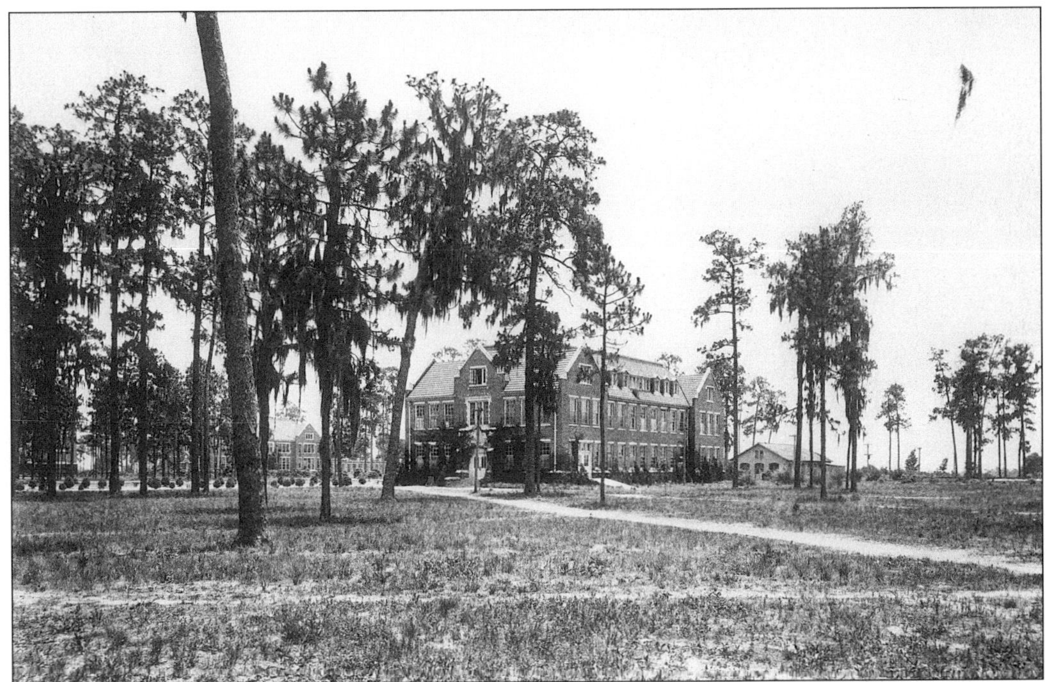

Floyd Hall on campus in 1919 had an ivy covering that was meant to imitate older universities. The team's fourth head coach, A.L. Busser from Wisconsin, had a 7-8 record in his three seasons (1917–1919). World War I and an influenza epidemic depleted the student body, and the team played only one game in 1918, a 14-2 loss to Camp Johnson. (Courtesy Florida State Archives.)

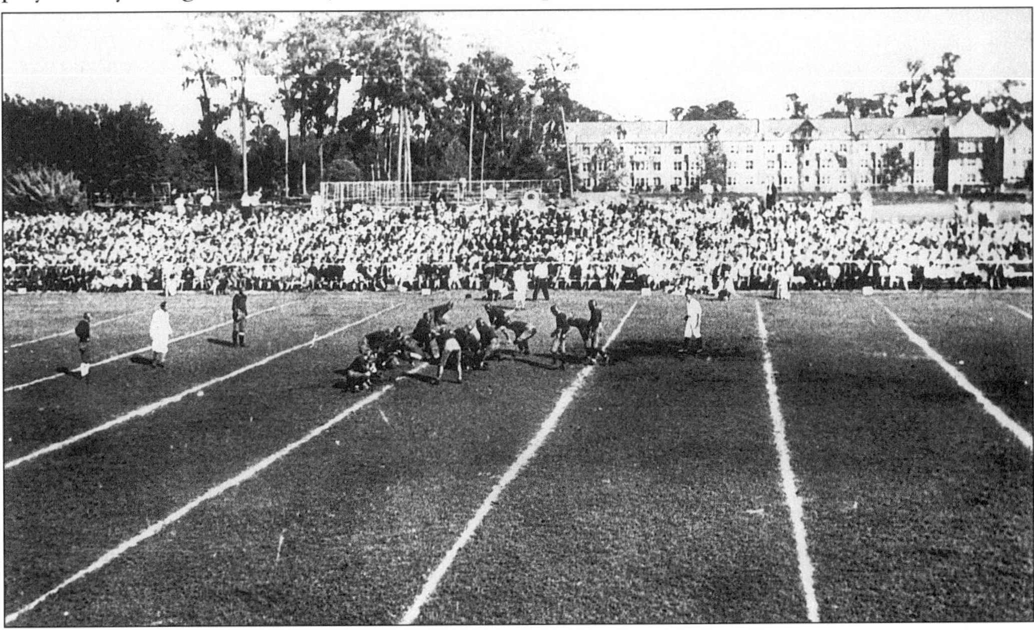

Early home football games like this one were played on Fleming Field, located just north of where today's football stadium stands. The Gators were undefeated on their home field in their first ten seasons, setting the stage for a similar home field advantage in the Swamp, beginning in 1990. (Courtesy of Florida State Archives.)

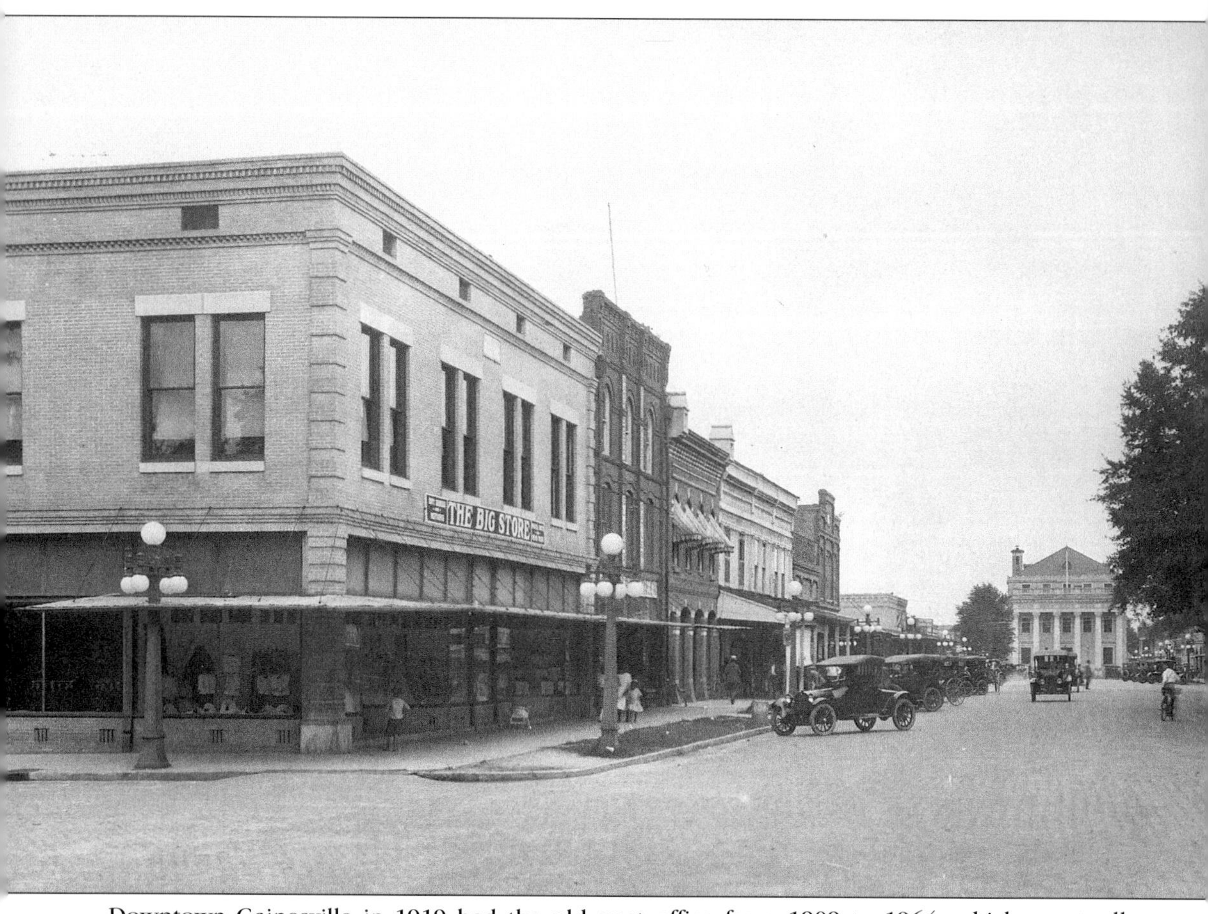

Downtown Gainesville in 1919 had the old post office from 1909 to 1964, which eventually became Santa Fe Junior College *c.* 1966 and the Hippodrome State Theatre in 1980. It anchored S.E. 2nd Place and became the center for an extensive downtown revival in the 1990s. (Courtesy Florida State Archives.)

Two

1920–1927: Coaches Kline, Van Fleet, and Sebring

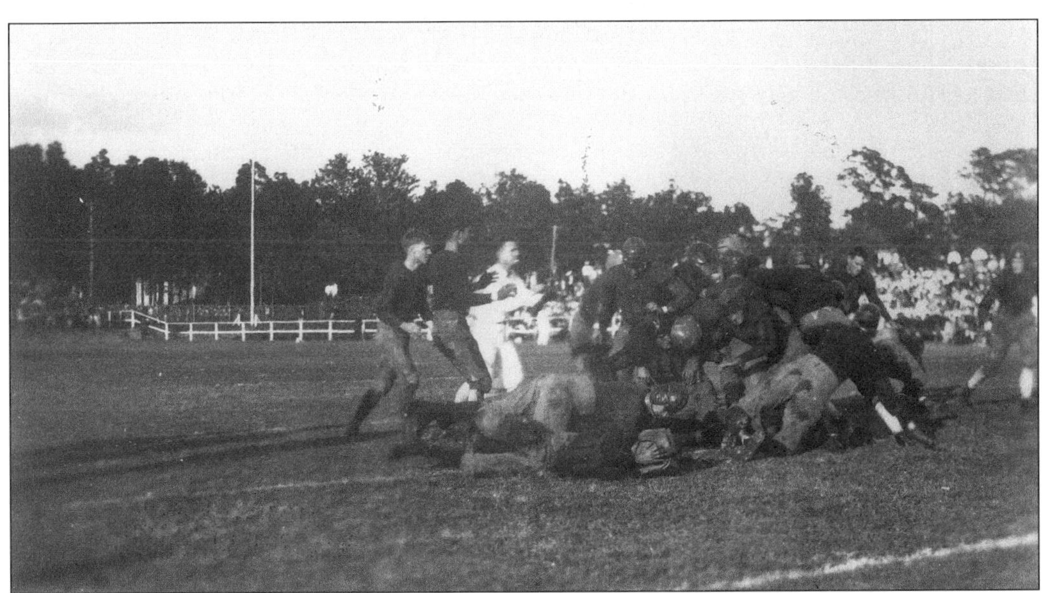

Football players in the 1920s did not always wear helmets. William Kline, the team's fifth head coach, had a 19-8-2 record in his three seasons (1920–1922). One of his victories included a 1-0 win over Rollins, which did not show up for the game and had to forfeit. (Courtesy Elmer Harvey Bone Photographic Collection, University Archives, Dept. of Special Collections, George A. Smathers Libraries, Univ. of Florida.)

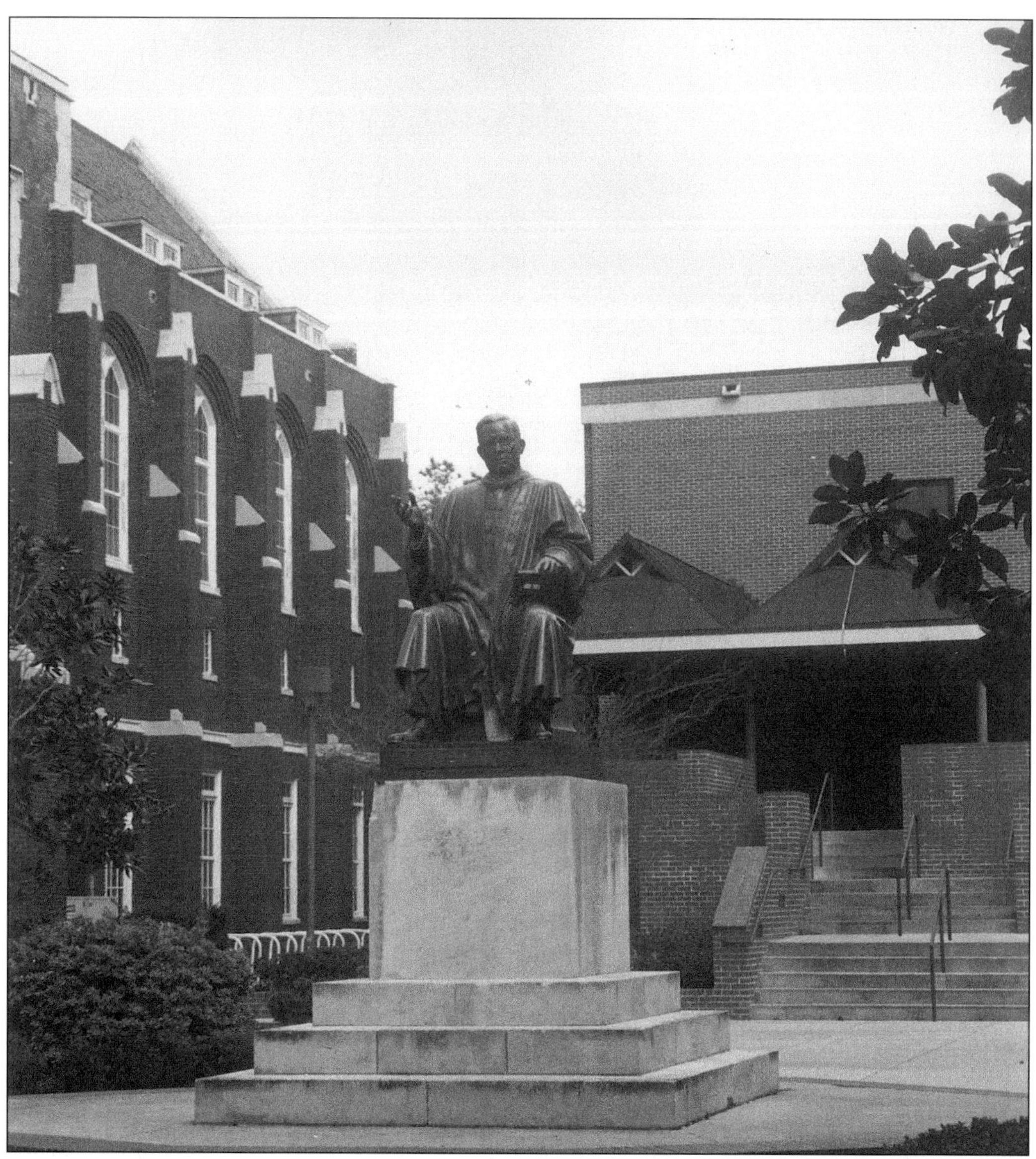

Dr. Murphree, the second president of UF, is honored in this statue near Peabody Hall and in the naming of Murphree Hall, a residence hall for undergraduates. He once said, "I consider football the most important sport in which a college student can engage." He also noted that "Football, the great college game of America, develops intuition, cultivates mental alertness, self-control and physical manhood. There is no other sport which develops these qualities to the same extent as the American game of football. Only men of clean habits, and intellectual acumen can hope to make places on the great teams. For this reason the men on College teams, as a rule, represent the finest type of American student." (Courtesy University Archives, Dept. of Special Collections, George A. Smathers Libraries, Univ. of Florida.)

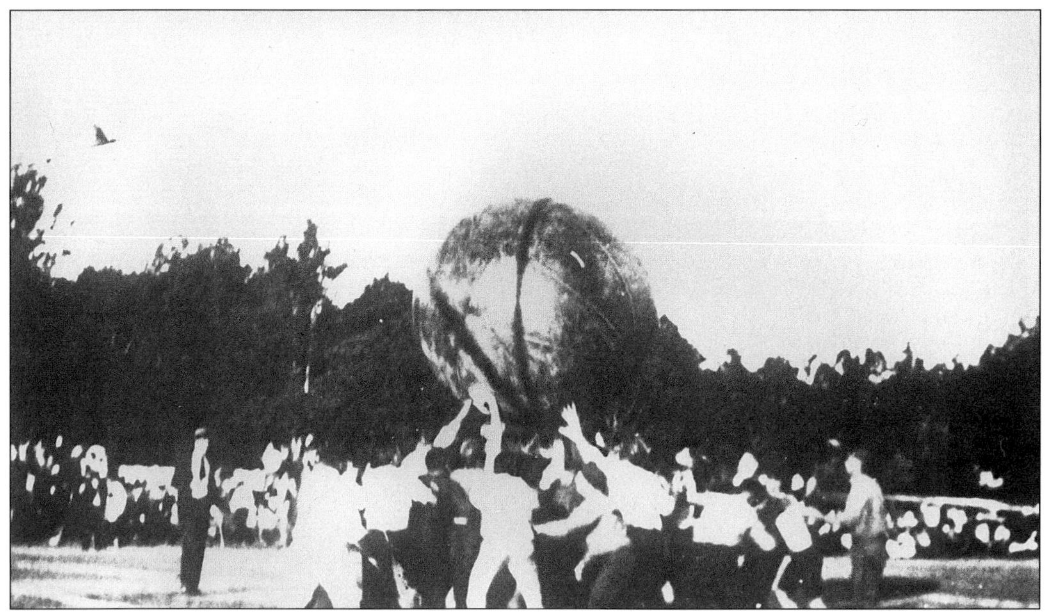

In a pushball intramural contest on campus, residents of Buckman Hall vied against those of Thomas Hall. Outdoor sports, including football, swimming, baseball, volleyball, and track, have always been popular at UF. Intramural sports enable thousands of students to participate every week. (Courtesy Florida State Archives.)

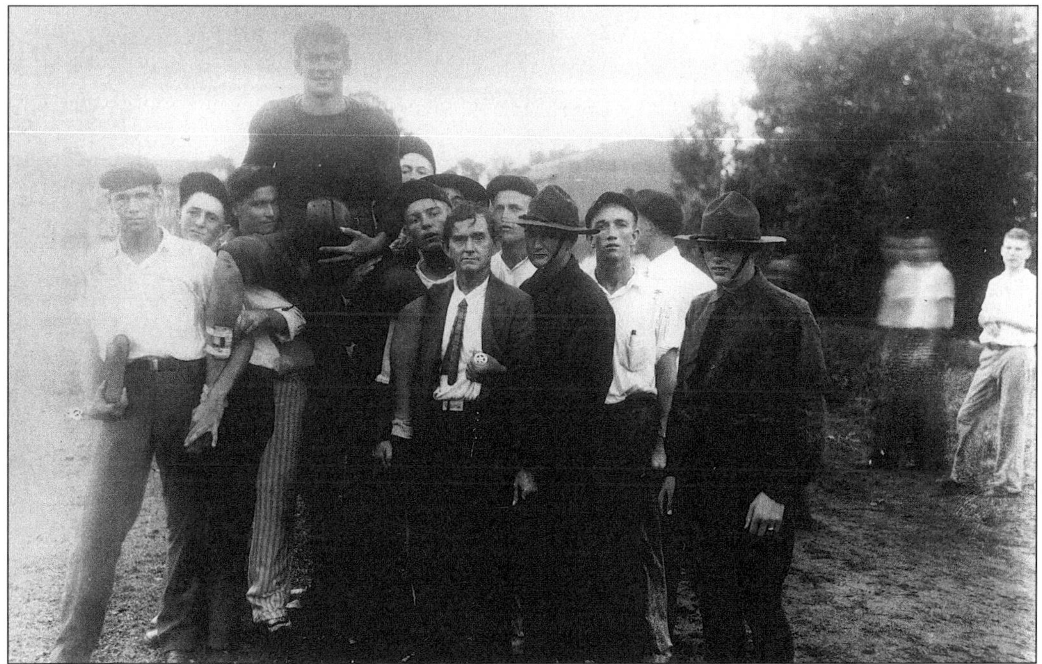

Players carry one of their own. One of the UF players at that time, Robert "Ark" Newton, who lettered for four years (1921–1924), may have been the greatest all-around athlete who ever played at the school. He played football, baseball, basketball, and track and earned 14 letters. (Courtesy Elmer Harvey Bone Photographic Collection, University Archives, Dept. of Special Collections, George A. Smathers Libraries, Univ. of Florida.)

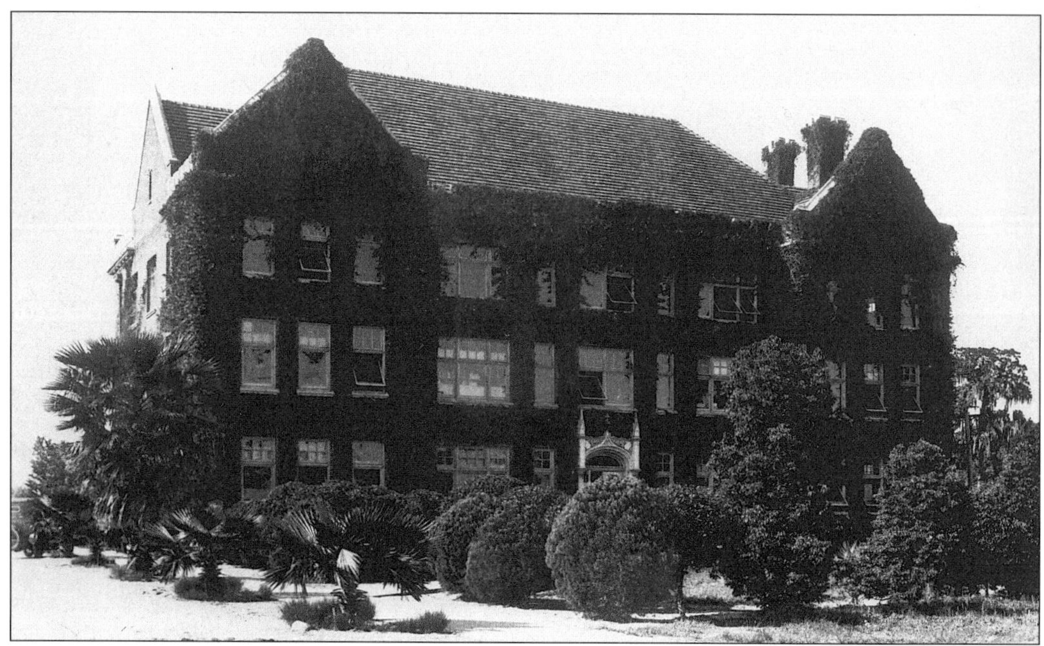

The Agricultural Experiment Station Building, built in the early 1920s, is shown later, covered in ivy. Major James Van Fleet, who was head of the school's ROTC program, coached the Gators for two seasons (1923–1924) and had a 12-3-4 record, drawing national attention to the team for the first time. Van Fleet went on to become a four-star general and international statesman. (Courtesy Florida State Archives.)

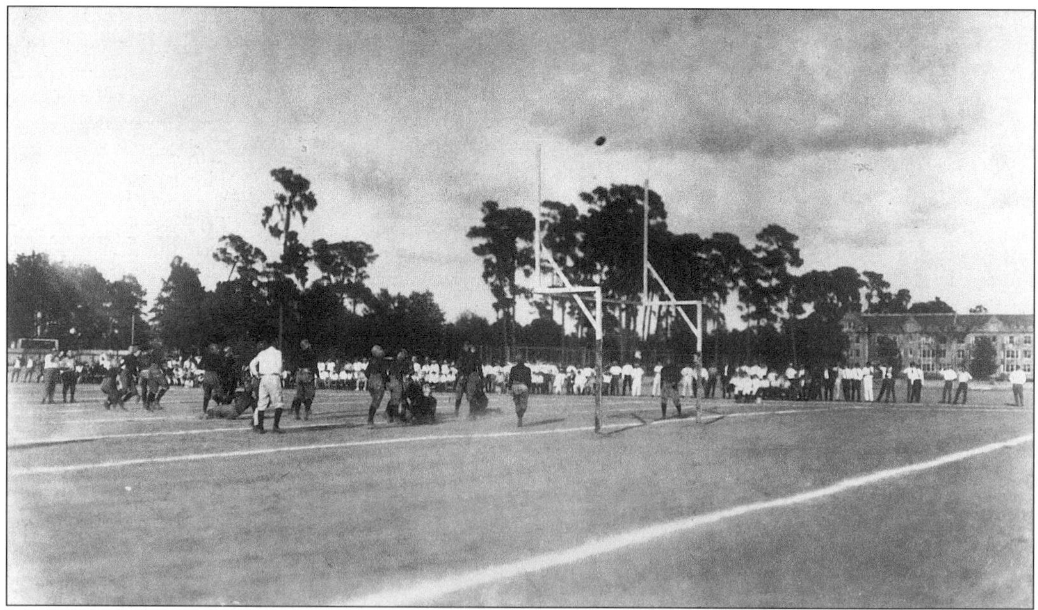

This 1924 football game was played at UF's Fleming Field. The 1925 Gator team was the first to win eight games in a season, finishing 8-2, the first season under the team's seventh head coach, H.L. Sebring. The team played a double-header that season, defeating both Southern College and Hampton-Sydney on the same day. (Courtesy University Archives, Dept. of Special Collections, George A. Smathers Libraries, Univ. of Florida.)

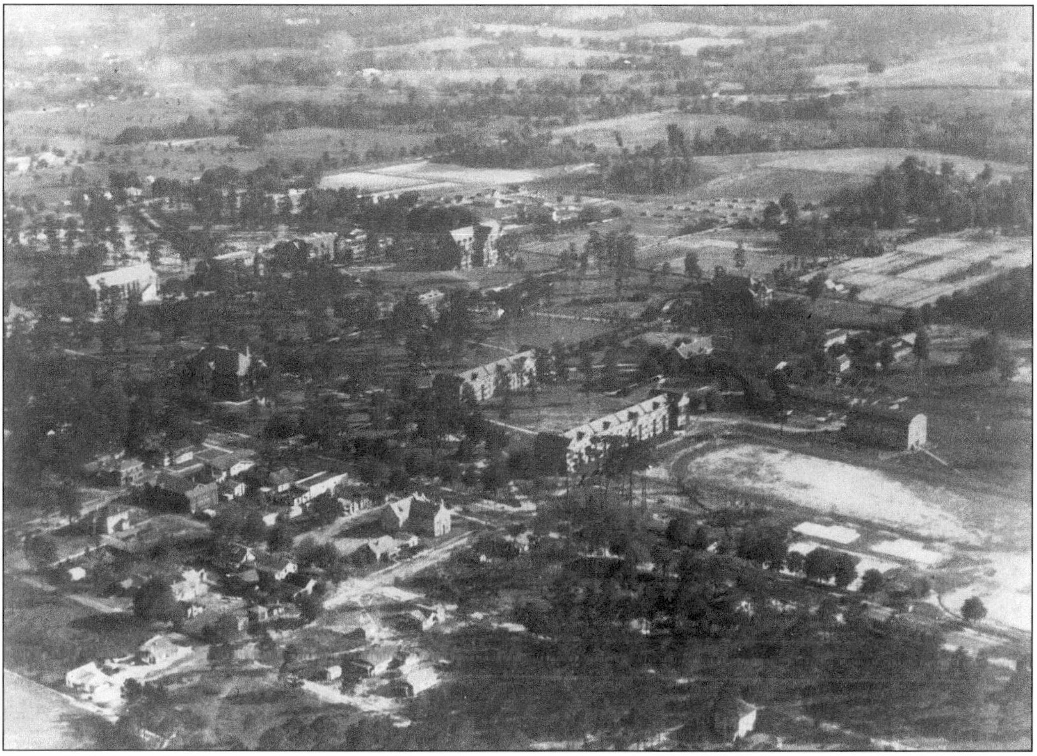

The 1926 UF campus resembled the spread-out campus of today. Coach Sebring, who finished with a 17-11-2 record in three seasons (1925–1927), eventually became chief justice of the state supreme court. (Courtesy University Archives, Dept. of Special Collections, George A. Smathers Libraries, Univ. of Florida.)

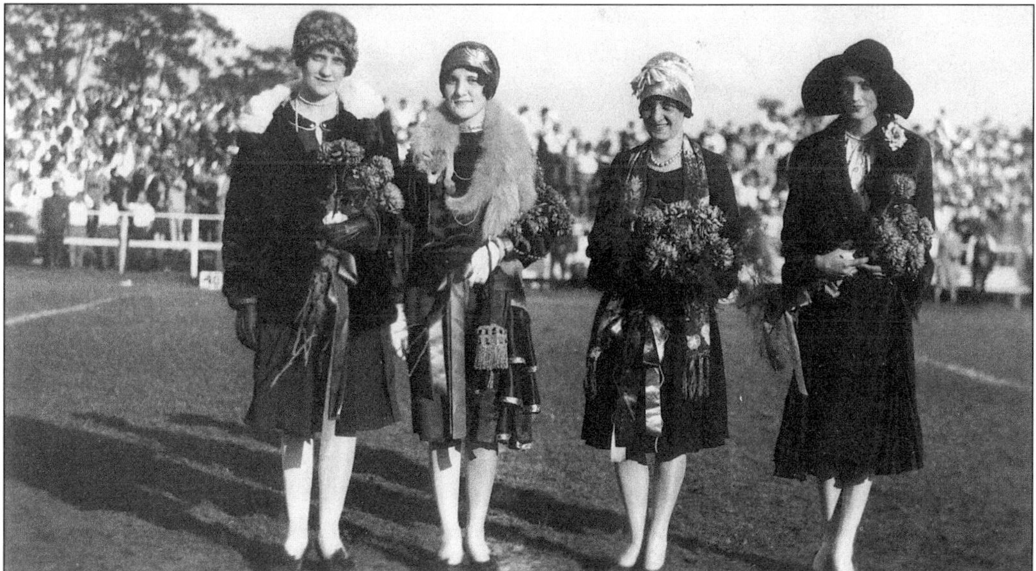

These four co-eds were at UF Homecoming in 1926, the third year of the tradition of inviting graduates back to campus to see old friends, compare success stories, and attend a football game. (Courtesy Florida State Archives.)

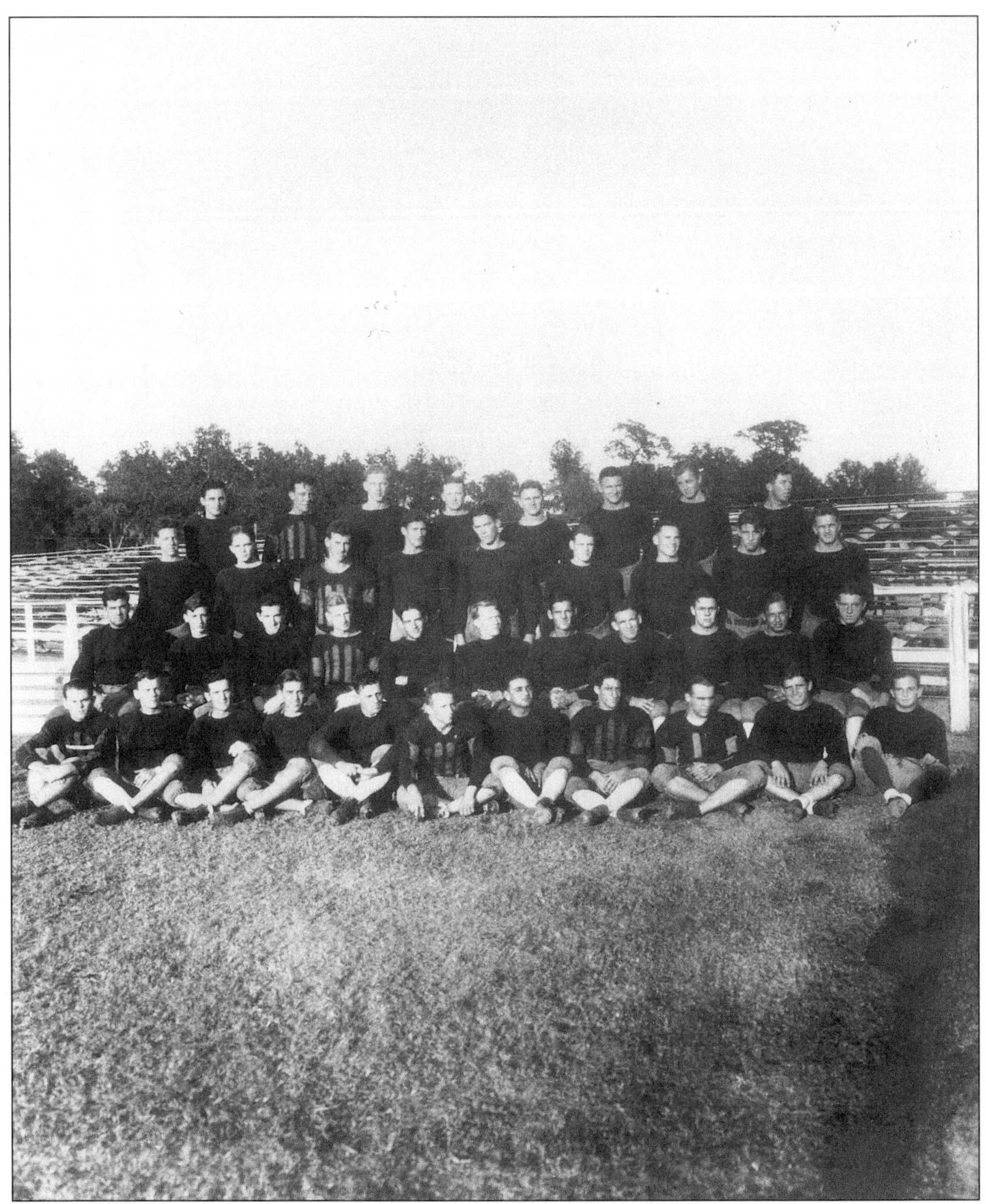

The 1927 freshmen team played its own schedule because freshmen were not allowed to compete against the varsity in the Southern Conference. The "Baby Gators" or "Scrubs" or "Omelet Squad," as they were called, were undefeated in 1926, a year in which the varsity team went 2-6-2, the only time in the 1920s when the team had a losing record. (Courtesy University Archives, Dept. of Special Collections, George A. Smathers Libraries, Univ. of Florida.)

Three

1928–1939: Coaches Bachman, Stanley, and Cody

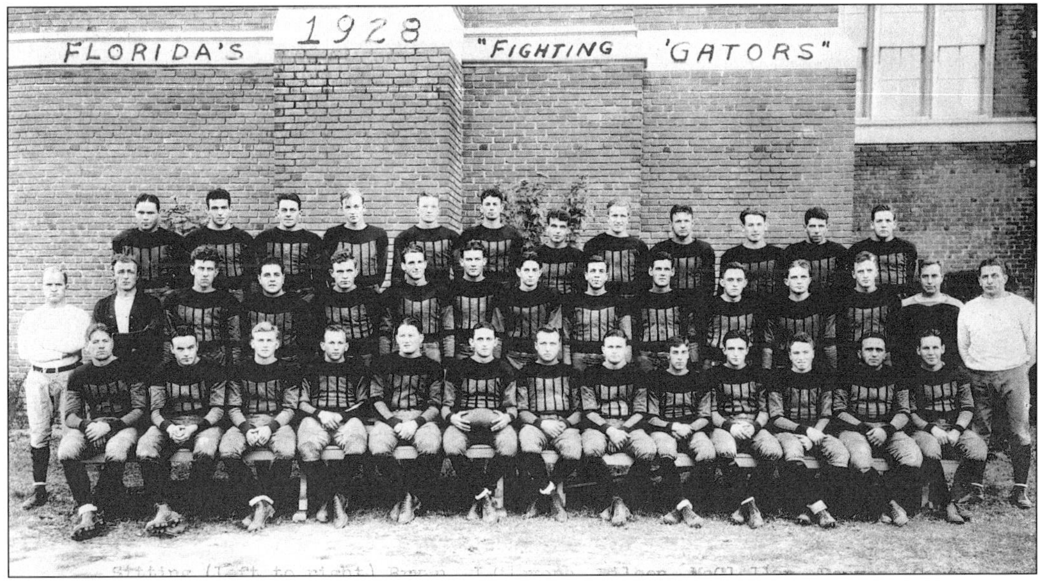

The 1928 team was coached by Charles Bachman, the eighth head coach of the Gators, who had a 27-18-3 record in five seasons (1928–1932). Bachman was one of five Gators selected for the National Football Foundation and College Hall of Fame, the others being players Dale Van Sickel, Steve Spurrier, Jack Youngblood, and Coach Ray Graves. That 1928 football team led the nation in scoring, compiled an 8-1 record, and lost only its final game to the Volunteers on a soggy field in Knoxville, Tennessee. (Courtesy Florida State Archives.)

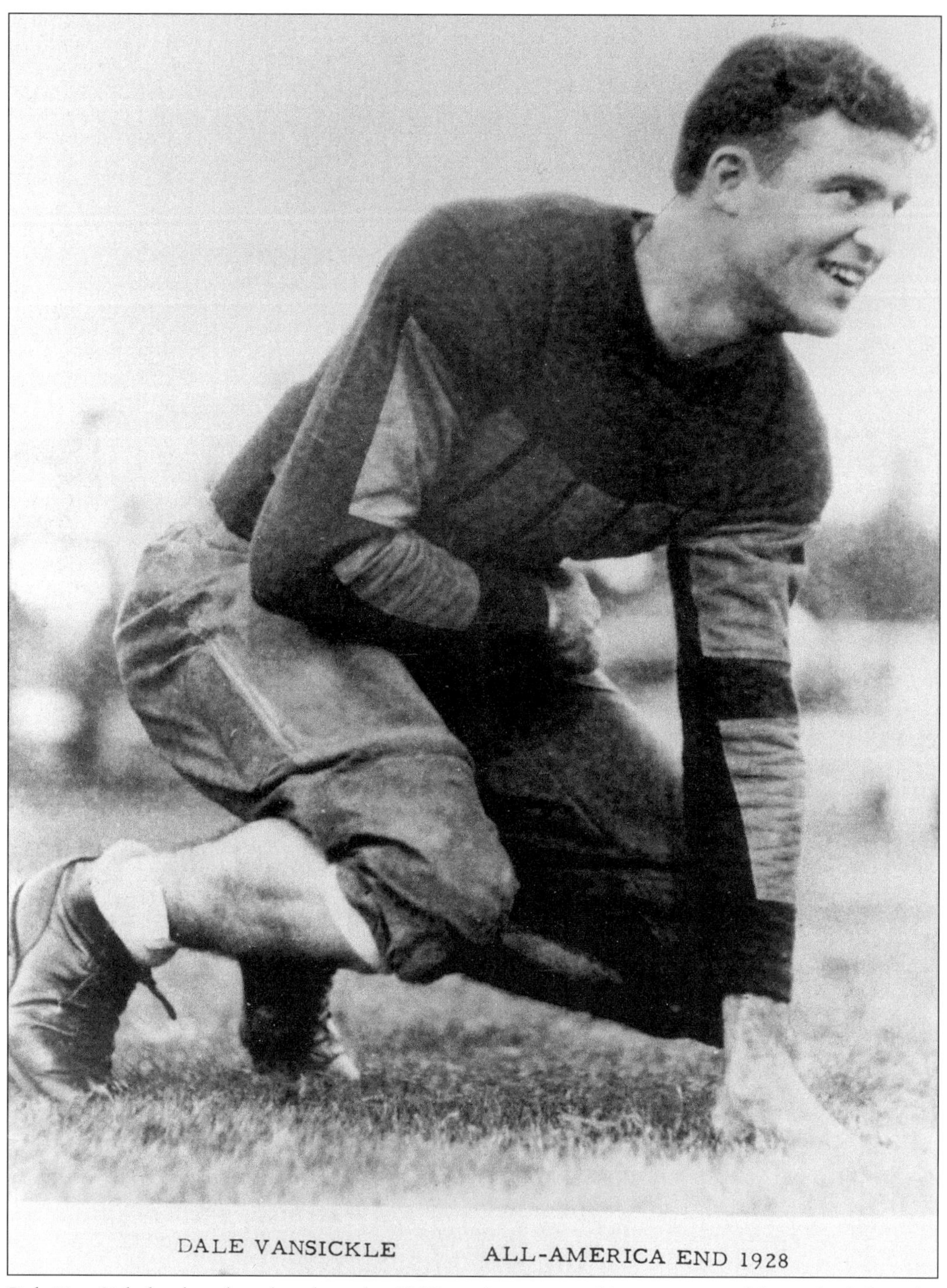

Dale Van Sickel, who played end on the 1928 varsity team and is seen second from the left in the top row in the previous photo, was UF's first football All-American. After college he became a stunt man in Hollywood, serving twice as president of the Motion Picture Stunt Men's Association and practicing his trade for almost 50 years. He died in his late sixties. (Courtesy UF News & Public Affairs.)

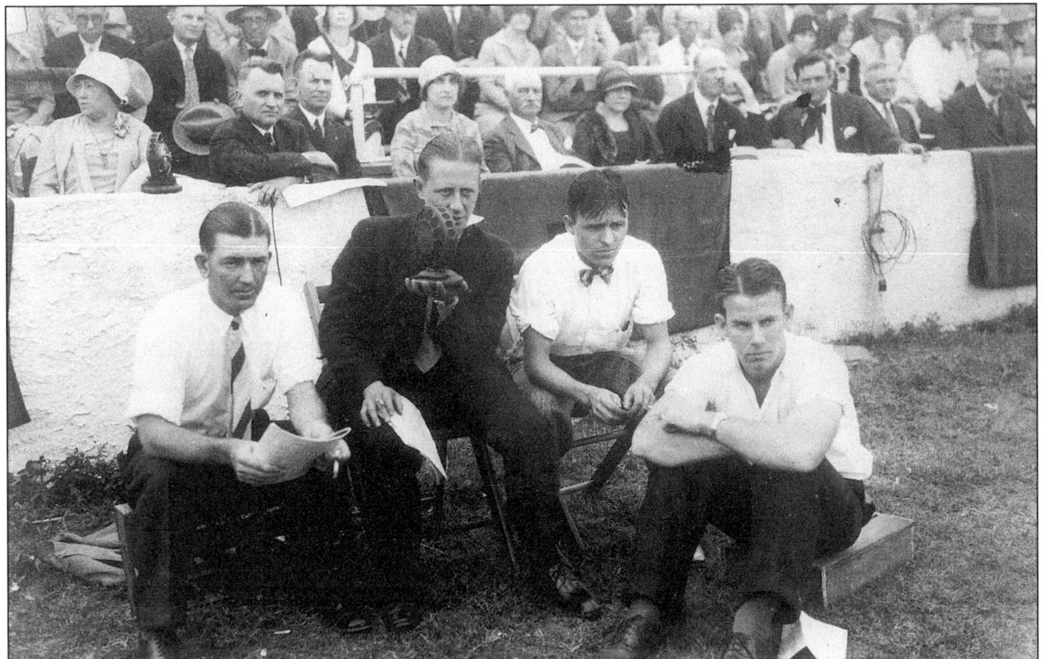

In a 1928 game, seated behind the game broadcasters, were the following, from left to right: (beginning with the fourth person) Governor Doyle Carlton, Mrs. John Tigert, Senator Duncan W. Fletcher, Mrs. Doyle Carlton, John Tigert (president of UF), and R.A. (Lex) Green. (Courtesy University Archives, Dept. of Special Collections, George A. Smathers Libraries, Univ. of Florida.)

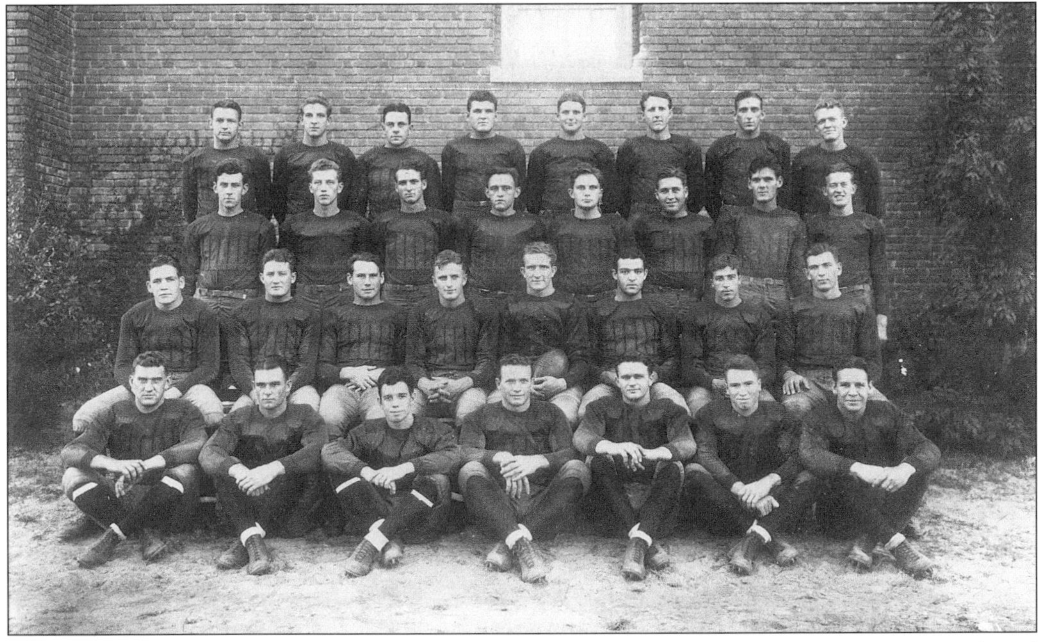

The 1929 squad had an 8-2 record, with its only losses being away-games with Georgia Tech and Harvard. Its final game, a victory in Miami over Oregon, was the first time the Gators played a team from the west coast. (Courtesy University Archives, Dept. of Special Collections, George A. Smathers Libraries, Univ. of Florida.)

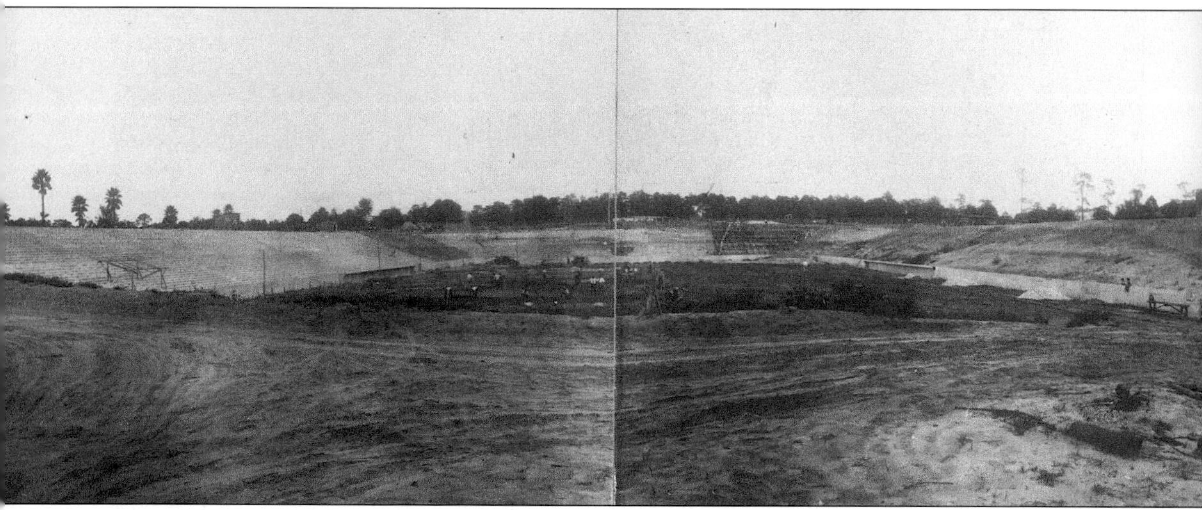

Florida Field, seen here during construction, was dedicated on November 8, 1930, as a sell-out crowd of 21,769 watched the Gators play, and lose to, Alabama, 20-0. The stadium's seating capacity, increased to a little under 22,000, would increase as the team improved over the years and attracted more fans. (Courtesy University Archives, Dept. of Special Collections, George A. Smathers Libraries, Univ. of Florida.)

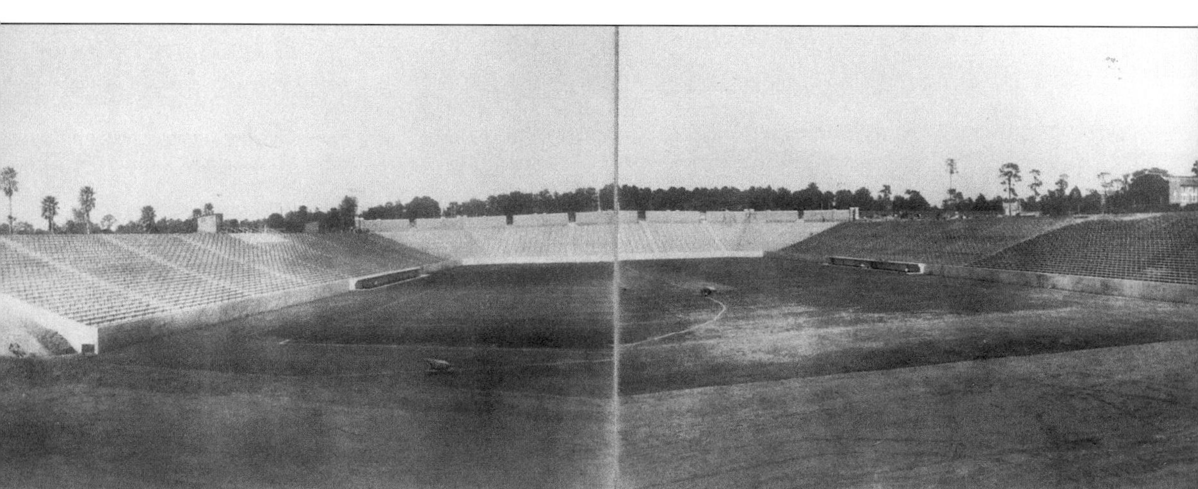

The finished stadium was the lower half of today's Florida Field. The student announcer in those early games was the legendary Red Barber, who became a baseball broadcaster for the Cincinnati Reds, Brooklyn Dodgers, and New York Yankees. His UF microphone is in the National Baseball Hall of Fame in Cooperstown, New York. (Courtesy University Archives, Dept. of Special Collections, George A. Smathers Libraries, Univ. of Florida.)

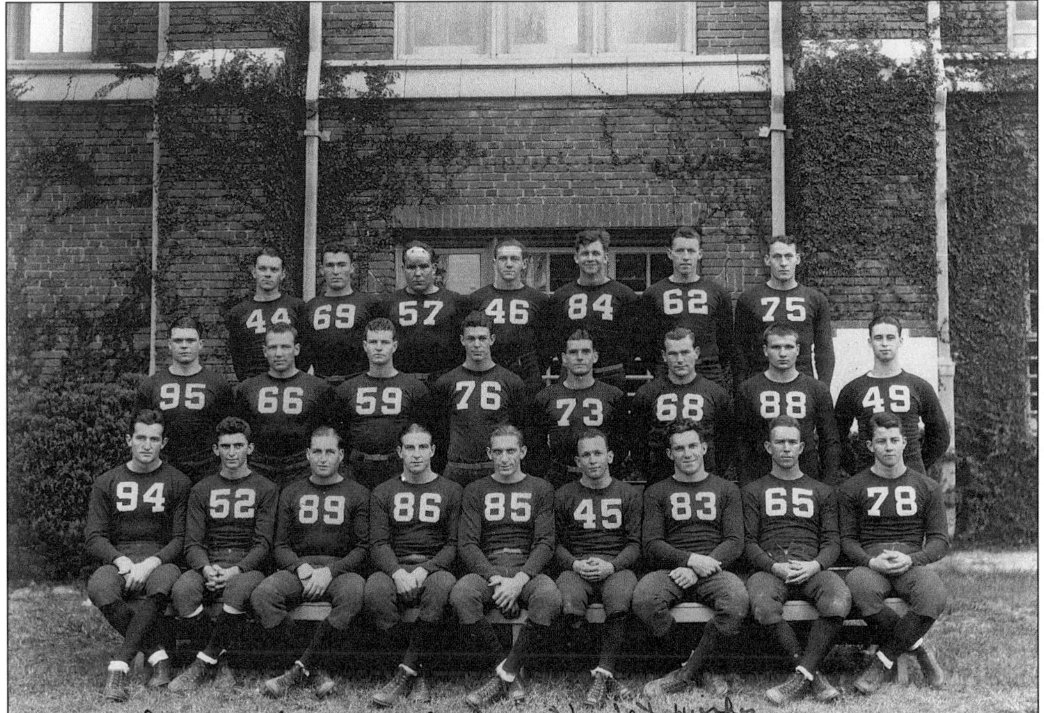

The captain of the 1931 squad, #85, end Ed Parnell of Stuart, received an honorable mention on the All-Southern Conference team, one of the few positives for a team that went 2-6-2 that year. (Courtesy University Archives, Dept. of Special Collections, George A. Smathers Libraries, Univ. of Florida.)

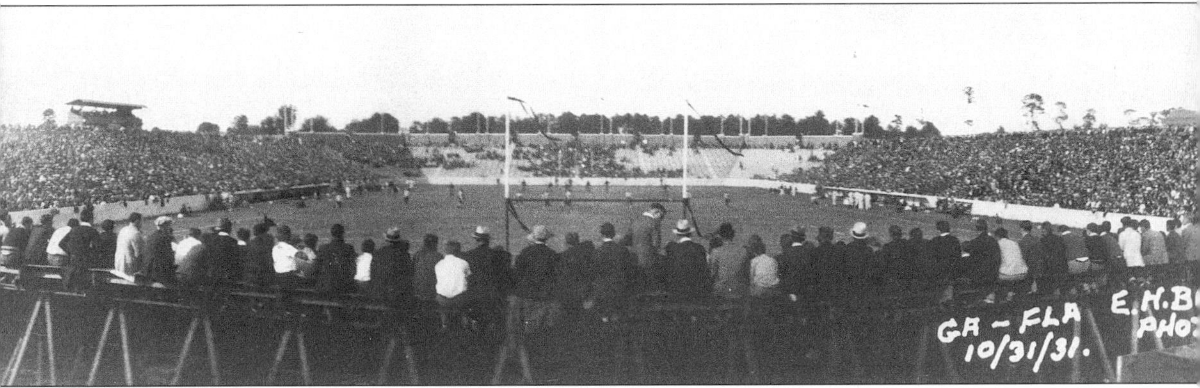

In 1931, the Georgia Bulldogs played the Gators at Florida Field for the first time, beating them 33-6. The Bulldogs, who usually played the Gators in Jacksonville, would not return to Gainesville until 1994. (Courtesy University Archives, Dept. of Special Collections, George A. Smathers Libraries, Univ. of Florida.)

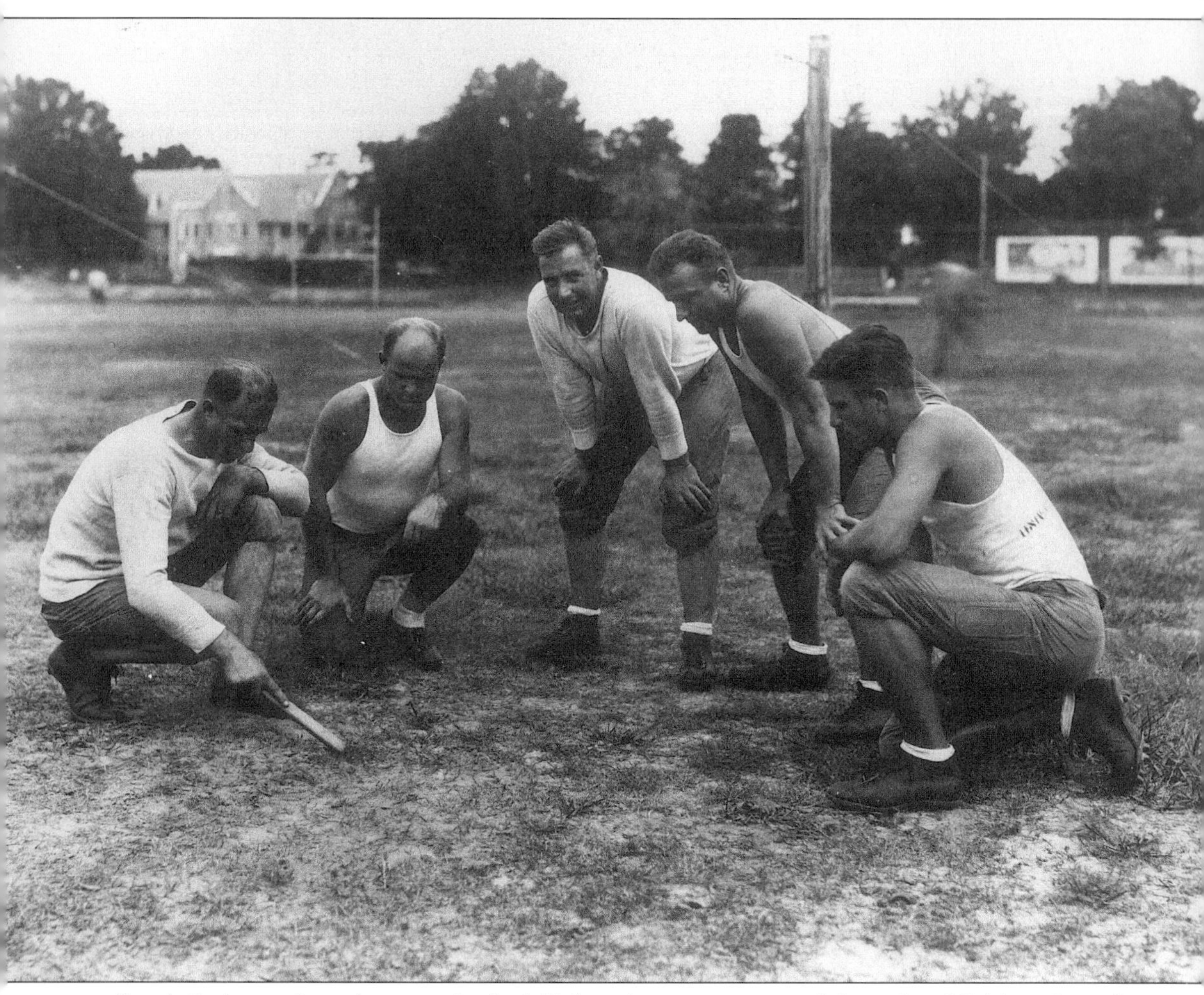

Coach Bachman (seen here on the far left) later became a successful coach at Michigan State for 14 years. He was replaced at UF by Dennis "Dutch" Stanley (third from the left), the team's ninth head coach, who managed only a 14-13-2 record in three seasons (1933–1935). (Courtesy University Archives, Dept. of Special Collections, George A. Smathers Libraries, Univ. of Florida.)

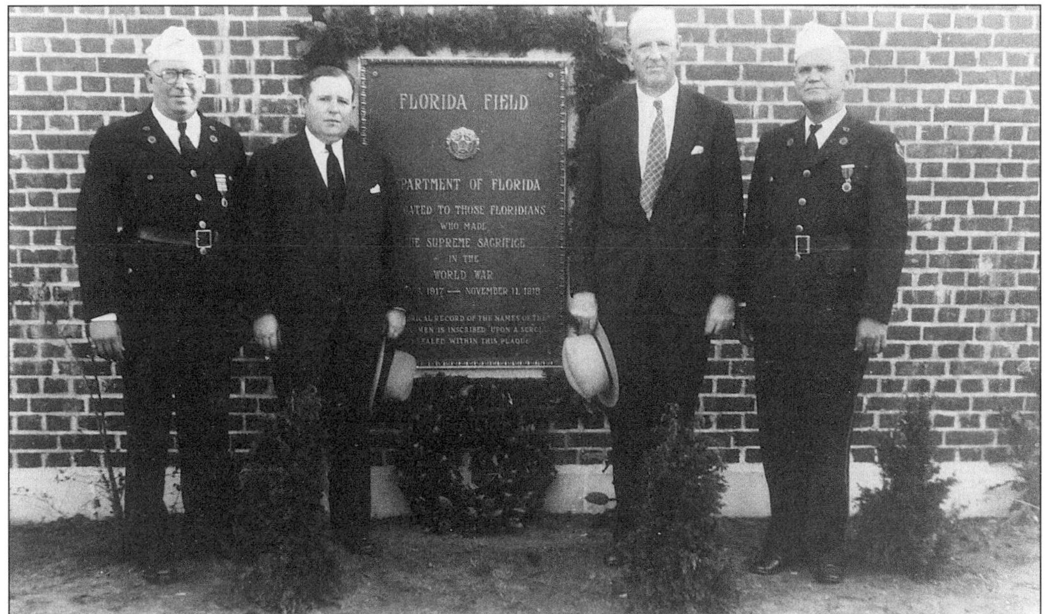

On October 13, 1934, Governor David Sholtz (second from the left) and UF President John Tigert (third from the left), with two American Legion officers, dedicated a plaque on the north wall of Florida Field during the Tulane game. Behind the plaque was a scroll listing those Floridians killed in World War I. (Courtesy University Archives, Dept. of Special Collections, George A. Smathers Libraries, Univ. of Florida.)

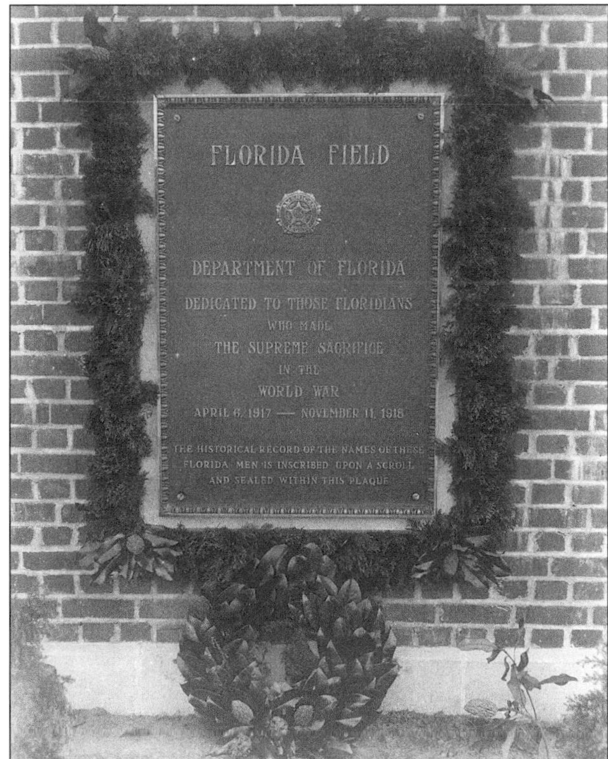

Pictured is a close-up of the plaque that was later reinstalled on the ground floor of the new entrance, which replaced the original red-brick north wall of Florida Field. (Courtesy Elmer Harvey Bone Photographic Collection, University Archives, Dept. of Special Collections, George A. Smathers Libraries, Univ. of Florida.)

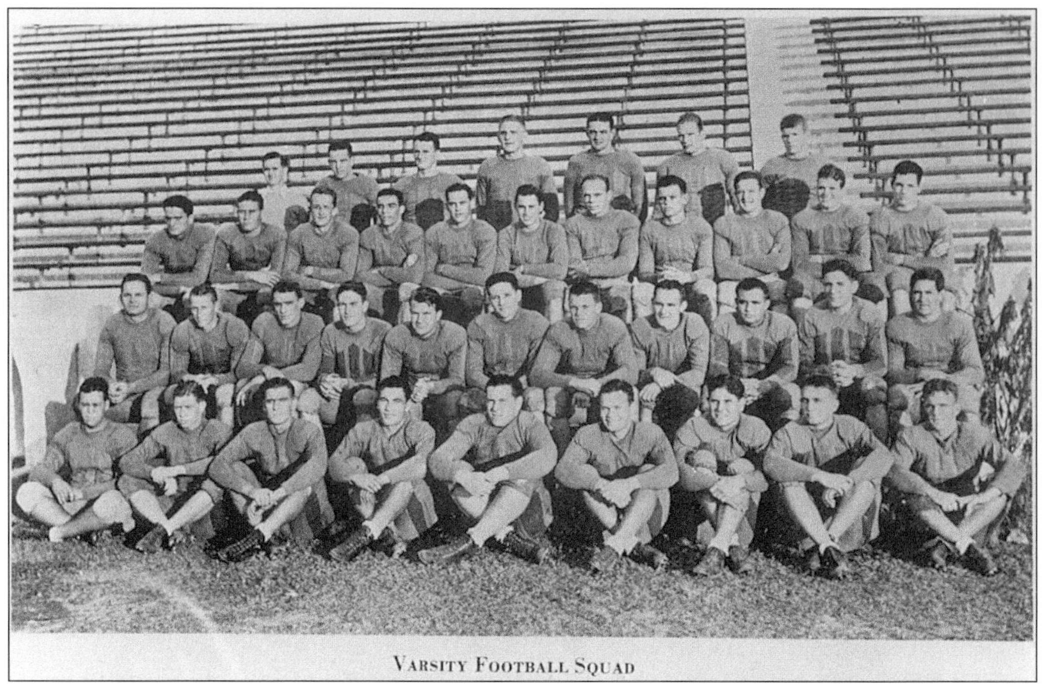

The 1935 team shown here could manage only a 3-7 record, after which Coach Stanley would be replaced. However, in its three wins that year against Stetson, Sewanee, and South Carolina, the team scored 76 points and held the opposition scoreless. (Courtesy UF News & Public Affairs.)

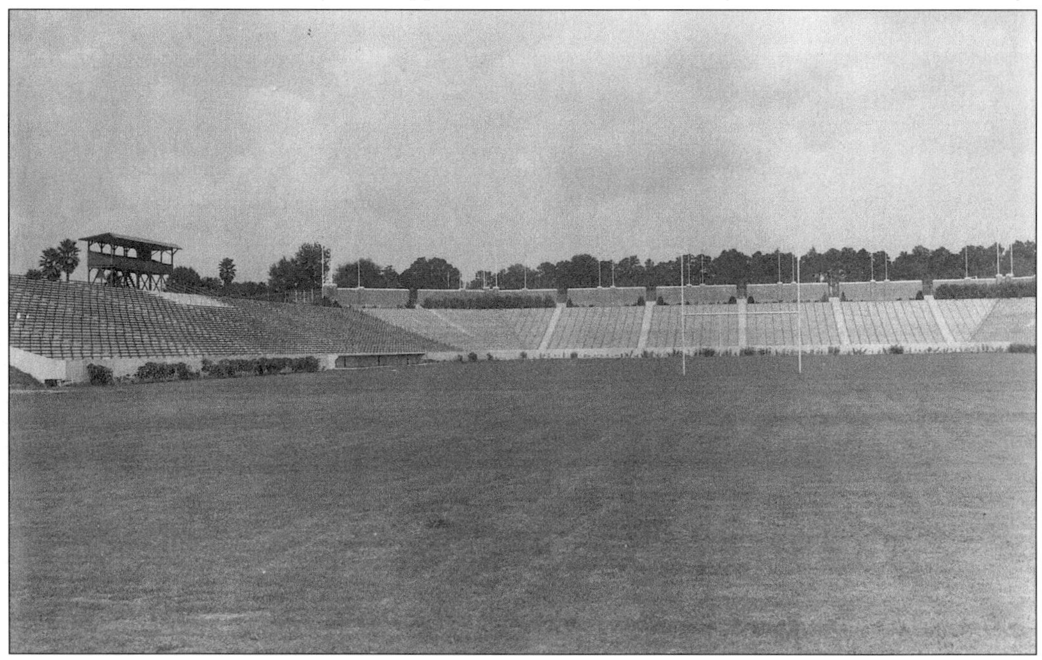

The stadium, shown in the mid-1930s, would later be greatly expanded as the team's winning records attracted more fans. However, the team's tenth head coach, Josh Cody, had a poor 17-24-2 record in four seasons (1936–1939). (Courtesy University Archives, Dept. of Special Collections, George A. Smathers Libraries, Univ. of Florida.)

Four

1940–1949: Coaches Lieb and Wolf

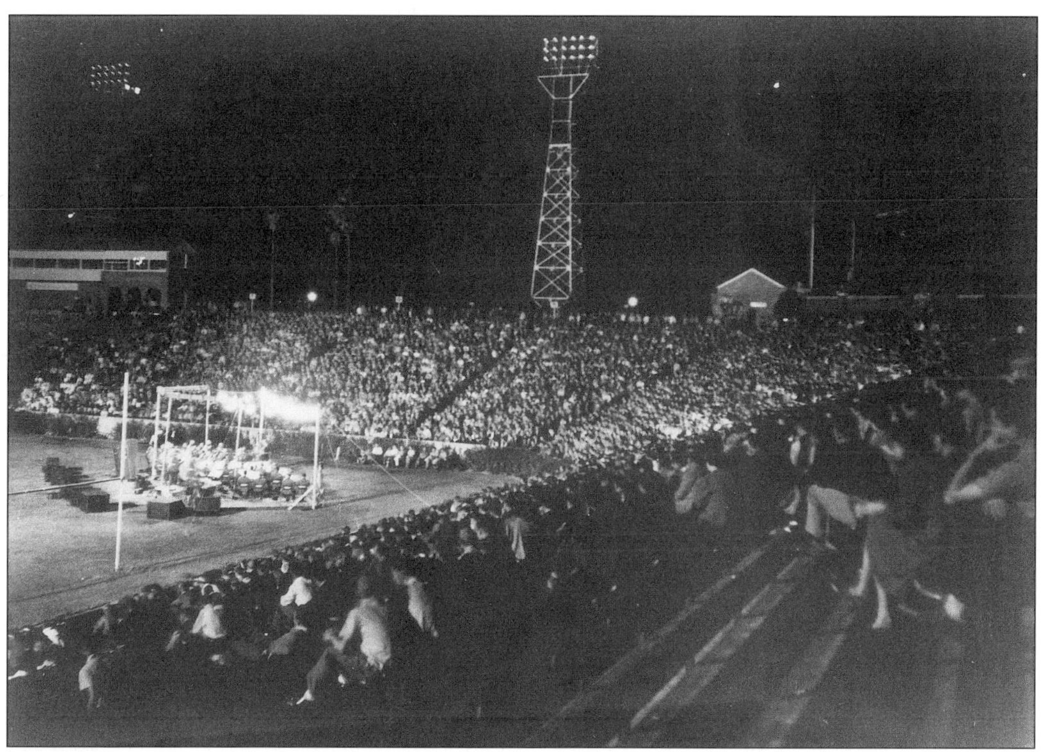

The US Marine band played during a night game on Florida Field in October 1940. Night games were played more and more to avoid the daytime heat. (Courtesy Elmer Harvey Bone Photographic Collection, University Archives, Dept. of Special Collections, George A. Smathers Libraries, Univ. of Florida.)

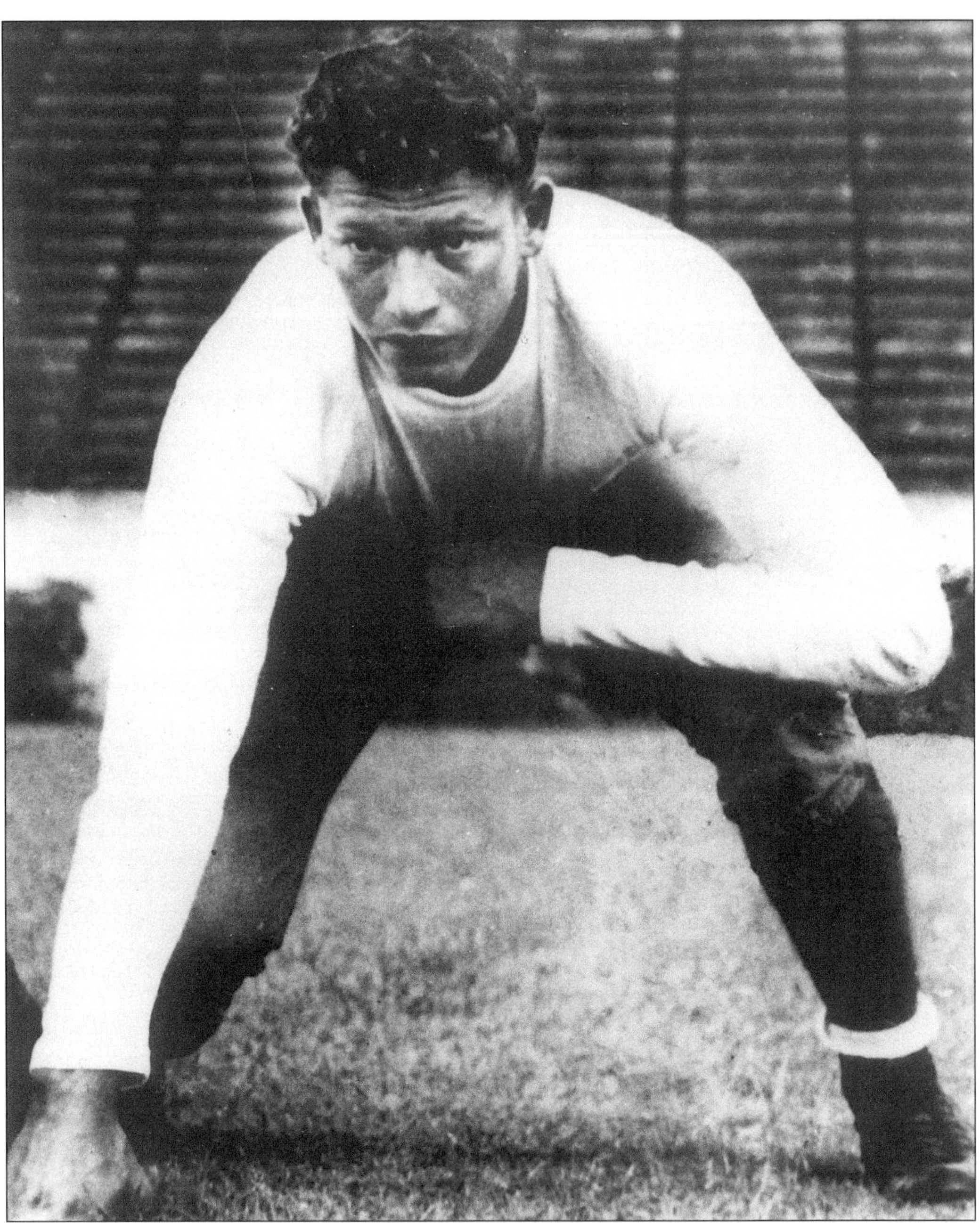

Forrest "Fergie" Ferguson, who started at end on both offense and defense for three years (1939–1941) and set receiving records that stood until the 1960s, won All-American honors (1941) as only the second Gator to do so (Dale Van Sickel was the first in 1928). Ferguson was a collegiate state boxing champion and won the National AAU javelin championship (1942) before entering the U.S. Army and serving in World War II. He died in 1954 of wounds he had suffered during the 1944 invasion of Normandy. He is honored today in the annual Forrest (Fergie) Ferguson Award, given to a senior player who displays outstanding leadership, character, and courage. (Courtesy University Archives, Dept. of Special Collections, George A. Smathers Libraries, Univ. of Florida.)

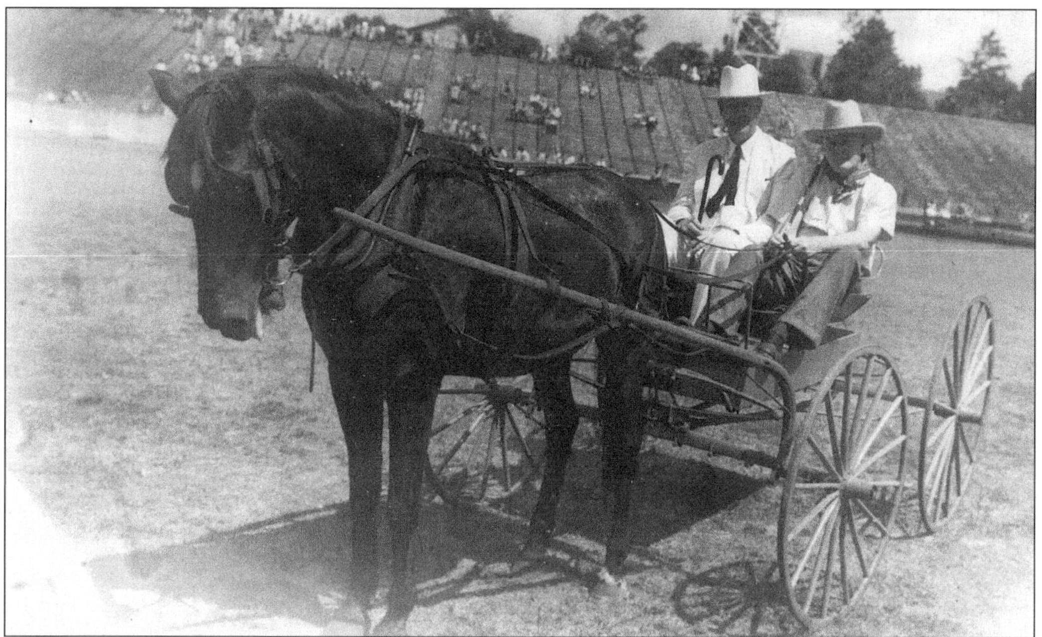

Dr. Tigert and Dean Hume rode in a horse-drawn buggy at Florida Field in 1943. Tom Lieb, the team's 11th head coach, had a 20-26-1 record in five seasons (1940–1945); there was no team in 1943, the mid-point of World War II. (Courtesy University Archives, Dept. of Special Collections, George A. Smathers Libraries, Univ. of Florida.)

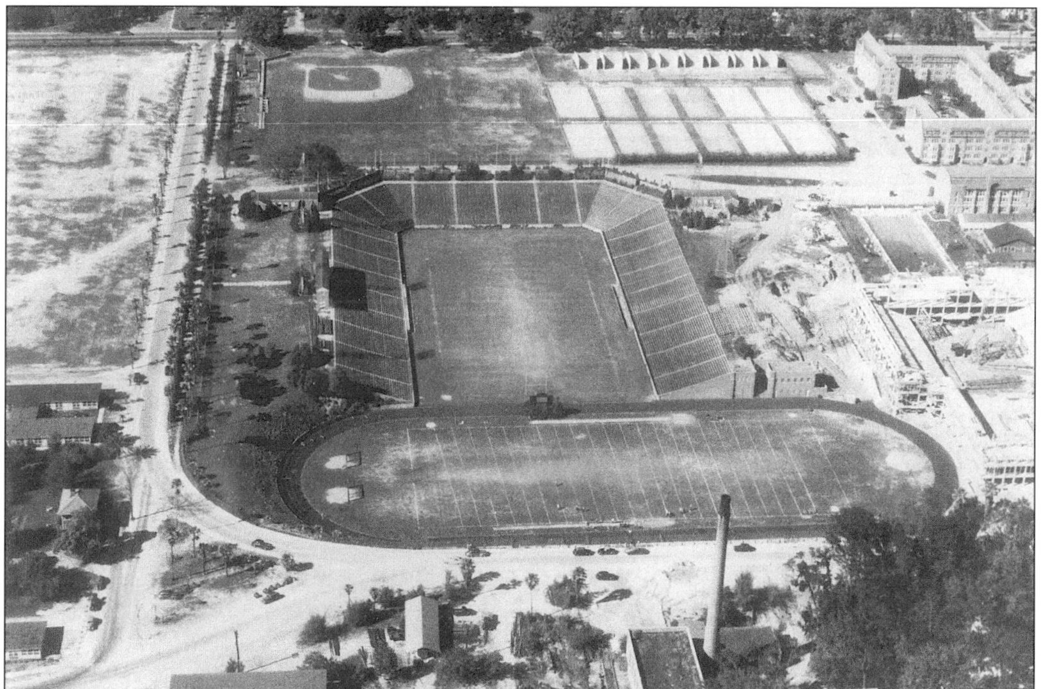

Florida Field was in the middle of an athletic complex consisting of a track field, baseball diamond, and tennis courts. (Courtesy University Archives, Dept. of Special Collections, George A. Smathers Libraries, Univ. of Florida.)

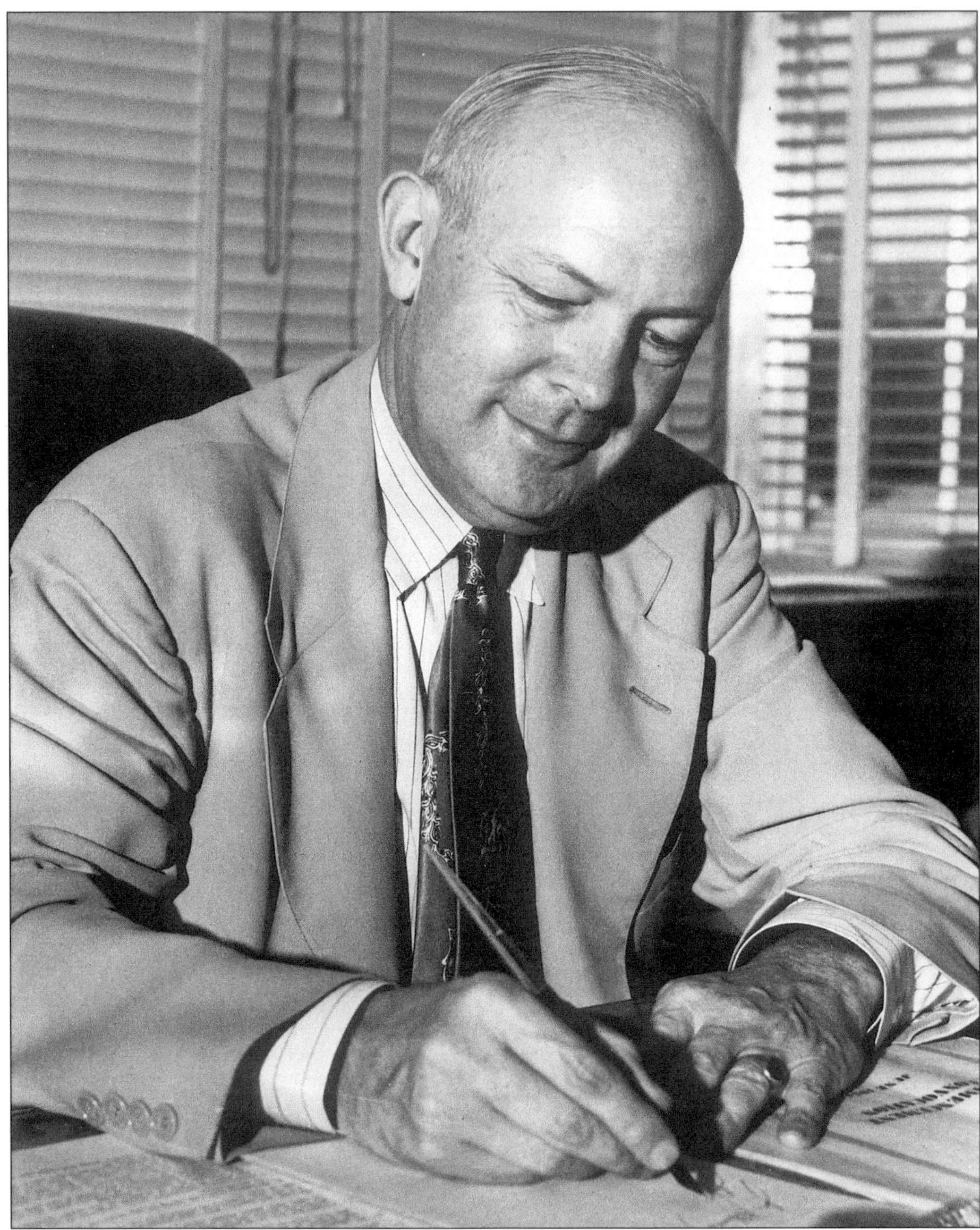

President J. Hillis Miller, who was president of UF from 1947 to 1953, was honored in the naming of the large complex of campus buildings devoted to health research and healing—the J. Hillis Miller Health Science Center. He lasted longer than the team's 12th head coach, Ray Wolf, who had a record of 13-24-2 in four seasons (1946–1949). (Courtesy Florida State Archives.)

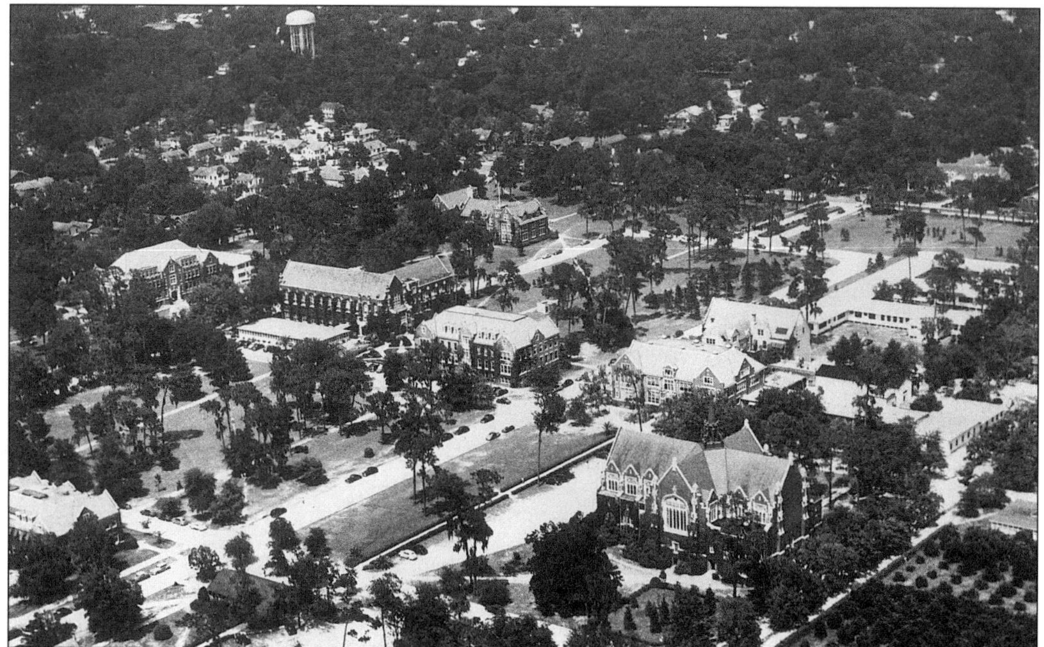

The UF campus in 1947 saw women enrolled in large numbers for the first time. Two years later, more than 2,000 women enrolled at UF. Women living on campus had a strict curfew and were not allowed to wear jeans and shorts, but they would eventually—in the 1990s—outnumber the male students. (Courtesy Florida State Archives.)

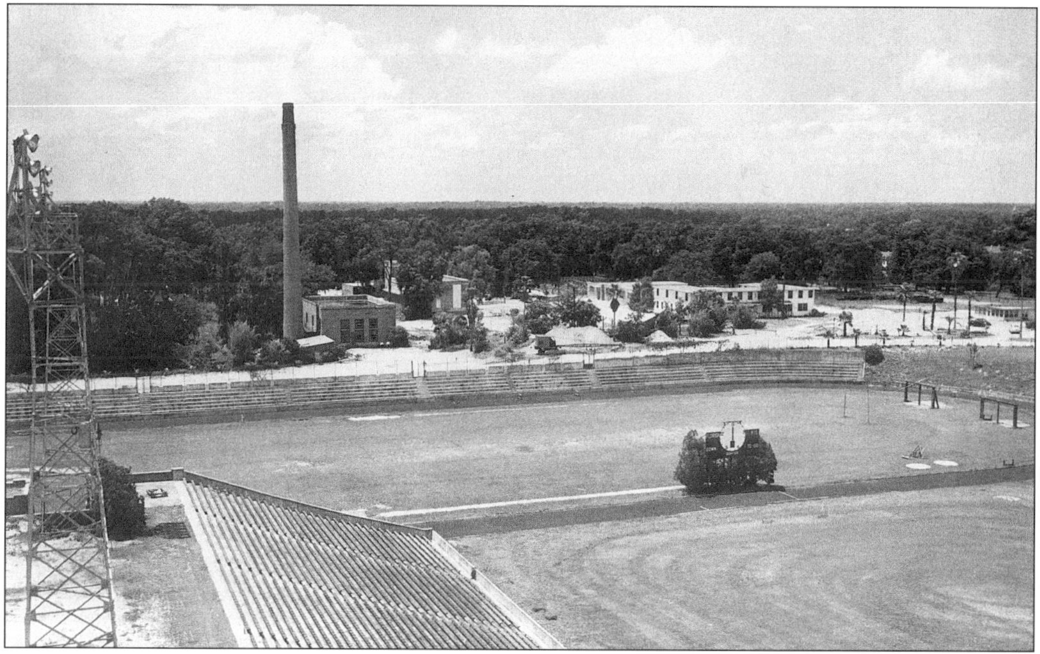

The south end zone of Florida Field had only a small scoreboard from the 1930s to the 1960s. In 1966, officials installed temporary bleachers to increase the capacity of the stadium to 62,800. That end zone seating area would later be enclosed and expanded in 1982, bringing the seating capacity of the stadium to 72,000. (Courtesy Florida State Archives.)

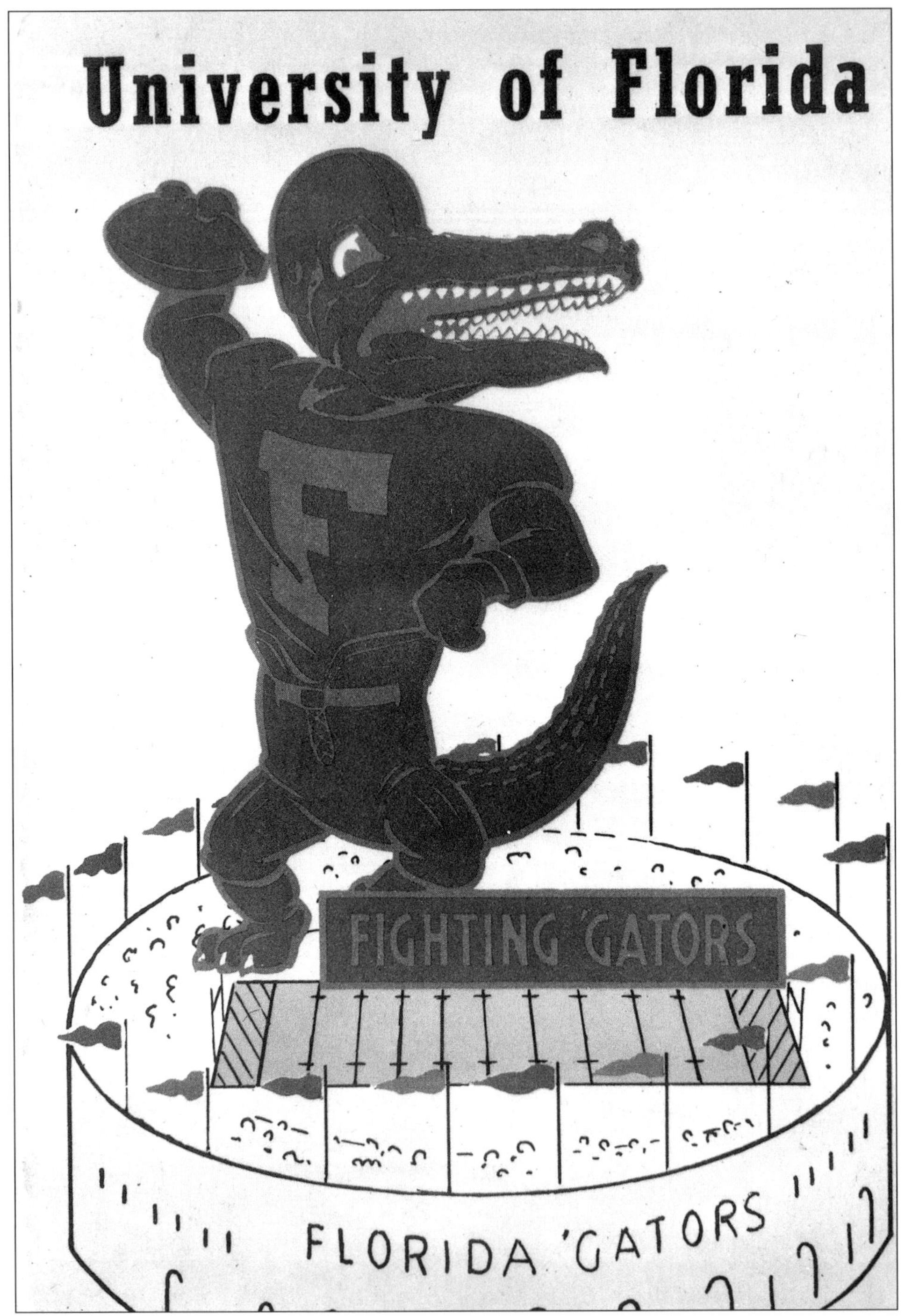

This early Gator mascot did not cause the problems that having a person, for example a Native American, would in terms of publicity and political correctness. The reptile was also honored in the name of the campus newspaper and the Gator Chomp, an up-and-down motion with both arms that fans in the stadium would do to intimidate the opposition. (Courtesy Florida State Archives.)

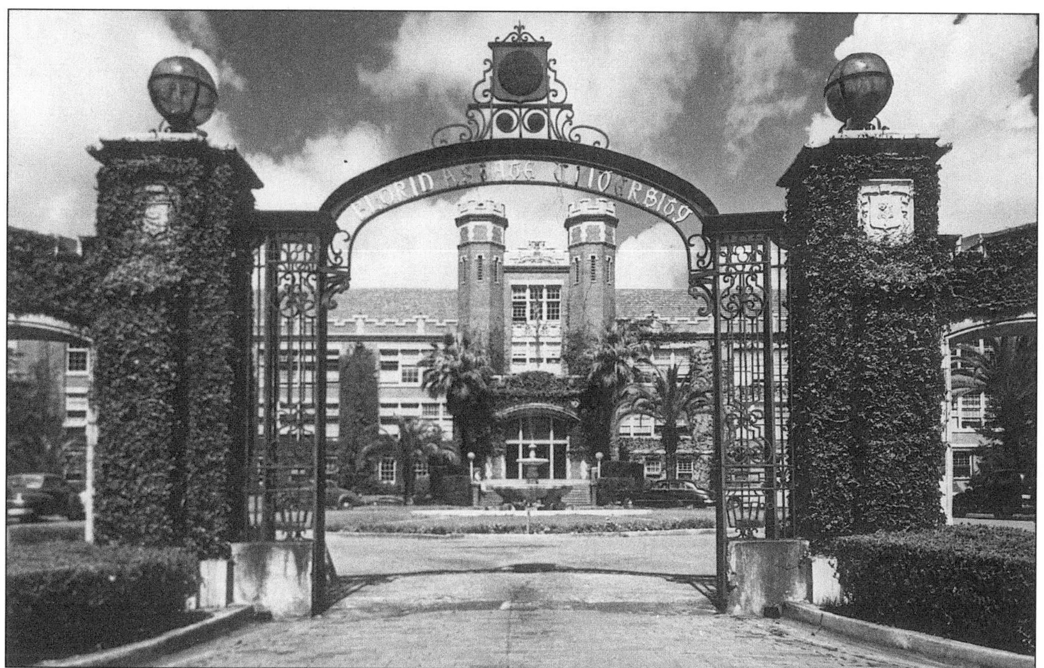

Florida State University (FSU) in Tallahassee began playing football in 1947, but some historians point out that the first Gator football victory was a 6-0 win over the men of Tallahassee's Florida State College, a school that later had only female students before eventually becoming the co-educational FSU. (Courtesy Florida State Archives.)

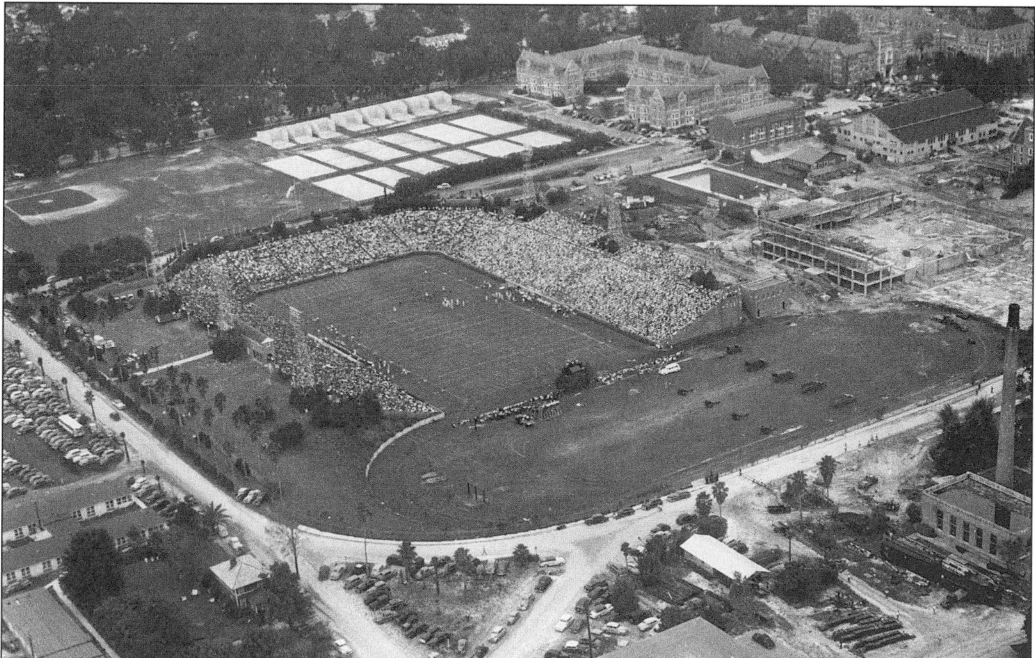

The increasing numbers of football fans who wanted to see the Gators play would soon lead to pressure to increase the size of the stadium. In 1950, its total capacity, including temporary bleachers, reached 40,116. (Courtesy Florida State Archives.)

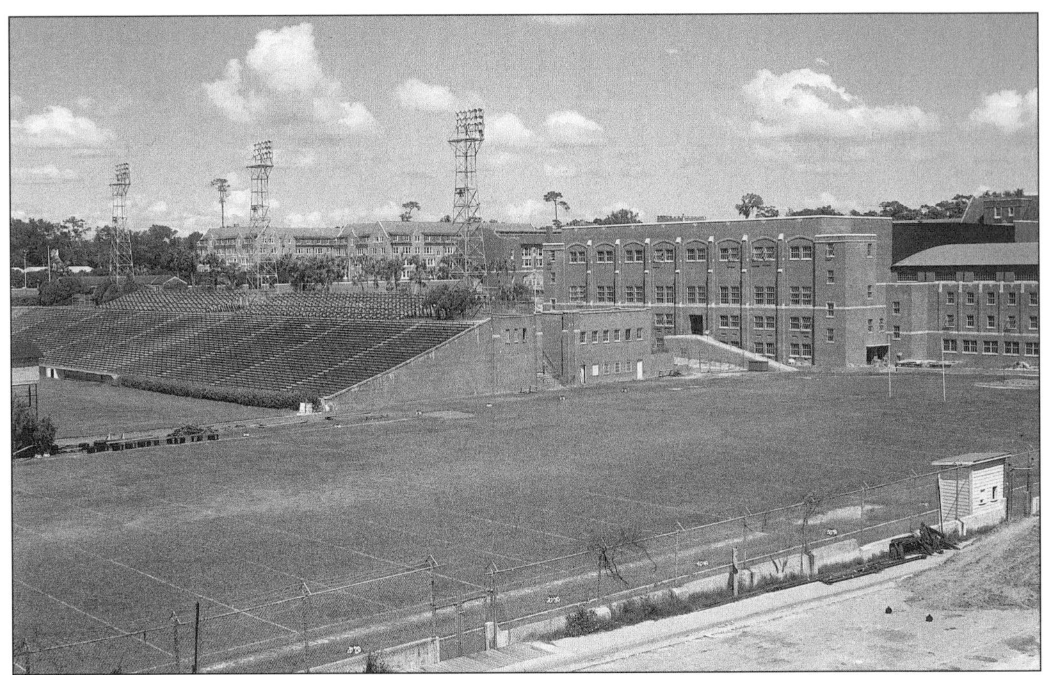

The expansion of Florida Field would force the track field to be placed farther away. The Women's Gymnasium to the east of the football stadium served as a gym, auditorium, movie theater, social hall, and chapel. When the school went co-ed in 1947, the women used the building for their athletic programs. (Courtesy Florida State Archives.)

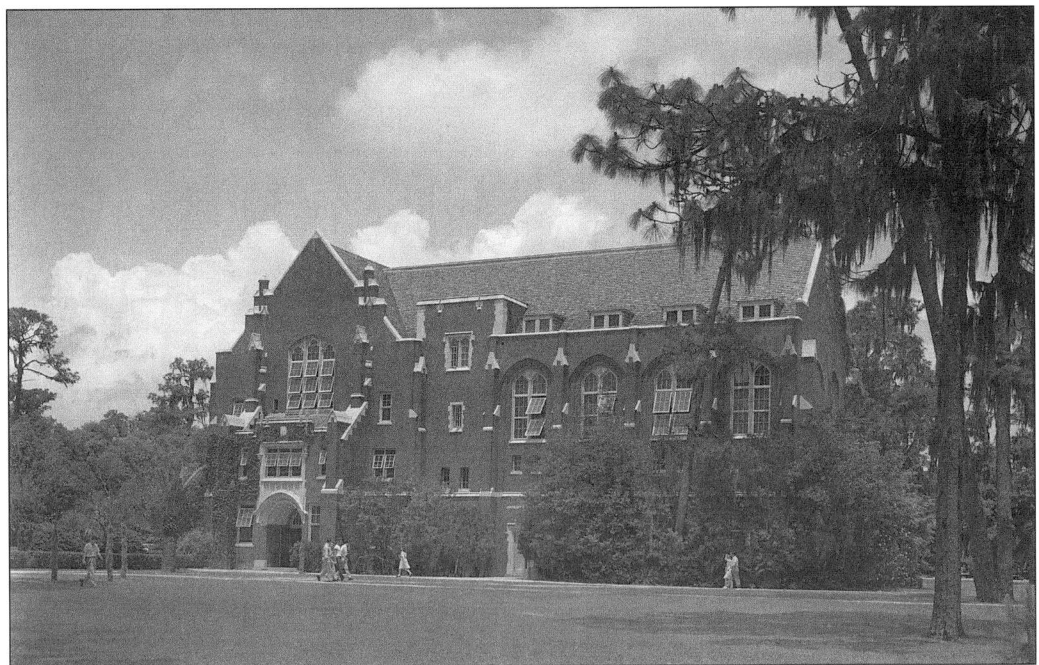

After World War II, as thousands of soldiers returned to America to resume their lives, UF went on an extensive building campaign, but officials kept the new buildings in a style similar to the older campus, for example the library, seen here in 1949. (Courtesy Florida State Archives.)

Five

1950–1959: Coach Woodruff

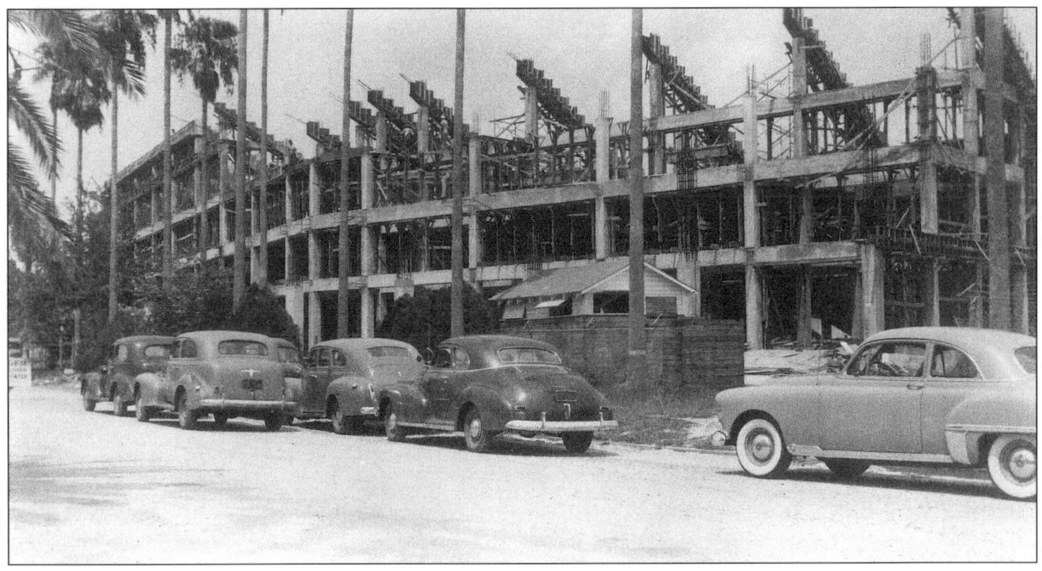

The addition of upper levels to the stadium in 1950 coincided with the arrival of Coach Bob Woodruff, the team's 13th head coach. He would have a 53-42-6 record in ten seasons (1950–1959). (Courtesy University Archives, Dept. of Special Collections, George A. Smathers Libraries, Univ. of Florida.)

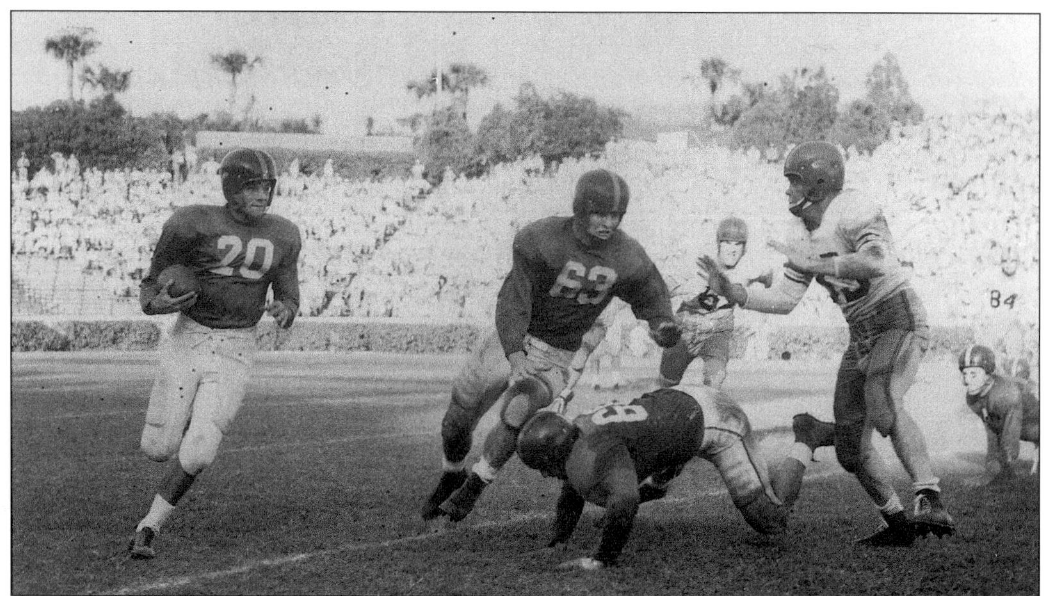

Halfback Loren Broadus (#20) runs in the 1950 Homecoming game with Auburn, a 27-7 win for the Gators. The 76 games of the UF-Auburn rivalry, going back to 1912, have been second only to the UF-Georgia rivalry in number of Gator games (77) through 1999. Auburn leads the UF series, 39 games to 35, with two ties. (Courtesy University Archives, Dept. of Special Collections, George A. Smathers Libraries, Univ. of Florida.)

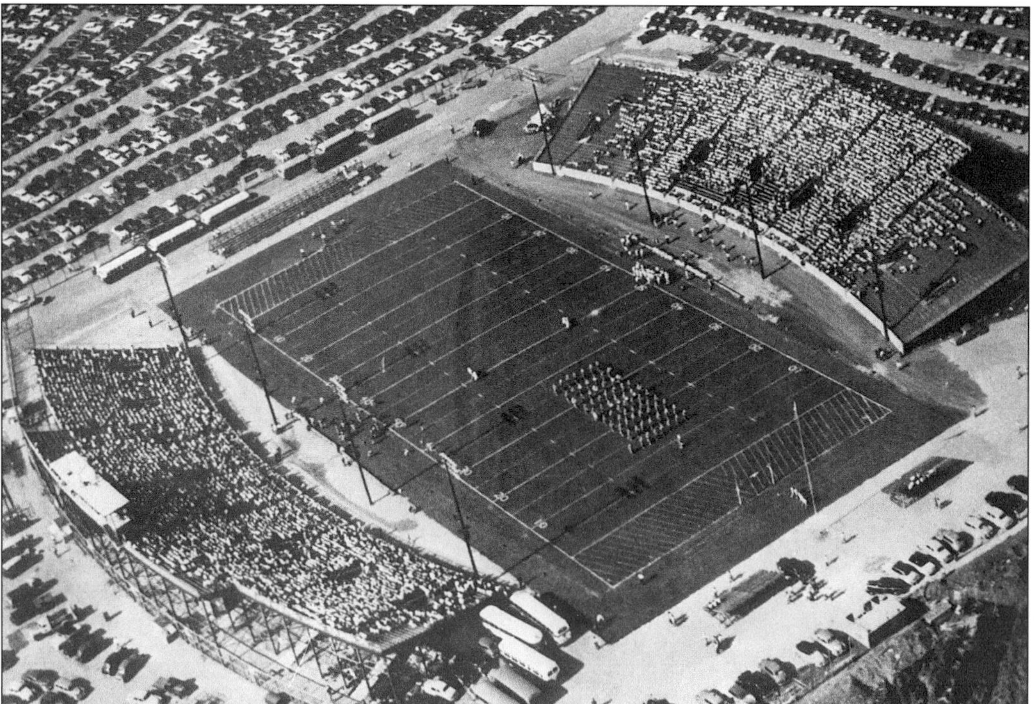

FSU's Campbell Stadium in Tallahassee was expanding in the 1950s, but it had to be larger still before the Gators would agree to play there, which did not happen until 1964. (Courtesy Florida State Archives.)

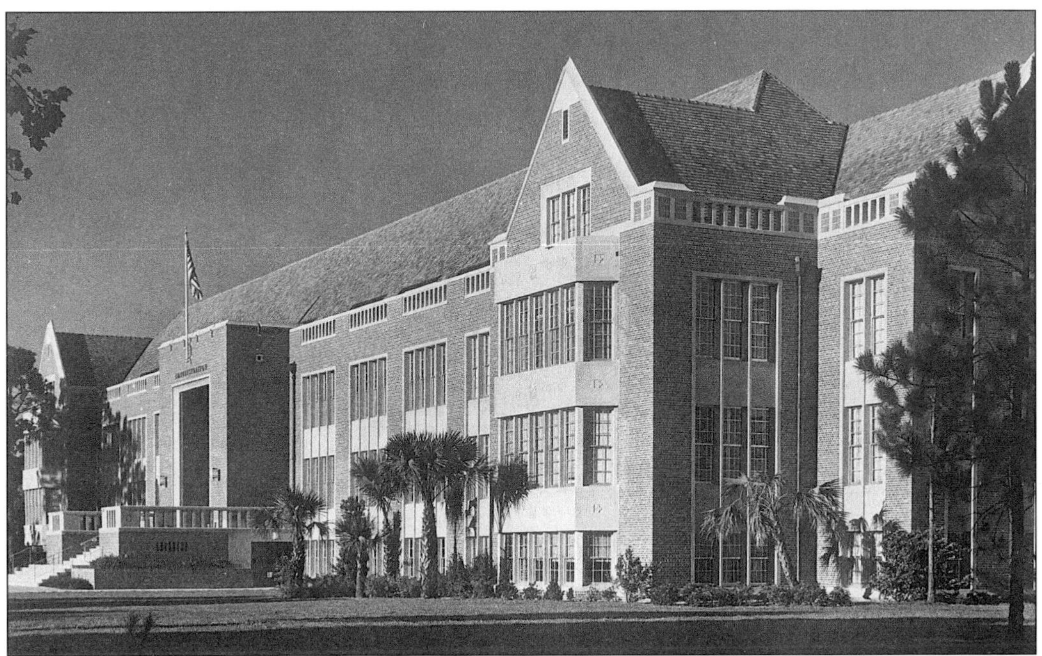

Tigert Hall, which was completed in 1950, honored John J. Tigert, UF president from 1928 until 1947. That four-story, brick building had the school's first computer, which the registrar used. (Courtesy Florida State Archives.)

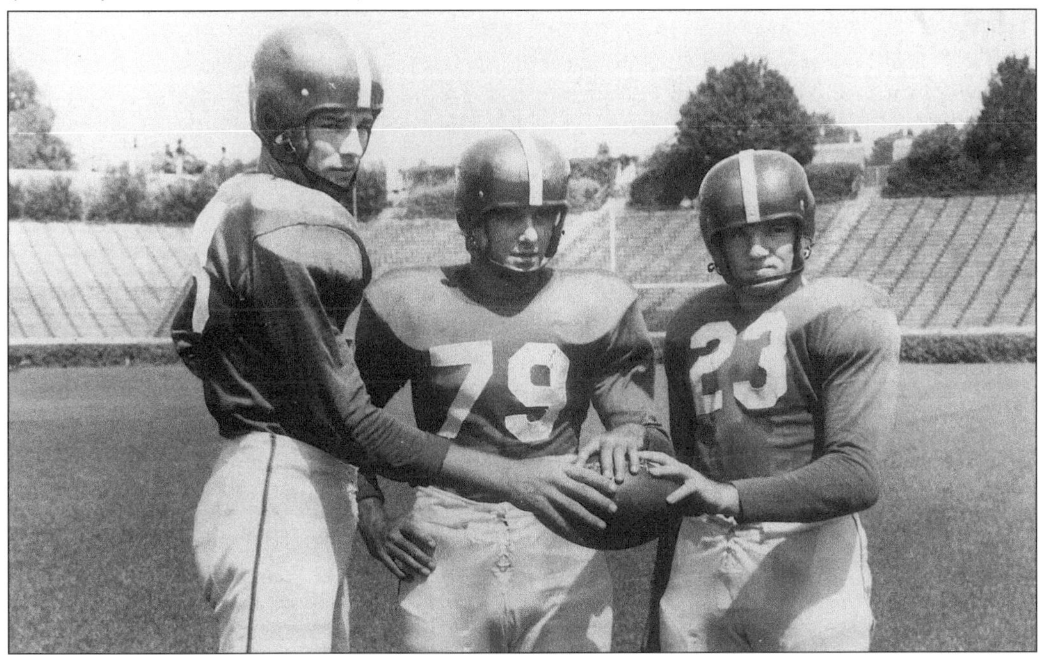

Three quarterbacks were on the 1950 team: Haywood Sullivan (on the left), Angus Williams (#79), and Kent Stevens (#23). The 6-foot-4-inch Sullivan, the first sophomore in the Southeastern Conference (SEC) to pass for more than 1,000 yards, went on to play baseball for the Boston Red Sox and Kansas City Athletics. (Courtesy University Archives, Dept. of Special Collections, George A. Smathers Libraries, Univ. of Florida.)

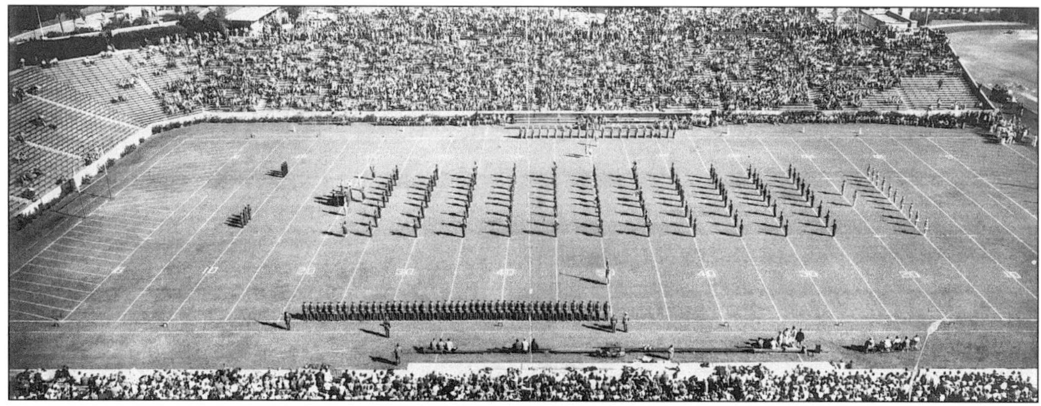

The UF Drill Team, shown here in a 1952 game against Kentucky, provided half-time entertainment. The 1952 Gator team was the school's first bowl team, beating Tulsa in Jacksonville's Gator Bowl, 14-13. (Courtesy University Archives, Dept. of Special Collections, George A. Smathers Libraries, Univ. of Florida.)

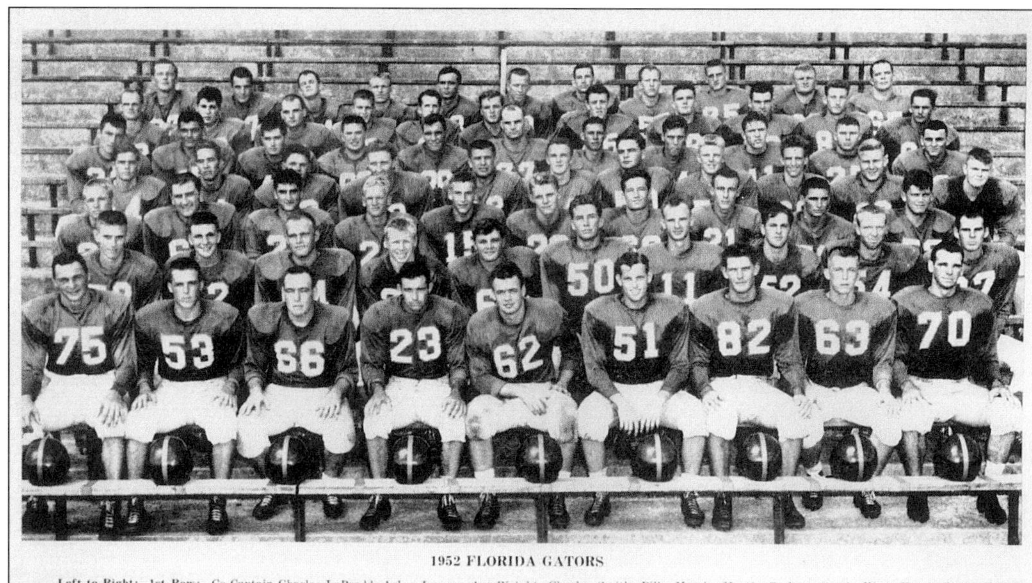

The 1952 Gator varsity squad included tackle Charlie LaPradd (#75, far left in front row), UF's third first-team All-American. That former Army paratrooper played both offense and defense on the school's first bowl team. He later became a football coach at FSU and then president of St. Johns River Community College in Palatka in the 1960s. (Courtesy UF News & Public Affairs.)

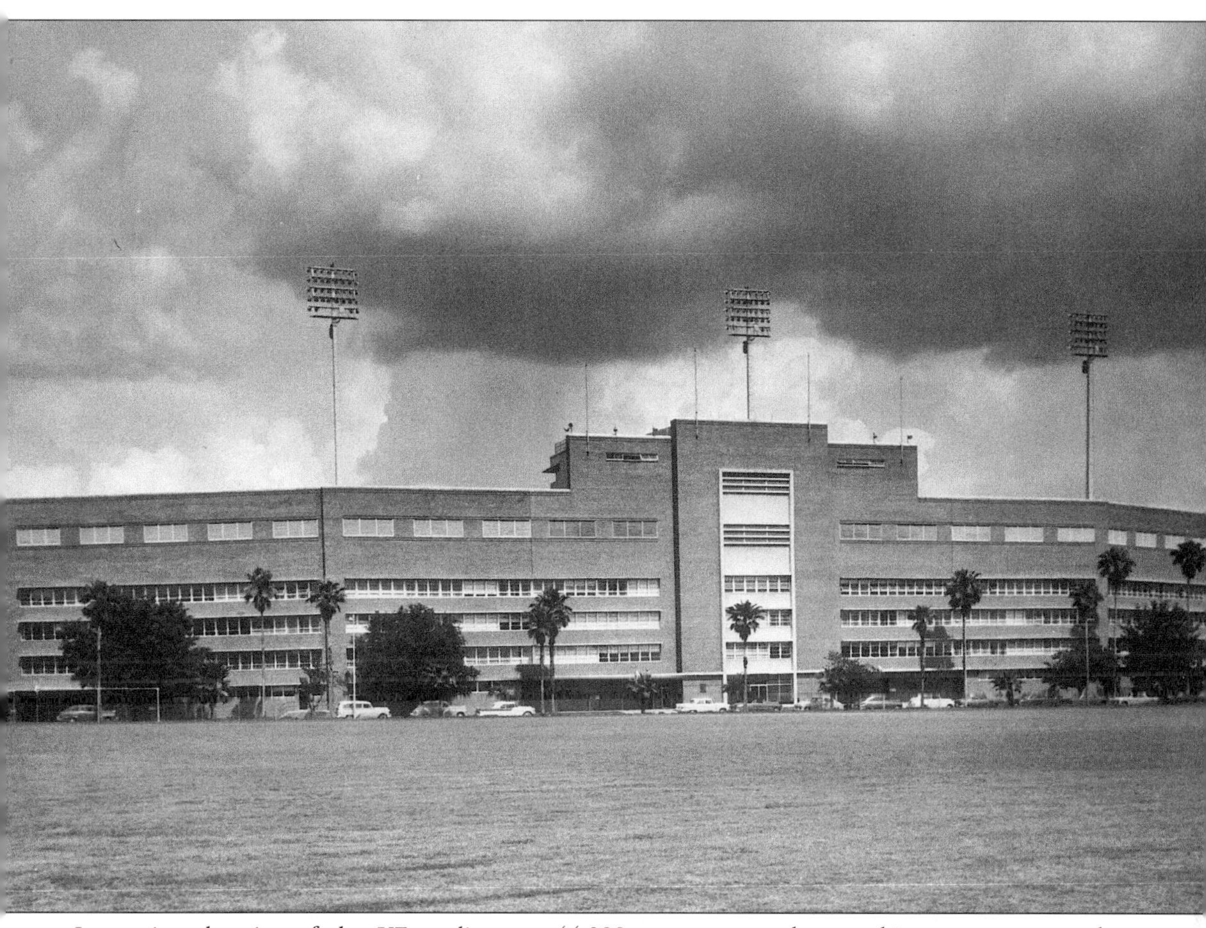

Increasing the size of the UF stadium to 44,000 seats attracted more big-name teams and increased revenues for the athletic department, which in turn helped all Gator sports. One of the toughest athletes playing at that time was Rick Casares (seen in the previous photo at the left end of the fifth row up from the bottom). He started at fullback for three years (1951–1953), and after UF, he played in the NFL for the Chicago Bears for ten years, scoring 59 touchdowns and rushing for 5,675 yards, which ranks third on Chicago's all-time rushing list. (Courtesy Florida State Archives.)

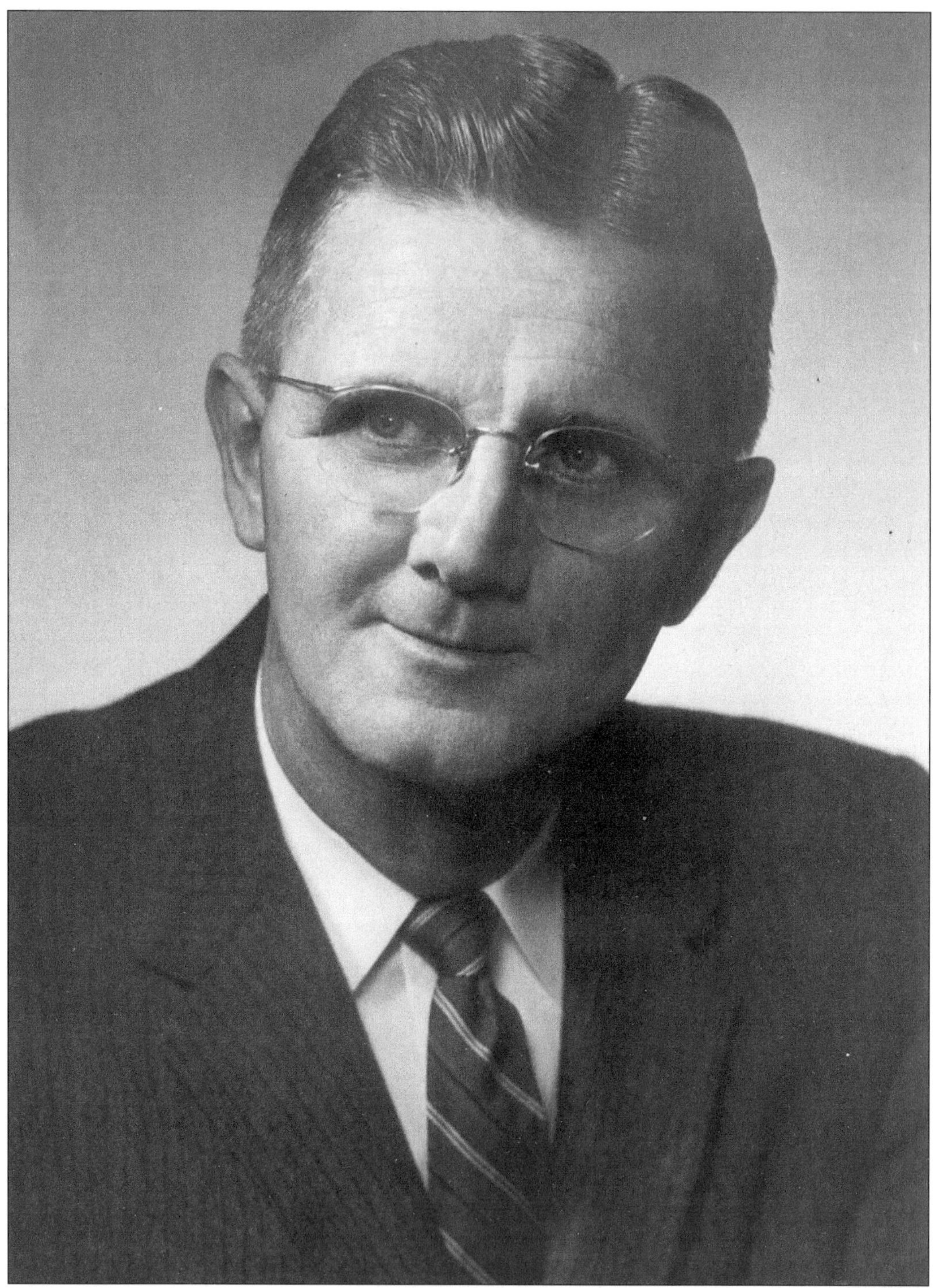

Dr. J. Wayne Reitz, who served as UF president from 1955 until 1967, was responsible for hiring head football coach Ray Graves, one of the most successful and popular UF coaches ever. The affable Graves was a welcome relief from the more conservative Woodruff, who emphasized defense over offense, something the fans did not approve of. (Courtesy Florida State Archives.)

Guard John Barrow, UF's fourth first-team All American, was also the SEC Lineman of the Year in 1956. He went on to play 15 seasons in the Canadian Football League before retiring to become general manager at Toronto. His son, Greg, lettered as a Gator tackle in 1980. (Courtesy UF News & Public Affairs.)

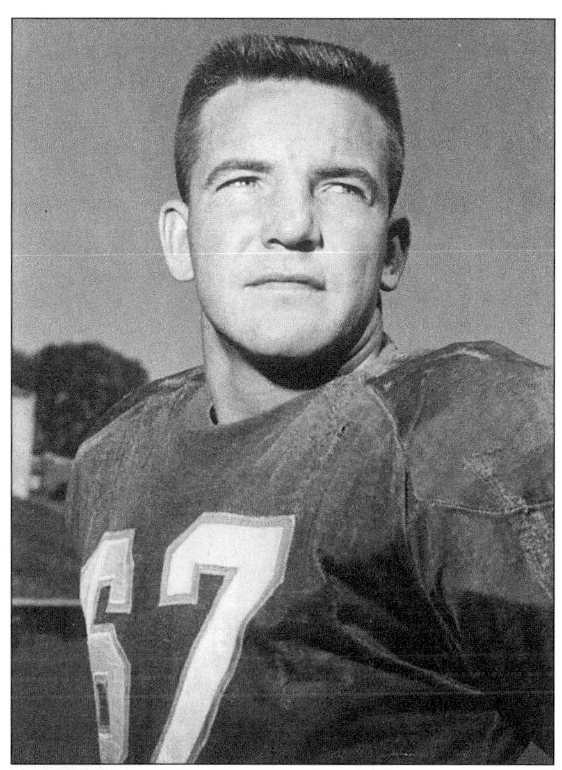

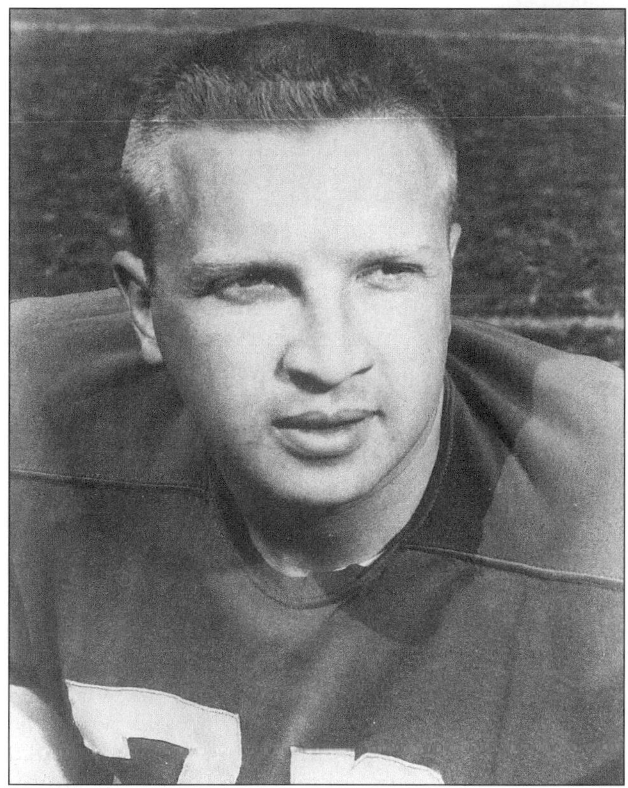

Defensive tackle Vel Heckman, who lettered for three years (1956–1958), became the second first-team All-American defensive player (Charlie LaPradd was first). While often known for its offensive firepower, Gator defensive teams have done very well, placing 23 different players on All-American teams and 29 in the NFL. (Courtesy UF News & Public Affairs.)

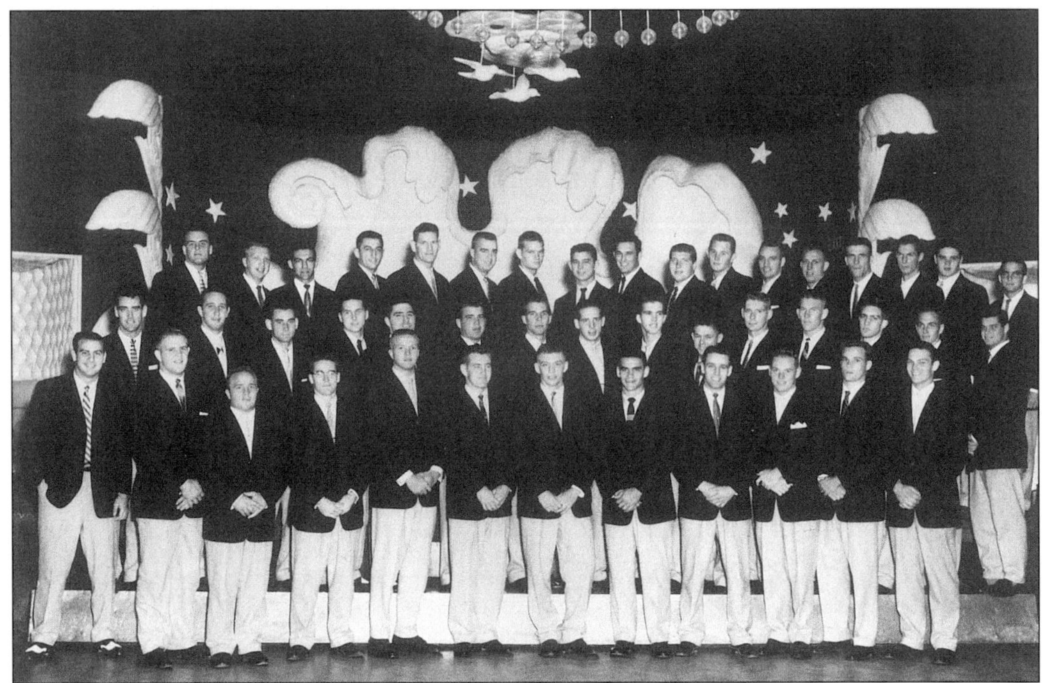

The 1956 team beat Georgia 28-0 and was ranked 12th after a five-game winning streak upped the team's record to 6-1-1. That winning streak was the Gators' longest in one season since the eight straight wins of the 1928 team. The team finished with a 6-3-1 record. (Courtesy University Archives, Dept. of Special Collections, George A. Smathers Libraries, Univ. of Florida.)

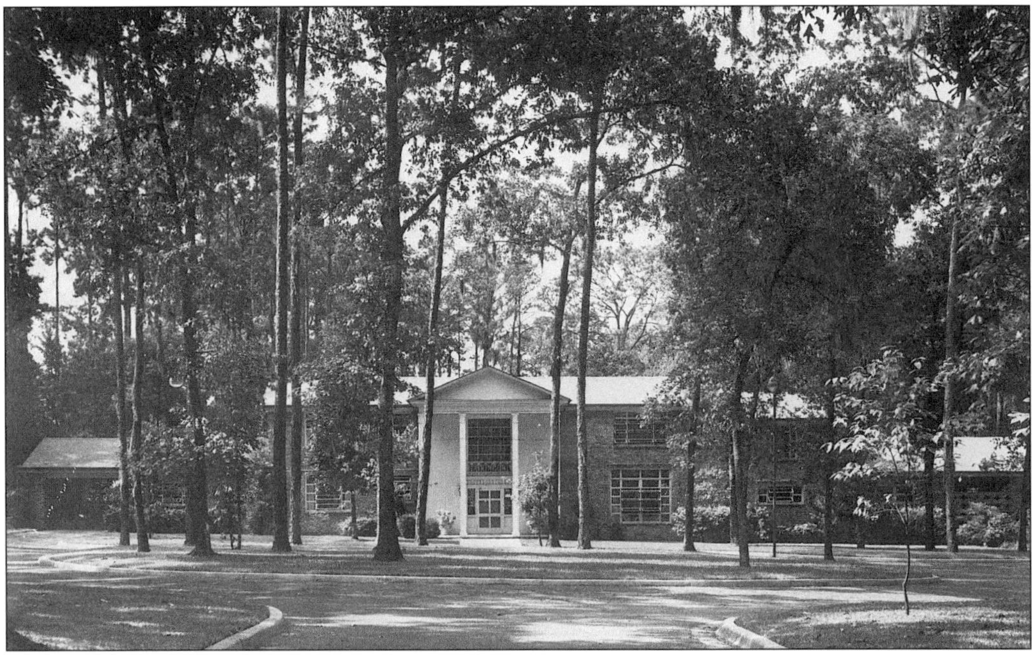

The UF president's house, which was within walking distance of the football stadium, became the site of many post-game celebrations, especially in the 1990s, as the Gators were almost unbeatable in the Swamp. (Courtesy Florida State Archives.)

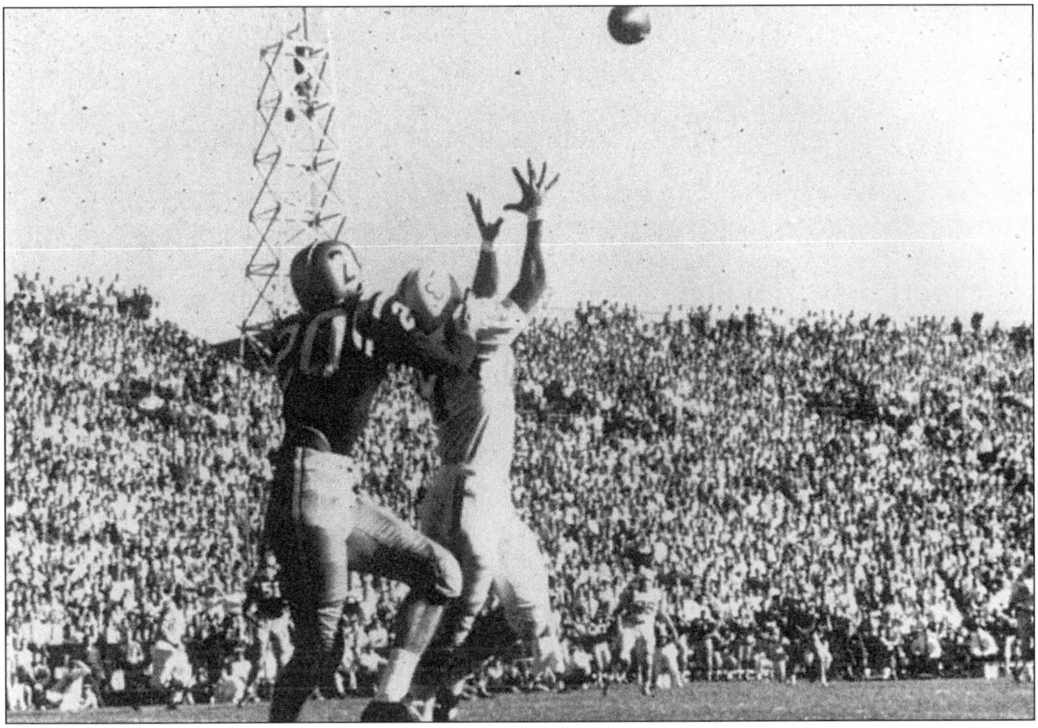

Dave Hudson's interception of an FSU pass in the first UF-FSU game (1958) led to a Gator victory, 21-7, in what would become UF's fiercest rivalry in the 1990s. (Courtesy University Archives, Dept. of Special Collections, George A. Smathers Libraries, Univ. of Florida.)

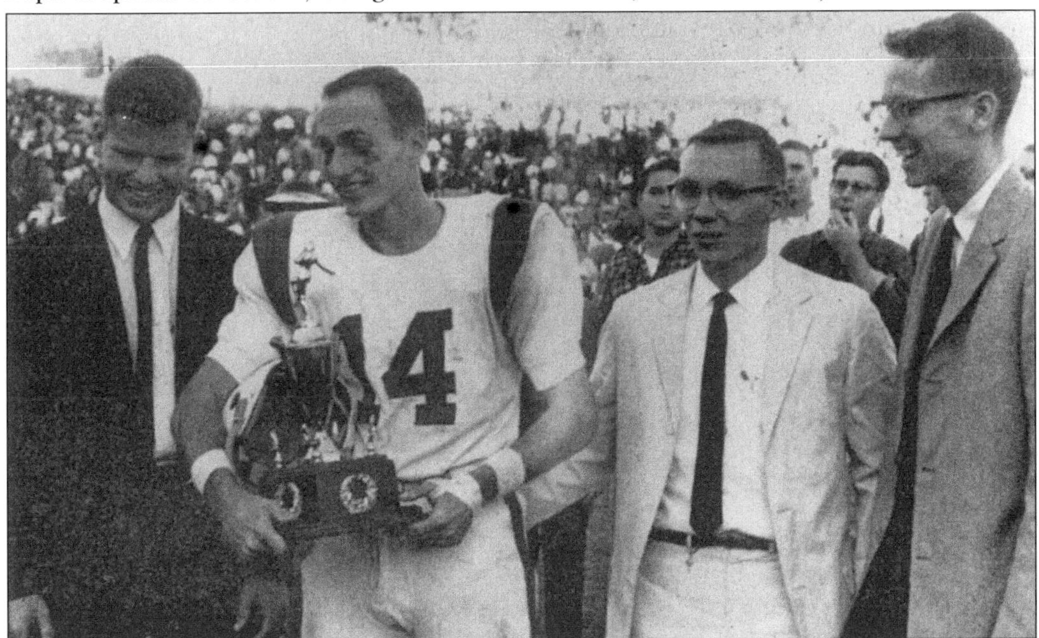

Junior-class officers presented UF quarterback Jimmy Dunn with the MVP award after the 1958 FSU game. He had run for two touchdowns and stopped an FSU player from scoring. (Courtesy University Archives, Dept. of Special Collections, George A. Smathers Libraries, Univ. of Florida.)

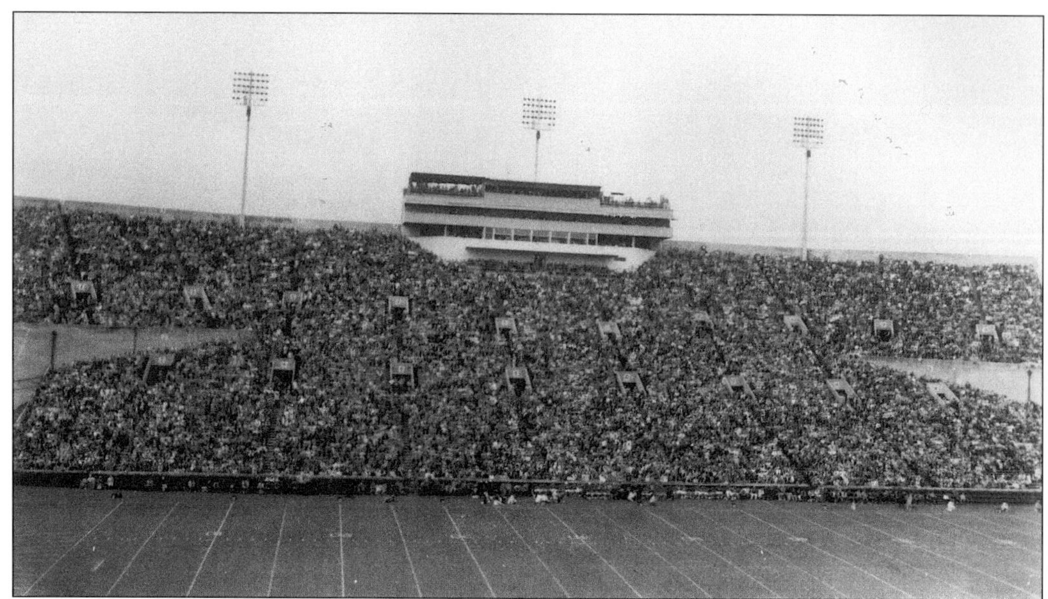

The addition of press boxes to the west side of the stadium in the 1950s gave reporters a modern facility from which they could report the game. The west side of the stadium houses a TV studio and the photo department of information services. (Courtesy University Archives, Dept. of Special Collections, George A. Smathers Libraries, Univ. of Florida.)

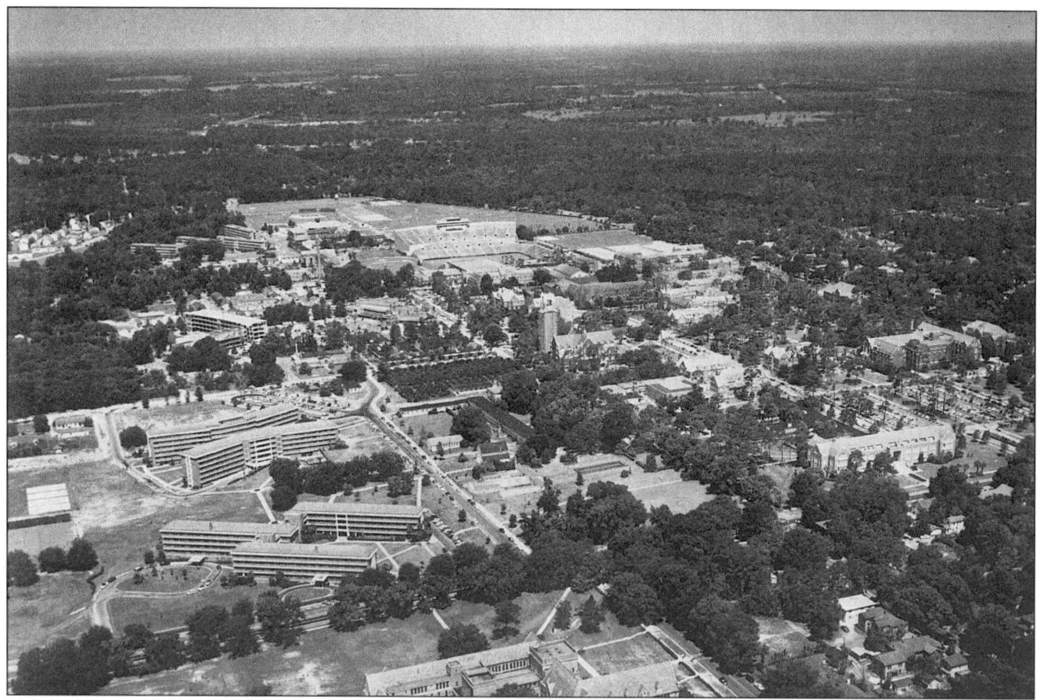

The UF campus continued to be full of trees as it expanded with more buildings. Today the 2,000-acre campus has 875 buildings, including 158 with classrooms and labs. The northeast part of the central campus has been named a Historic District on the National Register of Historic Places. (Courtesy Florida State Archives.)

Six

1960–1969: Coach Graves

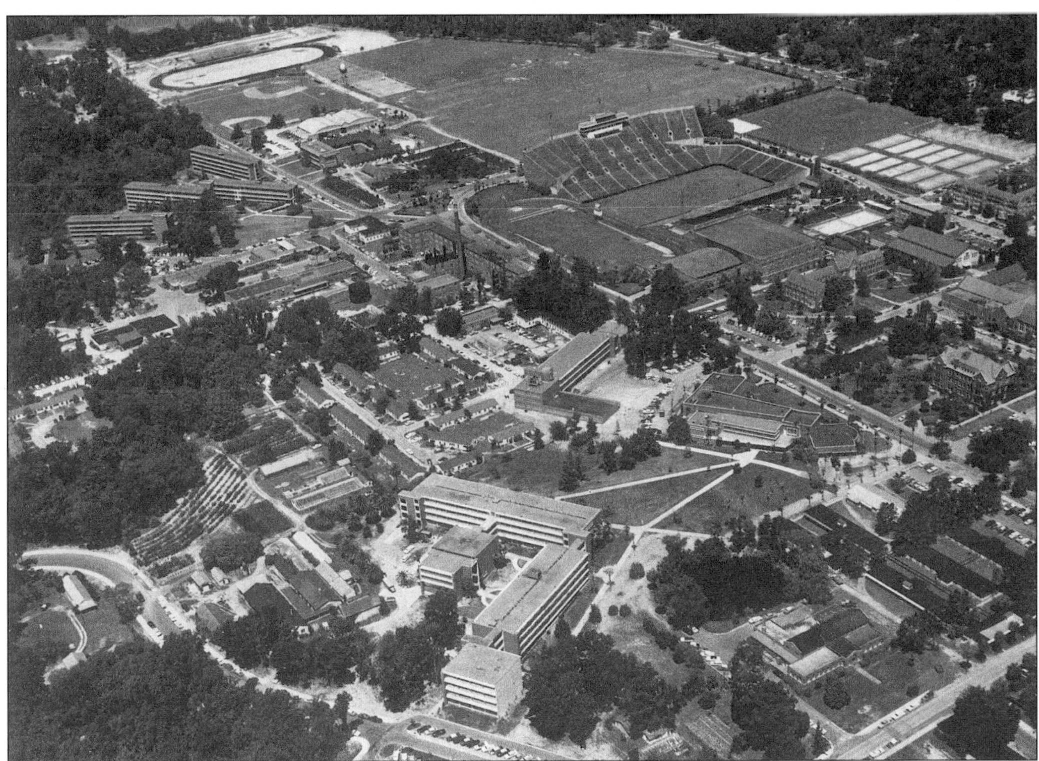

The UF campus in 1960 saw the hiring of Ray Graves, the team's 14th head coach, who would have a record of 70-31-4 in ten seasons (1960–1969). He took the team to five bowl games and won four of them, losing only to Missouri by two points in the 1966 Sugar Bowl, 20-18. (Courtesy Florida State Archives.)

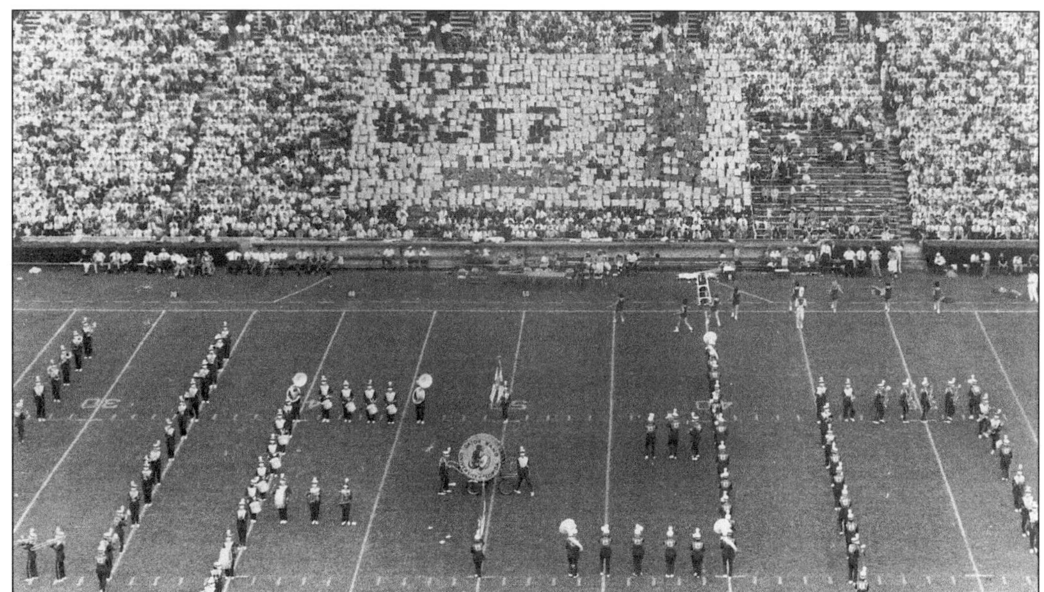

The halftime of a 1961 game at Florida Field had band members and cheerleaders performing at mid-field before a crowd that formed "pictures" in the stands by holding up different-colored cards. Here the students on the UF student side make a picture of a quarterback throwing the ball. (Courtesy Florida State Archives.)

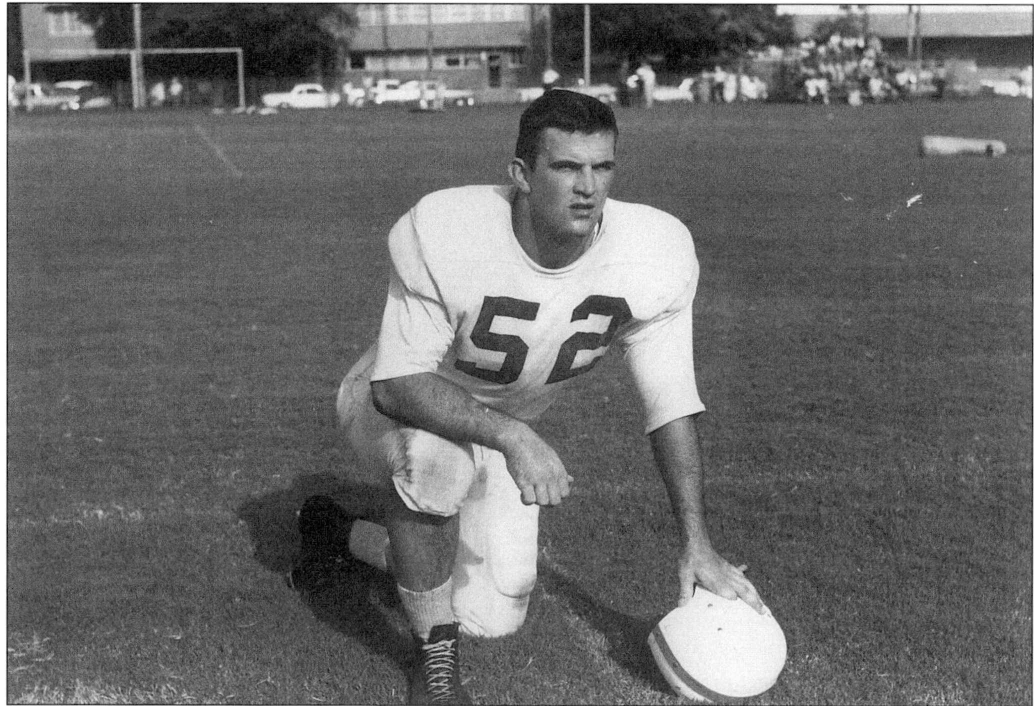

Center Bill Hood, an engineering major, was the 1960 Gator captain. The 1960 team went 9-2 for the most Gator wins in one season up to that point. They finished second in the SEC and played in only their third post-season bowl game ever, the Gator Bowl, in which they beat Baylor, 13-12. (Courtesy UF News & Public Affairs.)

Coach Graves talked with quarterback Mike McVay (#16) and halfback Don Deal (#21) at half-time. Graves had much experience to pass on. as a member of strong Tennessee teams (1939–41), a center and captain on the NFL's Philadelphia Eagles, line coach for the Tennessee Volunteers (1944–1945), and defensive assistant at Georgia Tech under Bobby Dodd (1947–1959). (Courtesy University Archives, Dept. of Special Collections, George A. Smathers Libraries, Univ. of Florida.)

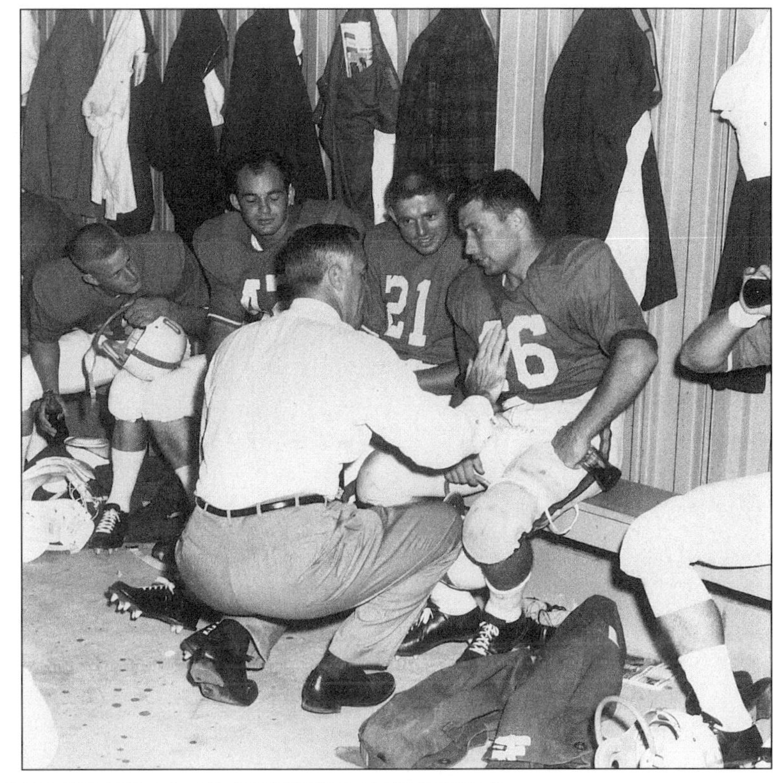

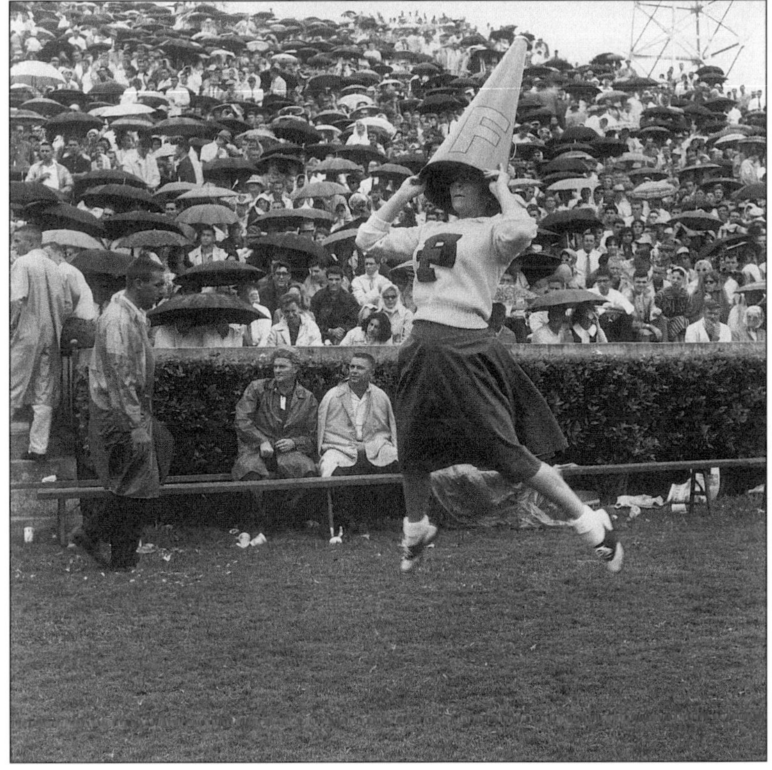

Cheerleaders in the rain in 1960 had a new use for their megaphones. Rain in the Swamp sometimes slowed the Gators, but not too much, especially in the high-powered offenses of the 1960s and 1990s. (Courtesy University Archives, Dept. of Special Collections, George A. Smathers Libraries, Univ. of Florida.)

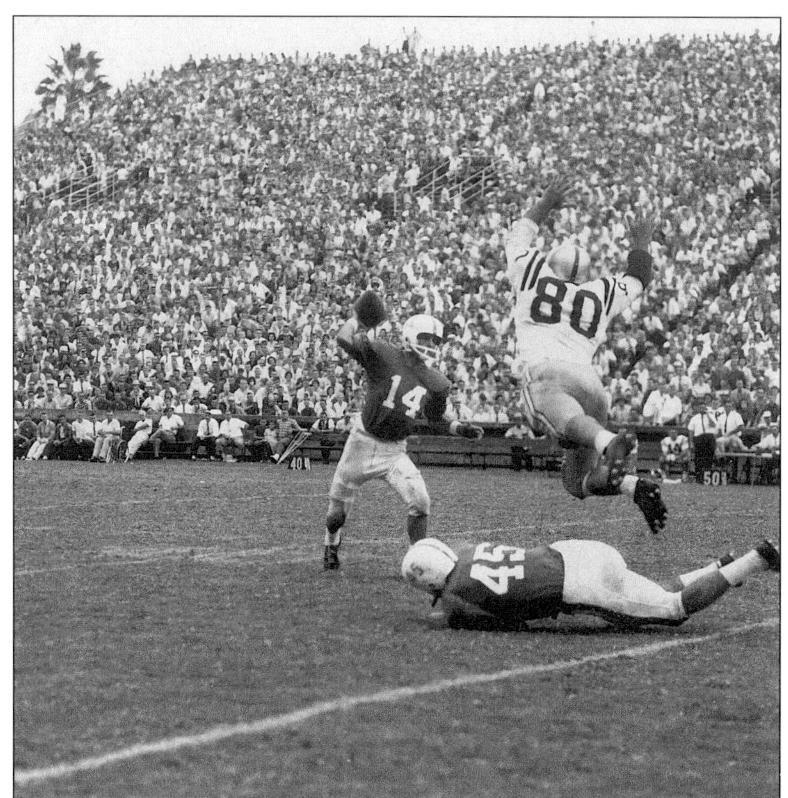

UF quarterback Larry Libertore threw a pass, after fullback Don Goodman blocked for him. Coach Graves introduced a high-scoring, passing offense, a system that produced prolific passers like Steve Spurrier and John Reaves, and wide receivers like Carlos Alvarez and Charles Casey. (Courtesy University Archives, Dept. of Special Collections, George A. Smathers Libraries, Univ. of Florida.)

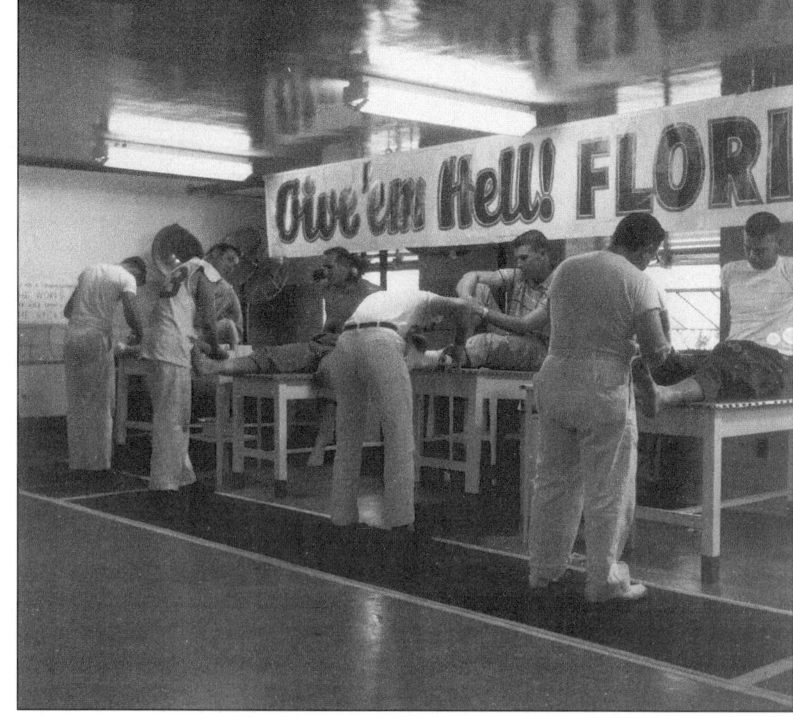

The UF training room was the place where trainers helped injured athletes recover from their injuries. (Courtesy University Archives, Dept. of Special Collections, George A. Smathers Libraries, Univ. of Florida.)

An early Gator mascot in 1961 would evolve into the modern-day Albert, to be joined by the female Alberta. Having an alligator for a mascot avoided the problems that other schools had, for example those that used a Native American for their mascot. (Courtesy University Archives, Dept. of Special Collections, George A. Smathers Libraries, Univ. of Florida.)

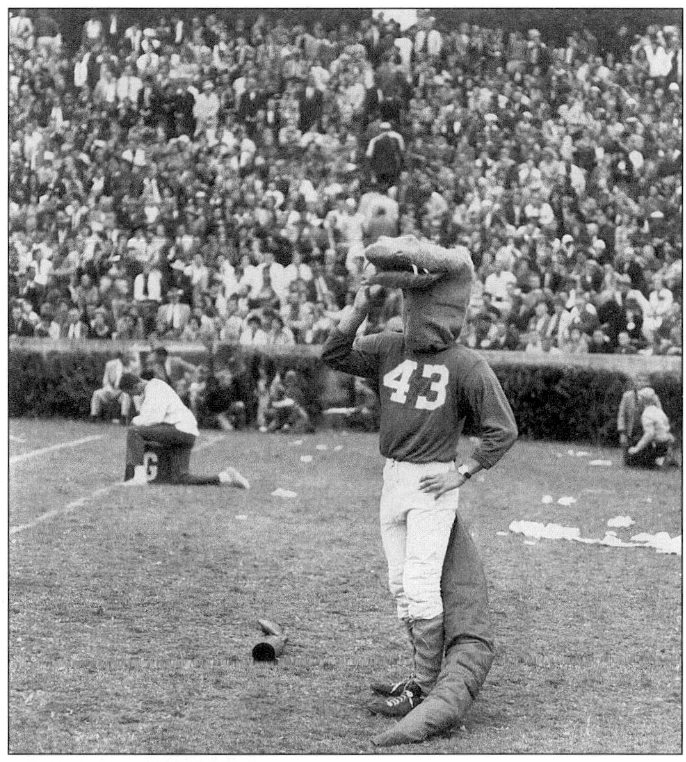

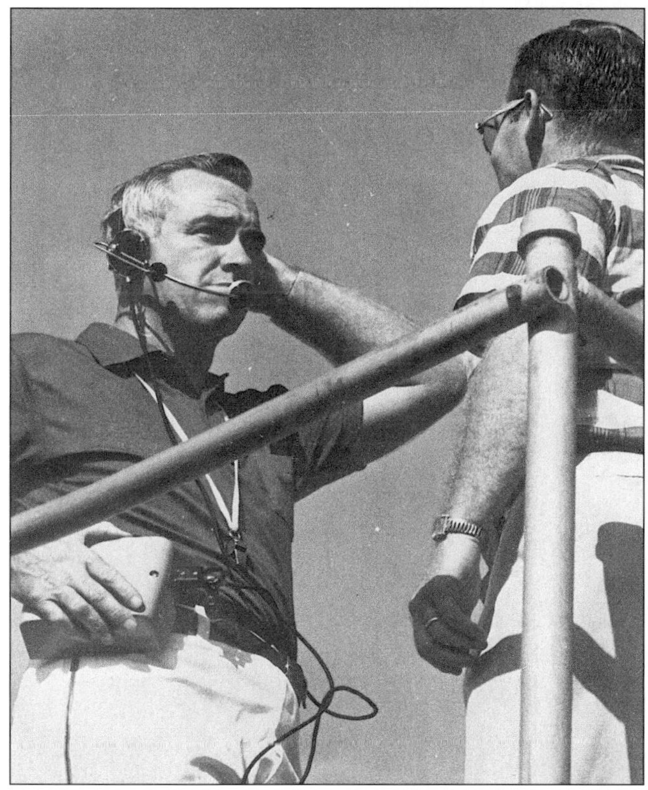

Coach Ray Graves, who compiled a record of 70-31-4 in ten years at UF (1960–1969), used a headset in the new tower over the practice field. After resigning as head coach and being replaced by Doug Dickey, Graves became athletic director at UF and directed all of the school's athletic programs in a fairness and honesty that always marked his style. (Courtesy Florida State Archives.)

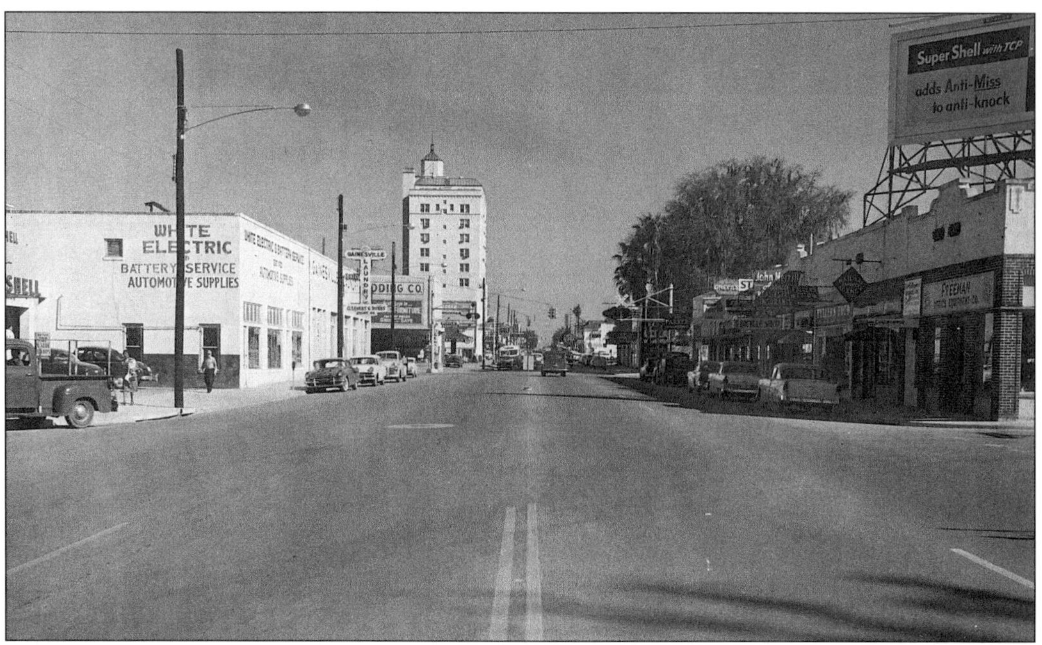

West University Avenue, down which homecoming parades have been marching since 1924, would be lined with thousands of spectators eager to see the many floats and bands. During "Gator Growl" each homecoming Friday evening, the seniors on the football field were introduced to the thousands of spectators at Florida Field. (Courtesy Florida State Archives.)

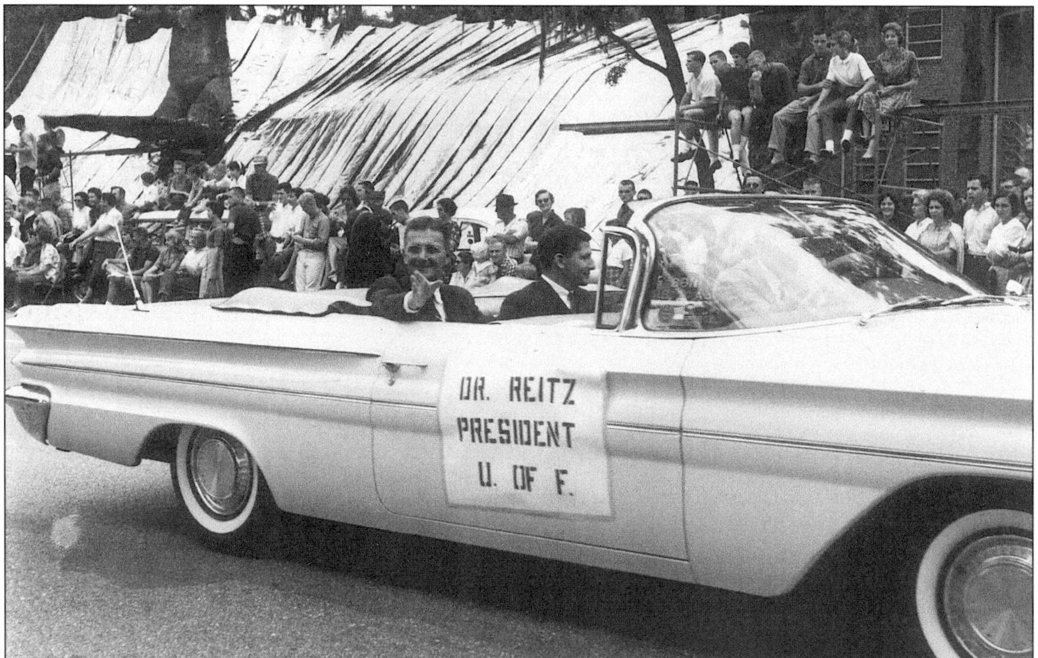

Dr. Reitz, shown here in the 1961 Homecoming parade, is honored in the naming of the student union after him. The UF presidents usually rode in that parade, which took place on the day before the football game. (Courtesy University Archives, Dept. of Special Collections, George A. Smathers Libraries, Univ. of Florida.)

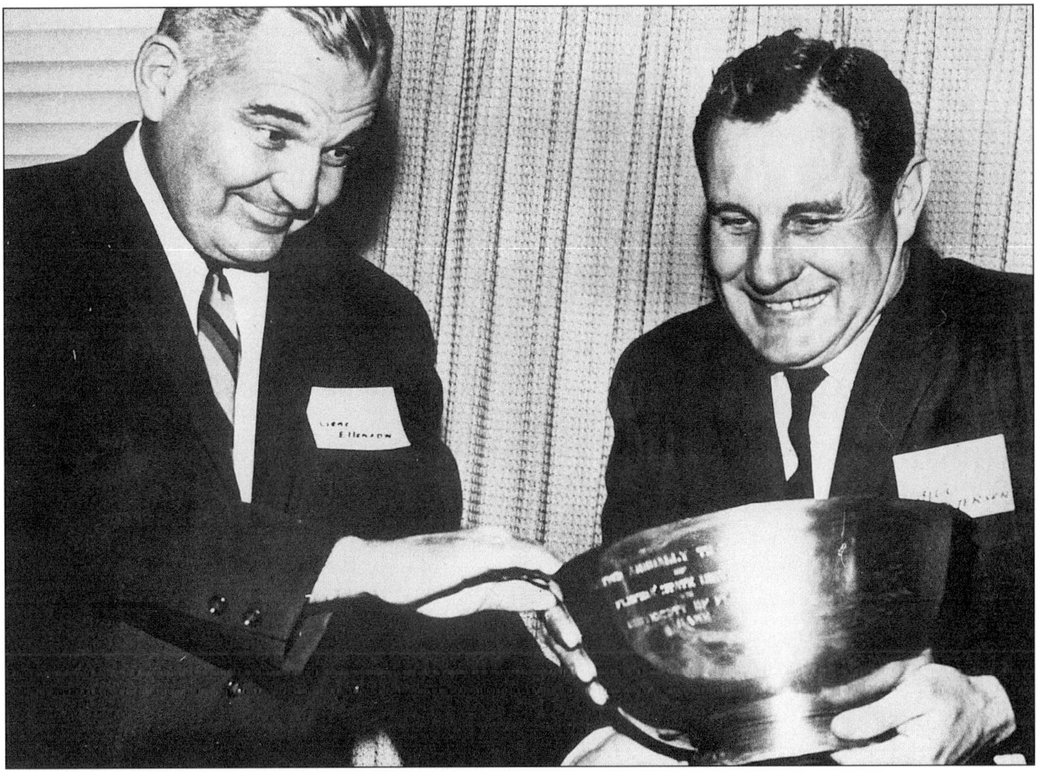

In 1961, Assistant UF Coach Gene Ellenson and FSU Coach Bill Peterson looked over the Governor's Cup that goes to the winner of the annual intra-state game. The Gators would not lose to FSU until 1964, although the two teams tied in 1961. (Courtesy Florida State Archives.)

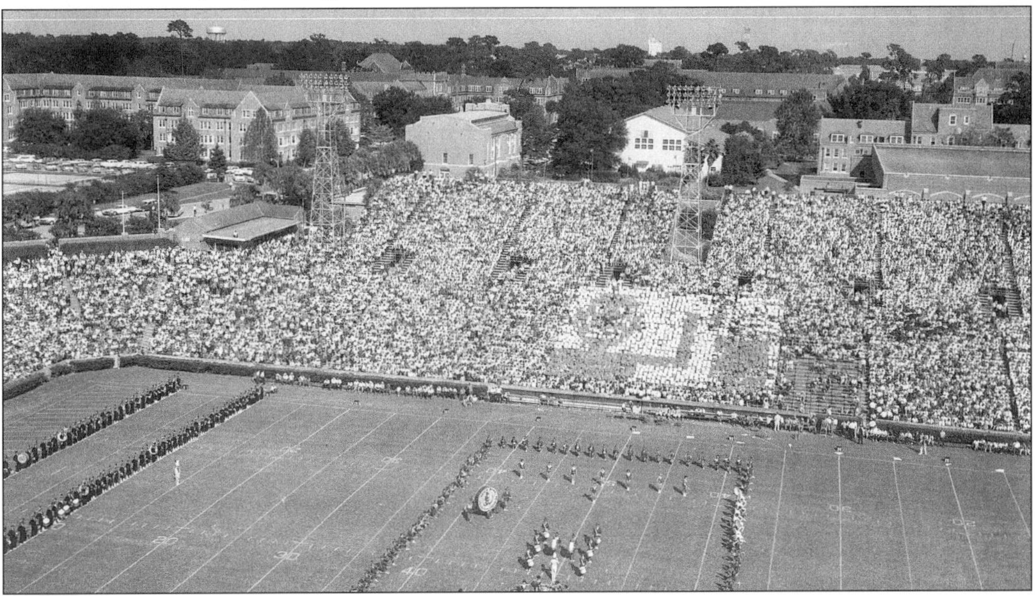

The UF-FSU players took a break in the 1961 game in Gainesville, one which ended in a tie and showed that FSU was approaching the high football level that UF had attained. (Courtesy Florida State Archives.)

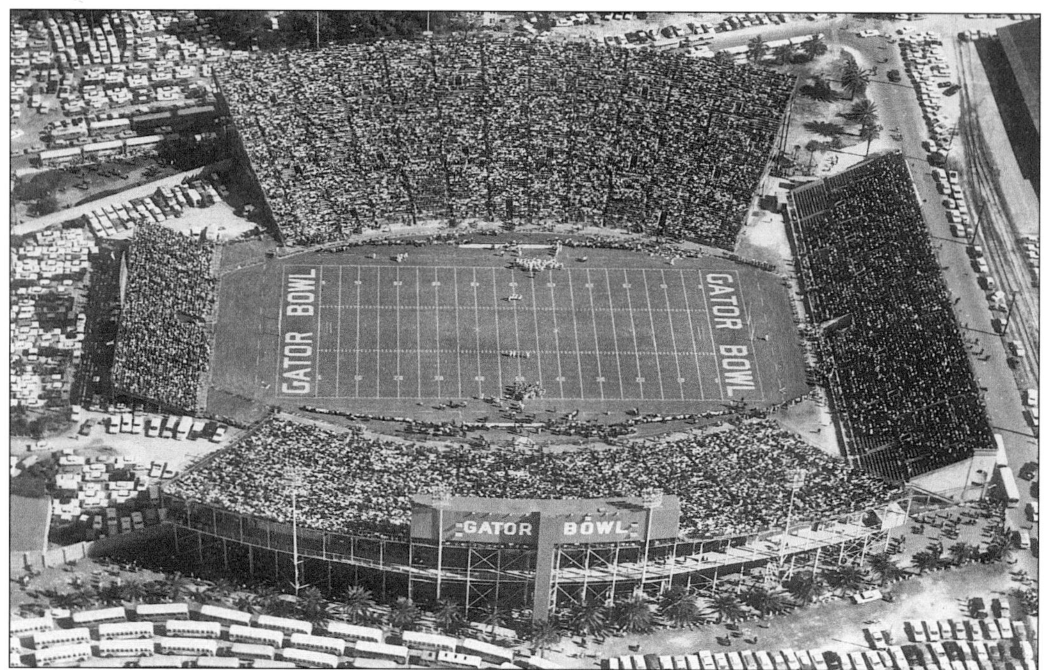

The Gator Bowl in Jacksonville would be the most popular bowl for the Gators, who played there eight times from 1953 to 1999, winning six times, including the team's first bowl ever, the 1953 win over Tulsa. (Courtesy Florida State Archives.)

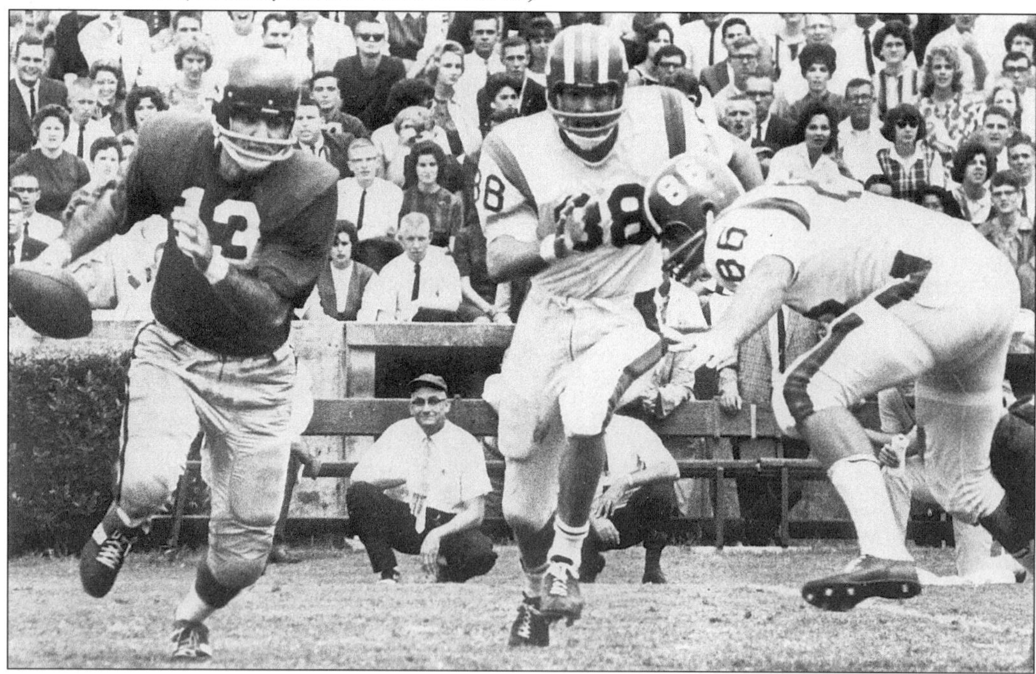

Gator defensive players Randy Jackson (#88) and Bob Lindsey (#86) go after the Richmond quarterback in a 1963 game in Gainesville. The Gators won that game and ended the season with a 6-3-1 record, including wins over Alabama, Georgia, Miami, and Florida State. (Courtesy Florida State Archives.)

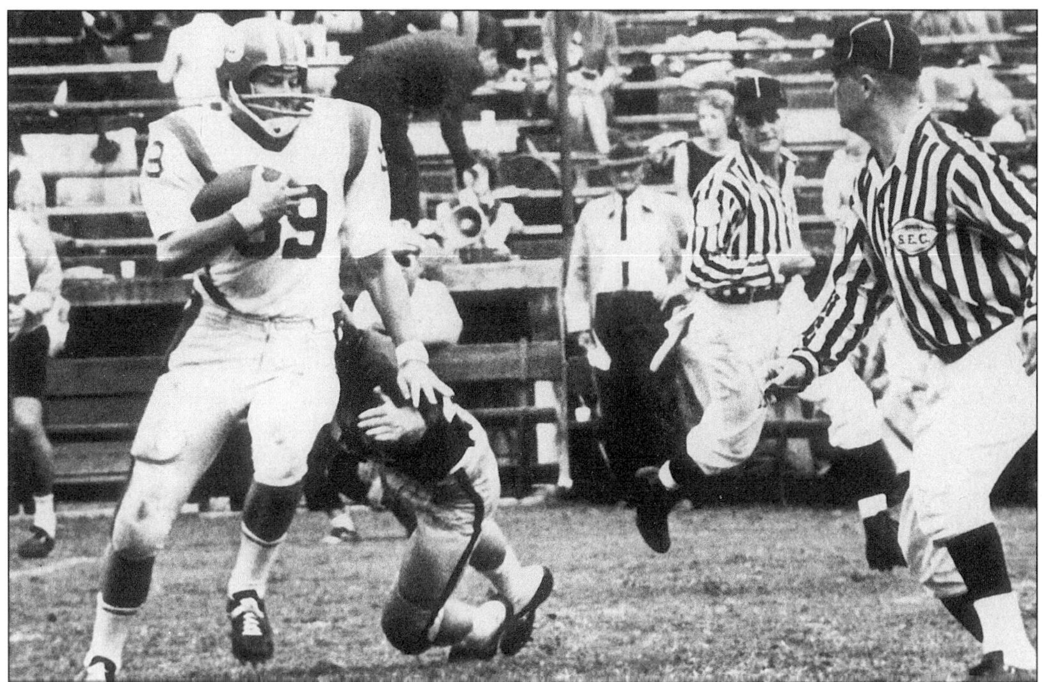

End Charles Casey, seen here running in the 1963 game against Richmond, won the 1965 Forrest K. (Fergie) Ferguson Award given annually to the senior football player whom his fellow lettermen vote as one who displays outstanding leadership, character, and courage. (Courtesy Florida State Archives.)

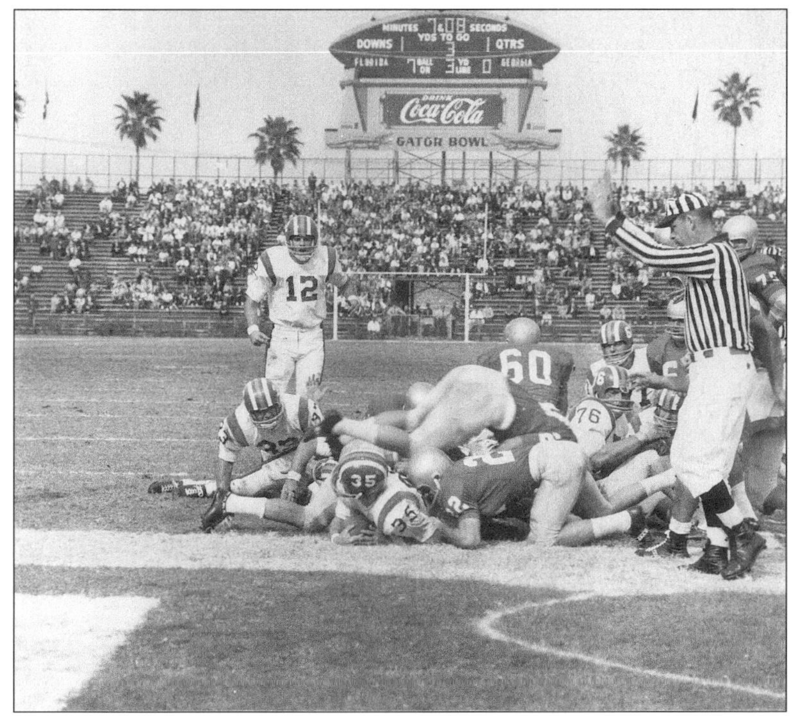

Fullback Larry Dupree, seen here scoring against Georgia in 1963, was the leading Gator rusher for three years (1962–1964) and led the SEC with 604 yards in 1962, averaging 5.2 yards a carry. His 66 yards of rushing and a touchdown pass helped the Gators defeat Penn State in the 1962 Gator Bowl, 17-7. (Courtesy University Archives, Dept. of Special Collections, George A. Smathers Libraries, Univ. of Florida.)

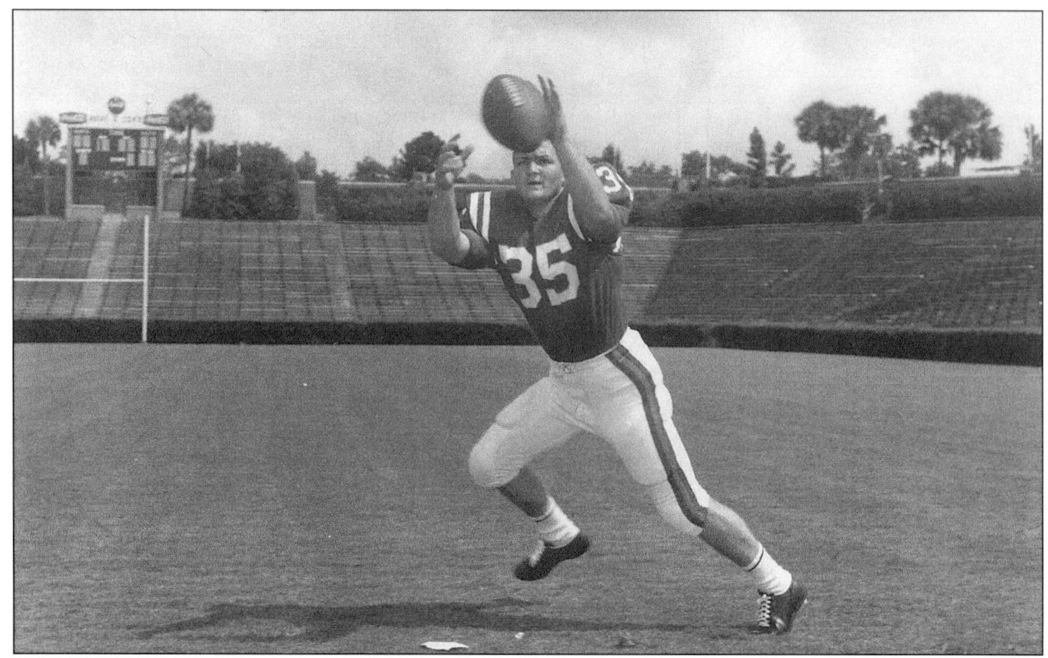

Larry Dupree, the first Gator running back to earn first-team All-America honors (1964), is second on the all-time Florida rushing list with 1,725 yards in his three seasons. He served as the captain of the 1964 team, which had a 7-3 record, scoring 181 points and holding their opponents to only 98. (Courtesy University Archives, Dept. of Special Collections, George A. Smathers Libraries, Univ. of Florida.)

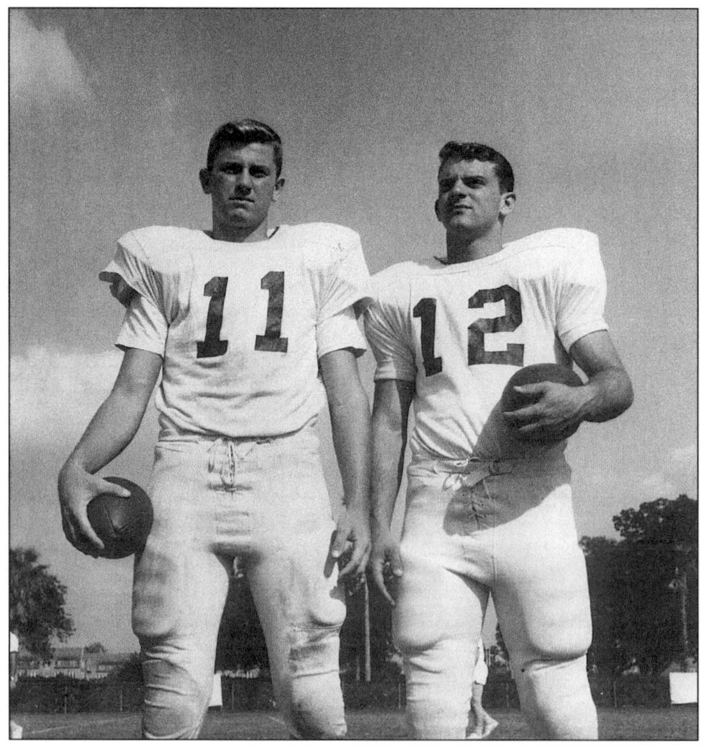

Sophomore Steve Spurrier (#11) and senior Tommy Shannon (#12) shared quarterbacking duties in 1964. A great player on the 1964 team, Bruce Bennett set UF's career-record for interceptions (13—which is now fourth on UF's list) and was a first-team All-American in 1965, before starring in the Canadian Football League for ten years. (Courtesy University Archives, Dept. of Special Collections, George A. Smathers Libraries, Univ. of Florida.)

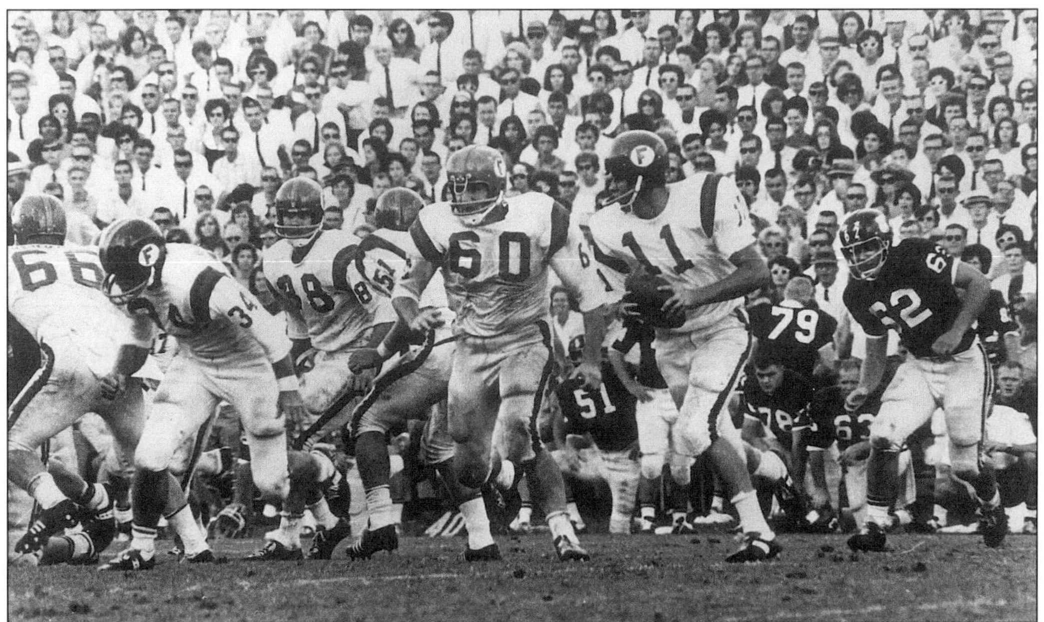

Steve Spurrier (#11) runs behind Larry Beckman (#66), Marquis Baeszler (#34), Randy Jackson (#88), Bill Carr (#51), and Jim Benson (#60) in 1964. Spurrier, Beckman, Carr, and Benson made the All-SEC team at least once in their Gator careers. (Courtesy University Archives, Dept. of Special Collections, George A. Smathers Libraries, Univ. of Florida.)

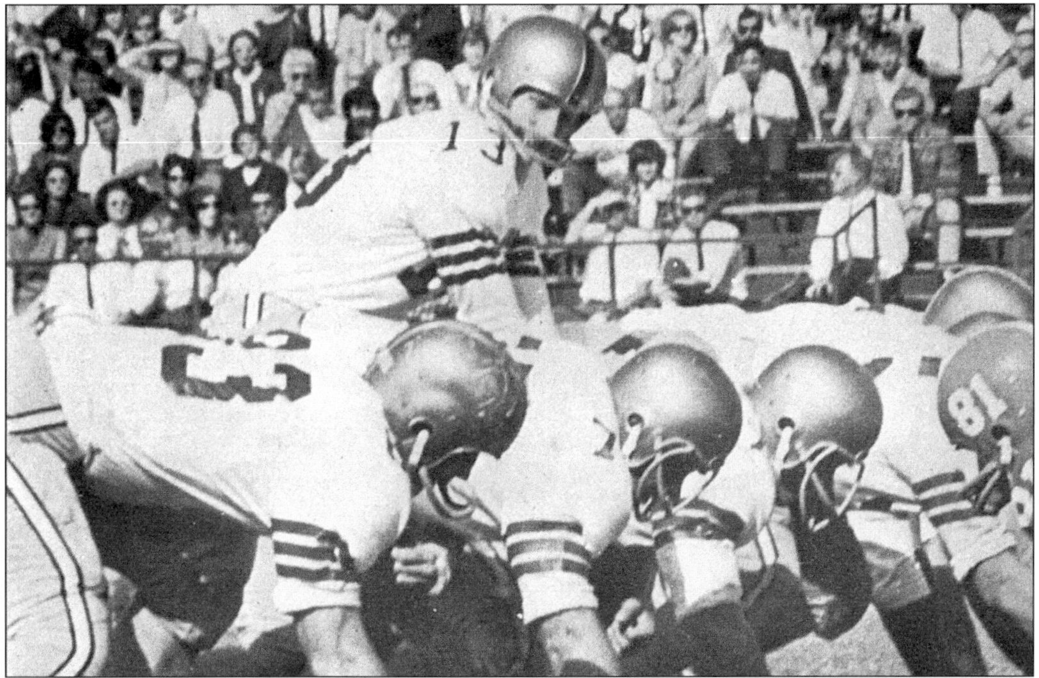

The Gators lost to FSU for the first time in 1964, the first time the UF-FSU game was played in Tallahassee. The Seminoles might have been angered when the Gator players wore "Go For Seven" on their jerseys, referring to the fact that the Gators had either won (five games) or tied (one game) in the previous six games. (Courtesy Florida State Archives.)

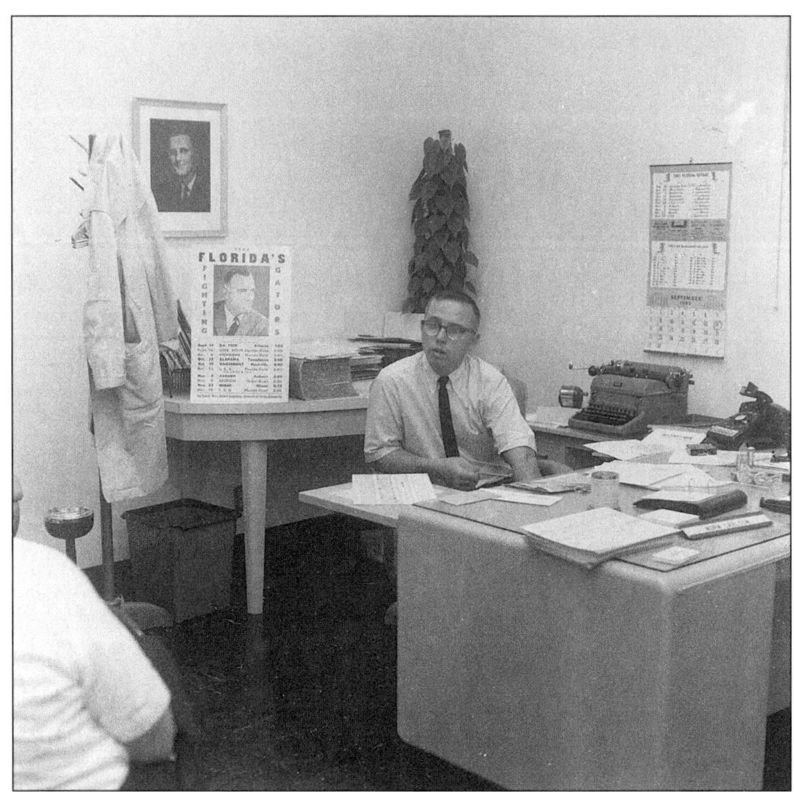

Norm Carlson, pictured here in 1964, earned his bachelor's degree at UF (1956), worked for the *Atlanta Journal Constitution* as a sportswriter (1956–1959), and served as sports information director at Auburn University (1959–1963). He has been UF's assistant athletic director in charge of Communications and has also been the sports information department's historian. (Courtesy UF News & Public Affairs.)

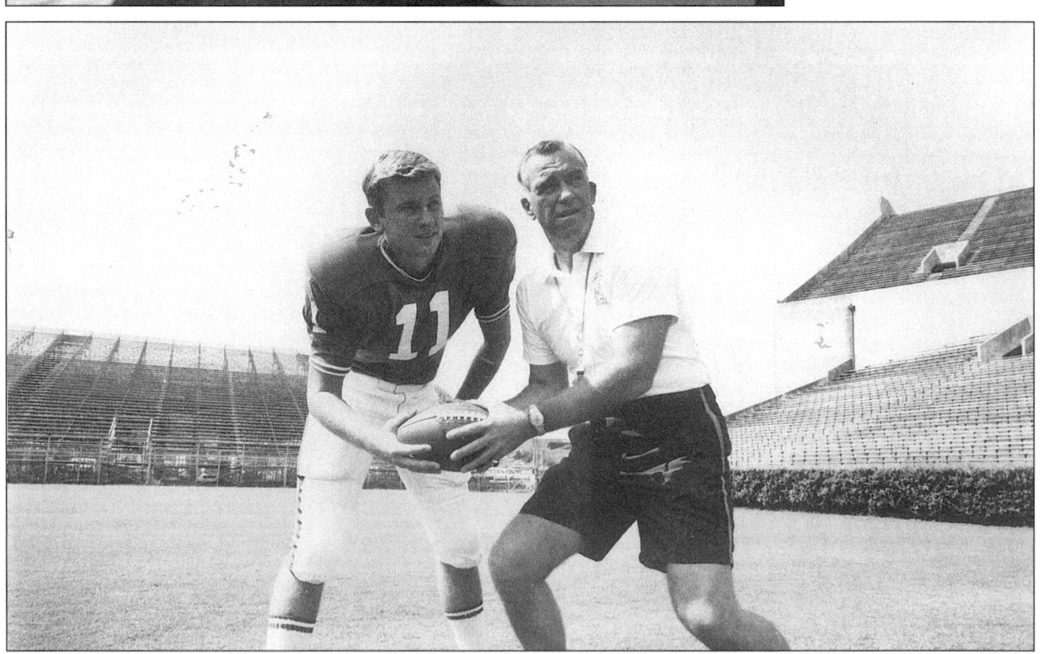

Spurrier and Coach Graves had a 7-4 record in 1965, but lost to Missouri, 20-18, in the Sugar Bowl. After Spurrier set five records in that game, he was named MVP, the first time in 32 years that the MVP was a player on the losing side. (Courtesy University Archives, Dept. of Special Collections, George A. Smathers Libraries, Univ. of Florida.)

Pepper Rodgers, seen here to the left of Coach Graves, was one of many Gator assistant coaches who went on to become head coaches at universities throughout the country. (Courtesy University Archives, Dept. of Special Collections, George A. Smathers Libraries, Univ. of Florida.)

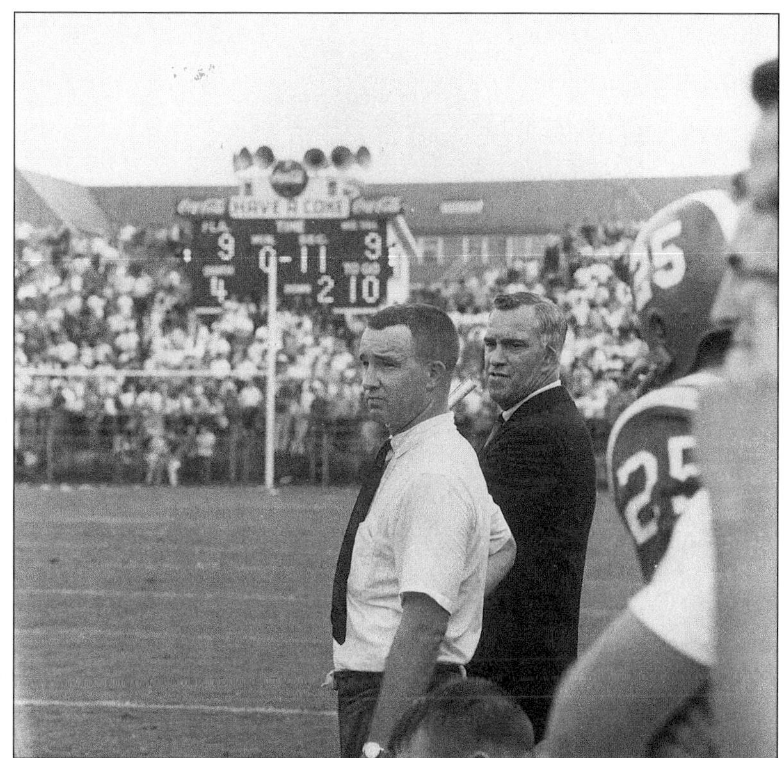

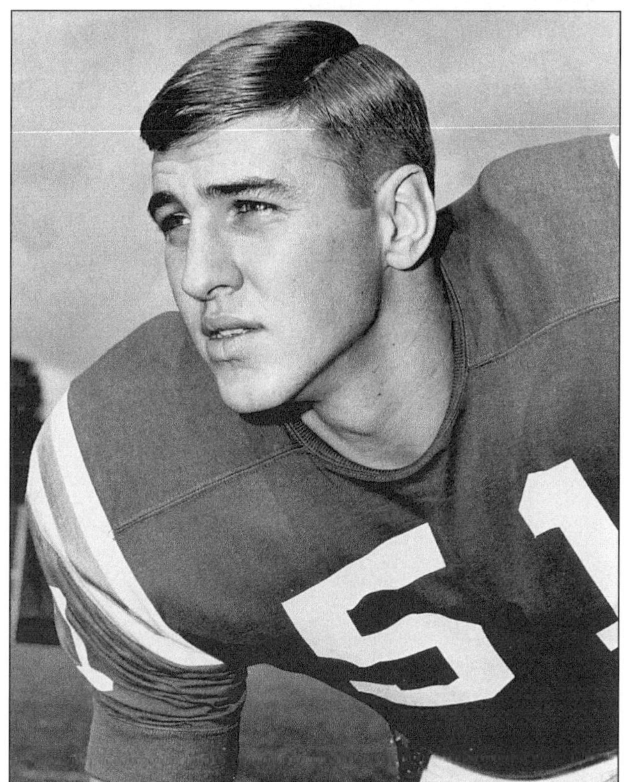

Center Bill Carr, who lettered at UF for three years (1964–1966), started at center in 32 consecutive games, earning All-American honors in his senior season. He was drafted by the New Orleans Saints in the NFL, but an ROTC commitment prevailed, and he served in the U.S. Army in Korea. He was later UF's athletic director for seven years (1980–1986). (Courtesy UF News & Public Affairs.)

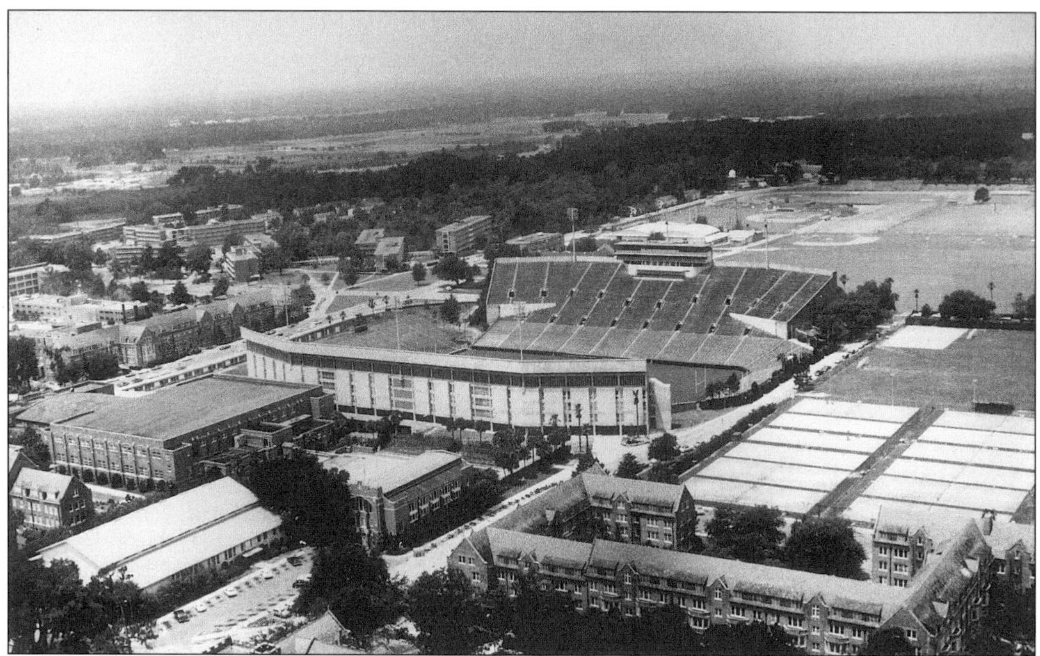

Florida Field's capacity was increased to 62,800 in 1966. An athletic dorm, Yon Hall, was also built for the players, although today the athletes live in residence halls throughout the campus as part of the school's commitment that the athletes are, first of all, students. (Courtesy University Archives, Dept. of Special Collections, George A. Smathers Libraries, Univ. of Florida.)

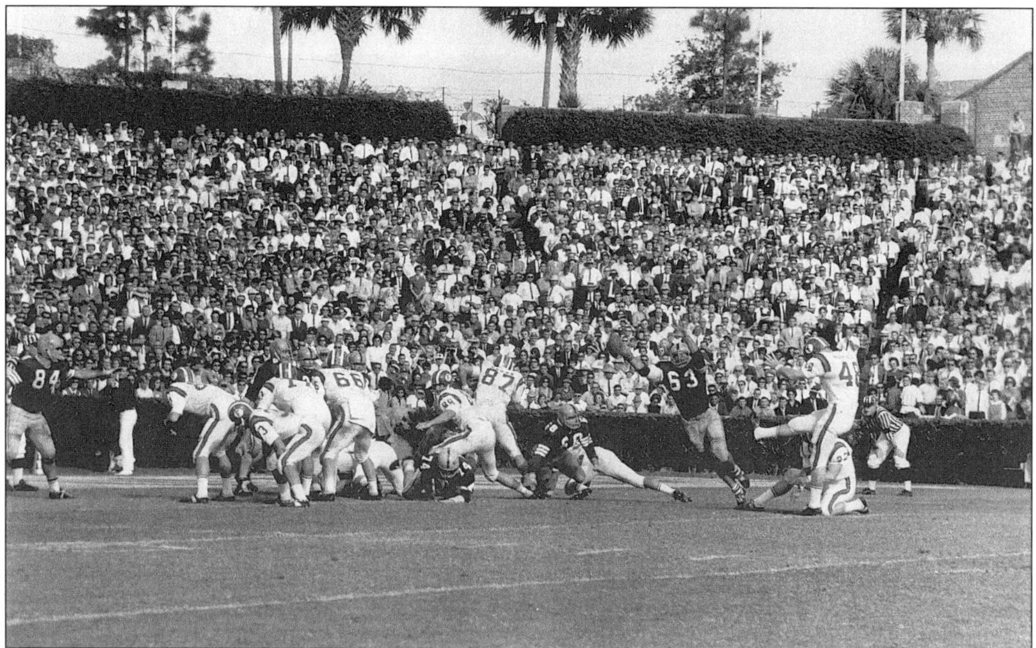

The stadium is shown here packed with fans watching Wayne Barfield (#48) kick a field goal in 1966 (the year that Steve Spurrier won the prestigious Heisman Trophy), easily beating out Purdue quarterback Bob Griese. (Courtesy University Archives, Dept. of Special Collections, George A. Smathers Libraries, Univ. of Florida.)

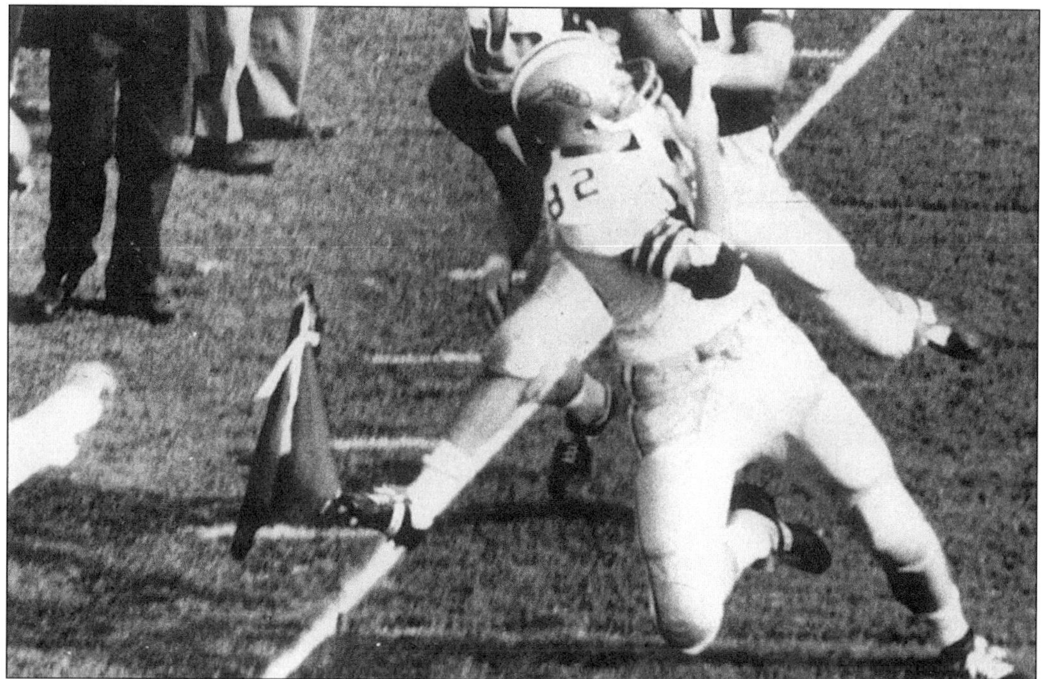

When UF played FSU in Tallahassee in 1966, the Seminoles' Lane Fenner seemed to catch the winning touchdown, but the field judge called him out of bounds. The "Lane Fenner Game" is one of the most controversial in the long series between the two teams. (Courtesy Florida State Archives.)

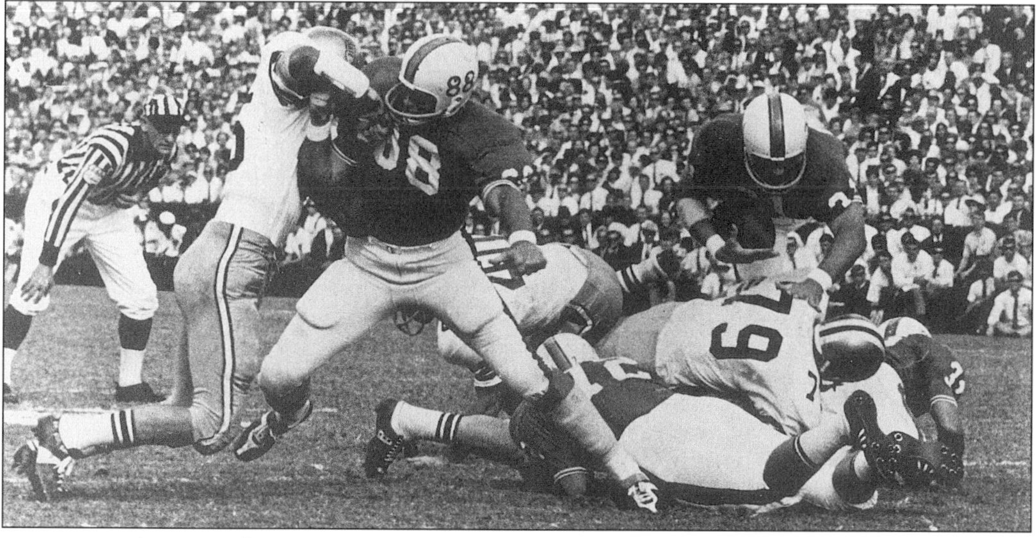

UF's Jim Yarbrough (#88) blocks for Tom Christian (#31) in 1967, a year in which UF had a disappointing 6-4 record. Yarbrough, who lettered three years (1966–1968) and was named to UF's Team of the Century as a tight end, later played in the NFL as an offensive tackle (1969–1977) for the Detroit Lions and Houston Oilers. (Courtesy University Archives, Dept. of Special Collections, George A. Smathers Libraries, Univ. of Florida.)

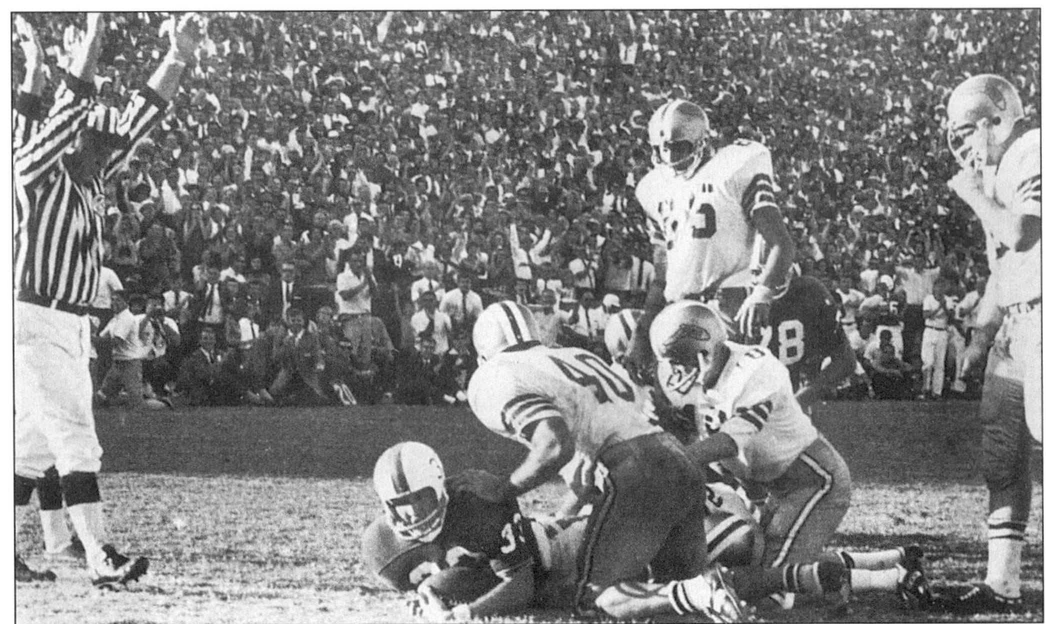

Fullback Larry Smith, seen here scoring in 1967, led the Gators in rushing for three years (1966–1968) and the SEC once (1966). He made first-team All-American (1968) and is currently seventh on the career yardage list for Gator runners (2,186 yards). He played in the NFL for the Rams (1969–1973) and Redskins (1974), before practicing law in Tampa. (Courtesy University Archives, Dept. of Special Collections, George A. Smathers Libraries, Univ. of Florida.)

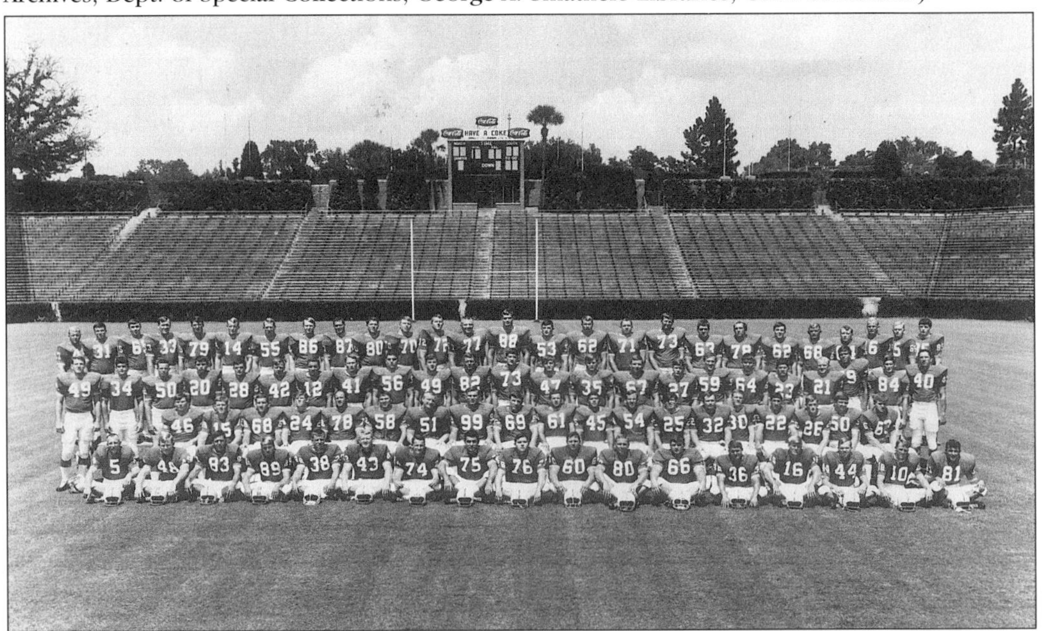

The 1967 team included wide receiver Richard Trapp (#44, third from the right in the first line). In the Georgia game that year, Trapp eluded seven would-be tacklers on a 52-yard touchdown run, a feat that Coach Graves called "the greatest individual effort I've ever seen on the football field." (Courtesy University Archives, Dept. of Special Collections, George A. Smathers Libraries, Univ. of Florida.)

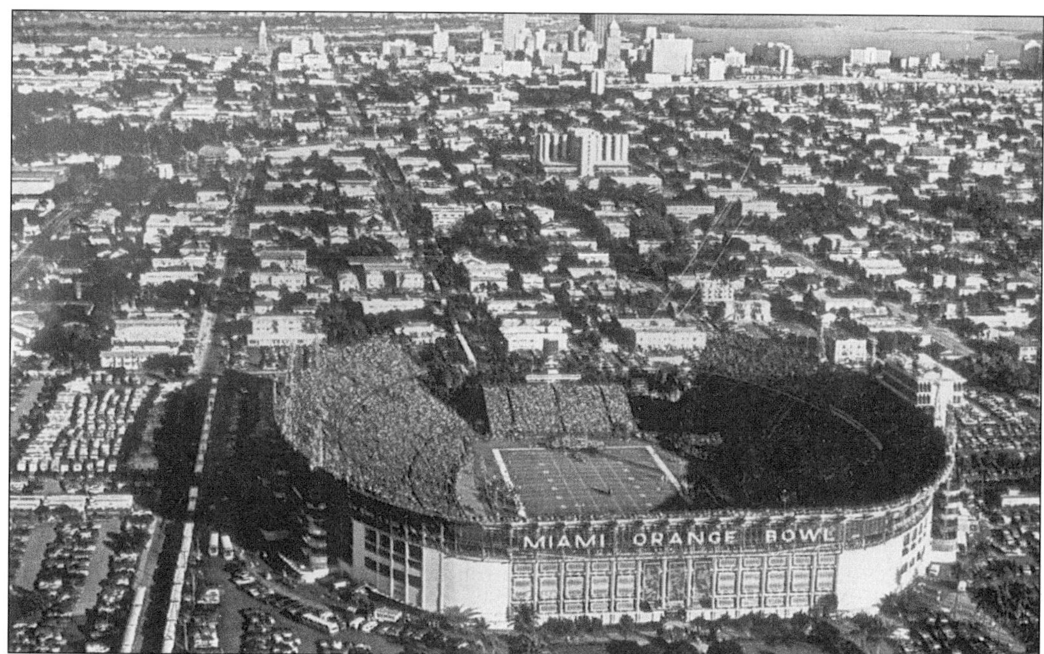

The Orange Bowl in Miami was where the Gators beat both Georgia Tech, 27-12 in 1967, and then Syracuse, 31-10 in 1999. In the first game, UF's Larry Smith set a bowl record for his 94-yard touchdown run, despite almost losing his pants along the way. (Courtesy Florida State Archives.)

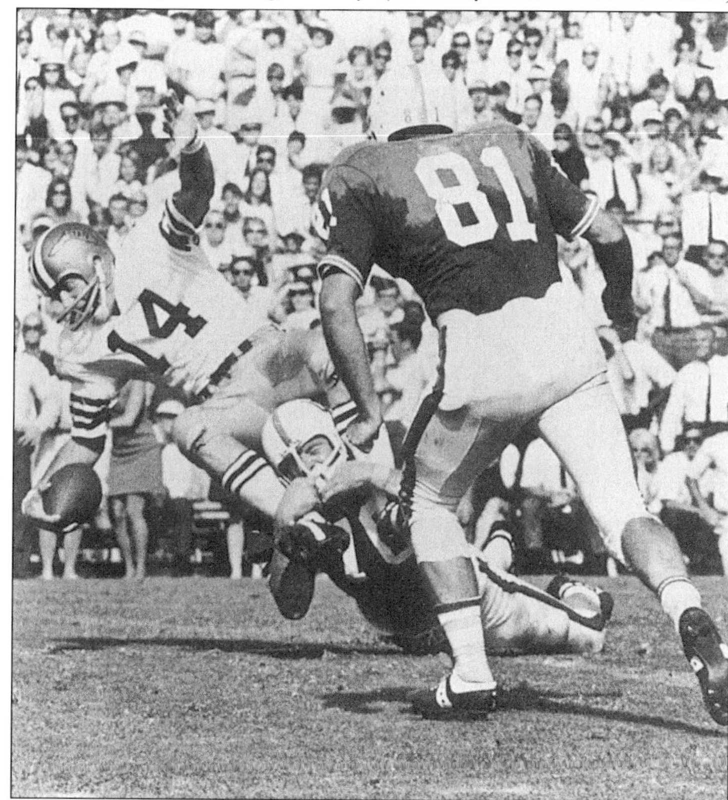

UF's Mike Healey (#70) and Britt Skirvanek (#81) tackle FSU's Bill Cappleman (#14) in the 1968 game between the Gators and the Seminoles, a game that would begin an eight-game win streak for UF. (Courtesy University Archives, Dept. of Special Collections, George A. Smathers Libraries, Univ. of Florida.)

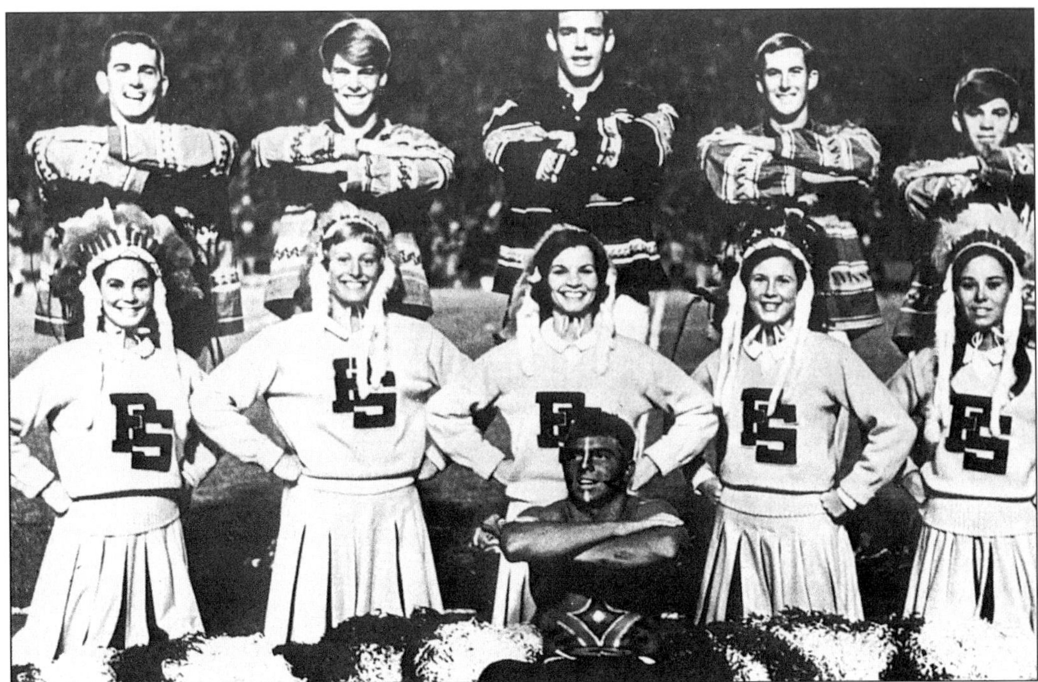

FSU's use of a Seminole mascot would be controversial in the 1990s when some thought that using a Native American for a mascot was inappropriate, whereas the Gator alligator mascot has never had that kind of controversy. (Courtesy Florida State Archives.)

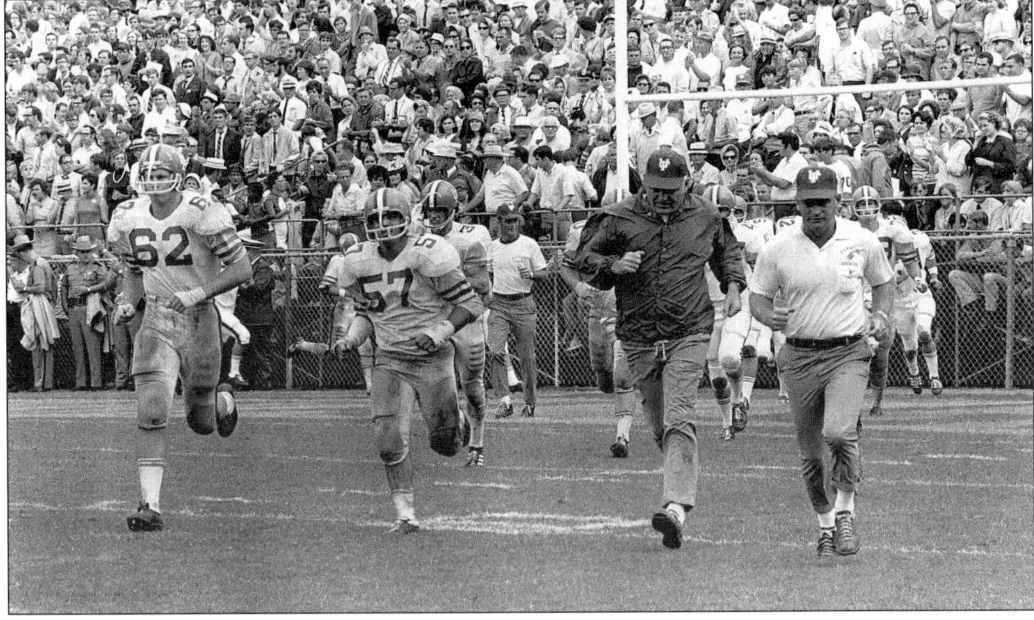

Coach Gene Ellenson, in the dark jacket, leads the team onto the field before another packed stadium in 1969. On the third offensive play of the season, UF's quarterback John Reaves threw a TD pass to fellow sophomore Carlos Alvarez, beginning a 9-1-1 season that would see the Gators score 329 points, the second highest in UF history to that point, while holding opponents to only 187. (Courtesy UF News & Public Affairs.)

Quarterback John Reaves was a first-team All-American (1971), set the SEC record for touchdowns (56), and finished as the all-time leading passer in the SEC and NCAA with 7,581 yards. He played in the NFL for the Eagles (1972–1974), Bengals (1975–1978), Vikings (1979), and Oilers (1981), as well as for Tampa in the USFL (1983–1985) under Coach Spurrier, before working as an assistant coach at UF (1990–1994). (Courtesy UF News & Public Affairs.)

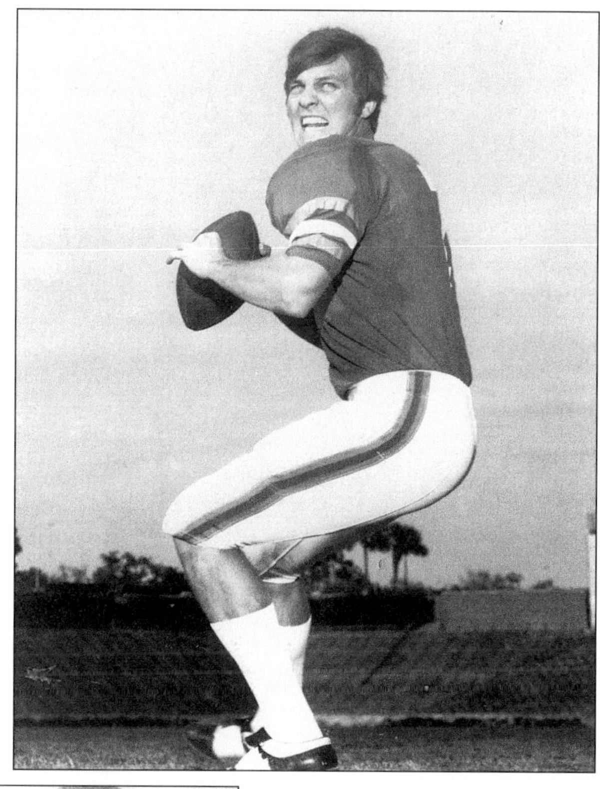

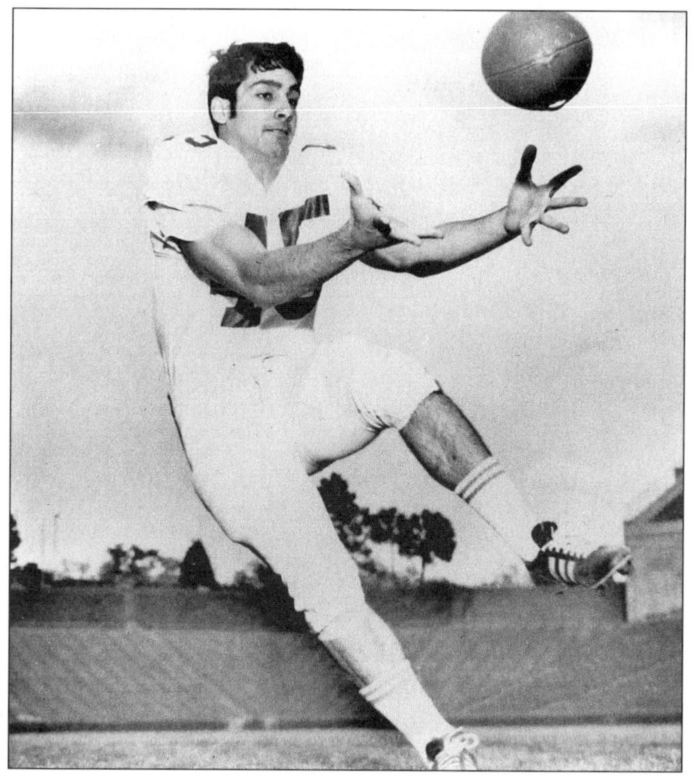

Carlos Alvarez, who lettered at Florida for three years (1969–1971), is the leading UF receiver with 172 catches, and is a wide receiver on the UF Team of the Century. His 88 catches in 1969 set a record that was only broken in 1999. He was a first-team All-American that year, after he caught 88 passes for 1,329 yards and 12 touchdowns, all still Gator records. He is a lawyer today in Tallahassee. (Courtesy UF News & Public Affairs.)

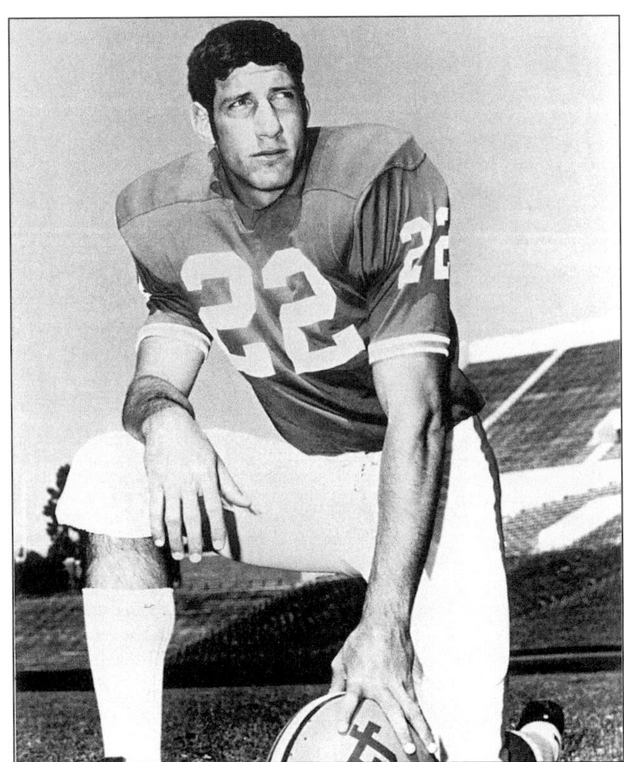

Defensive back Steve Tannen, a first-team All-American in 1969, is tied today for fifth place with Walter Mayberry, Wayne Fields, and Louis Oliver for career interceptions (11). He returned four punts for touchdowns during his Gator career (1967–1969), before playing in the NFL for the Jets (1970–1974) and becoming an actor in Hollywood and New York. He now works in the construction business in Los Angeles. (Courtesy UF News & Public Affairs.)

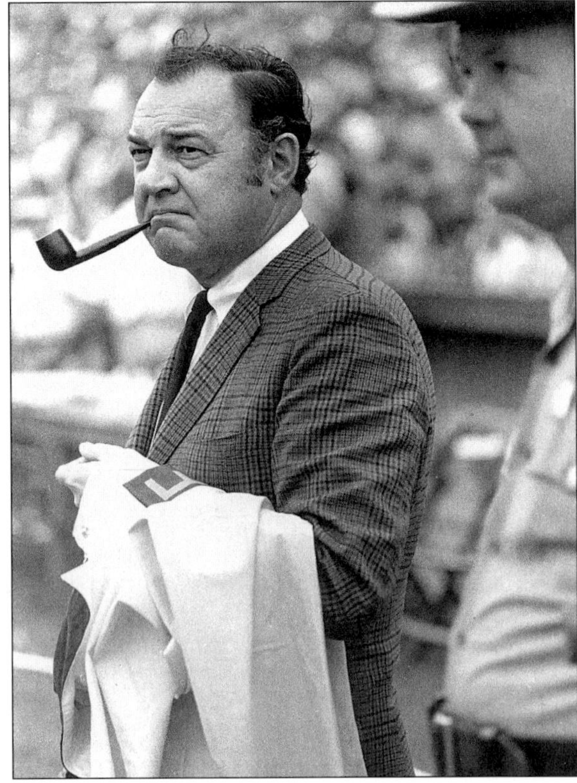

Governor Claude Kirk, shown here in 1969, would try to be neutral during the annual Gator-Seminole football clash, especially since the two teams each had thousands of fans throughout the state. (Courtesy University Archives, Dept. of Special Collections, George A. Smathers Libraries, Univ. of Florida.)

Seven

1970–1978: Coach Dickey

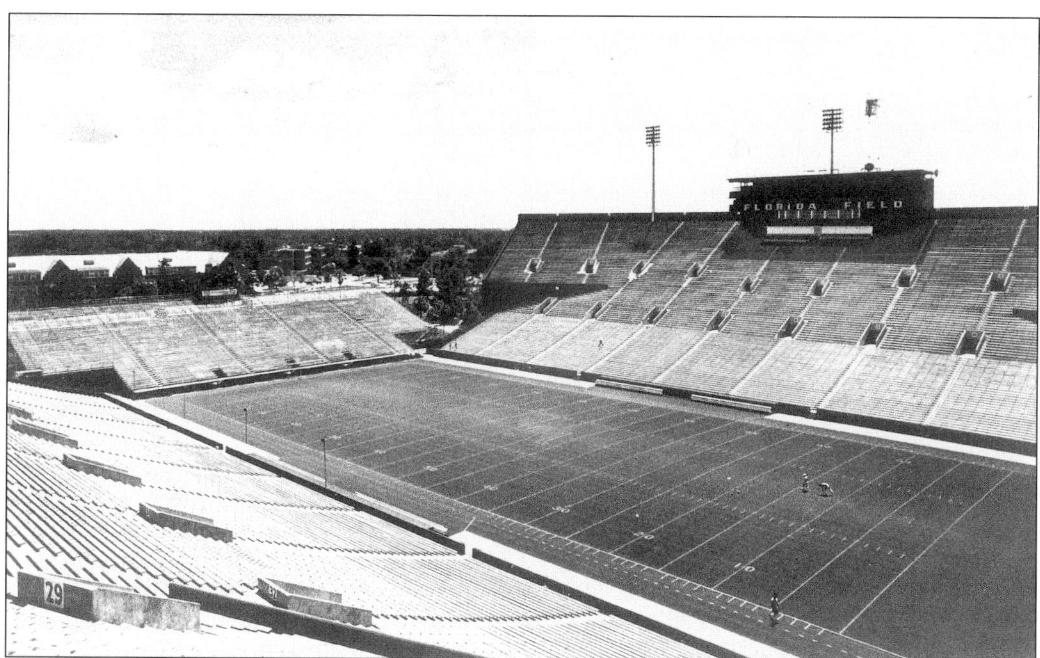

The UF stadium in the 1970s saw a change in the style of play, from the passing game of the Ray Graves era to one of running and the wishbone offense that Doug Dickey preferred. (Courtesy University Archives, Dept. of Special Collections, George A. Smathers Libraries, Univ. of Florida.)

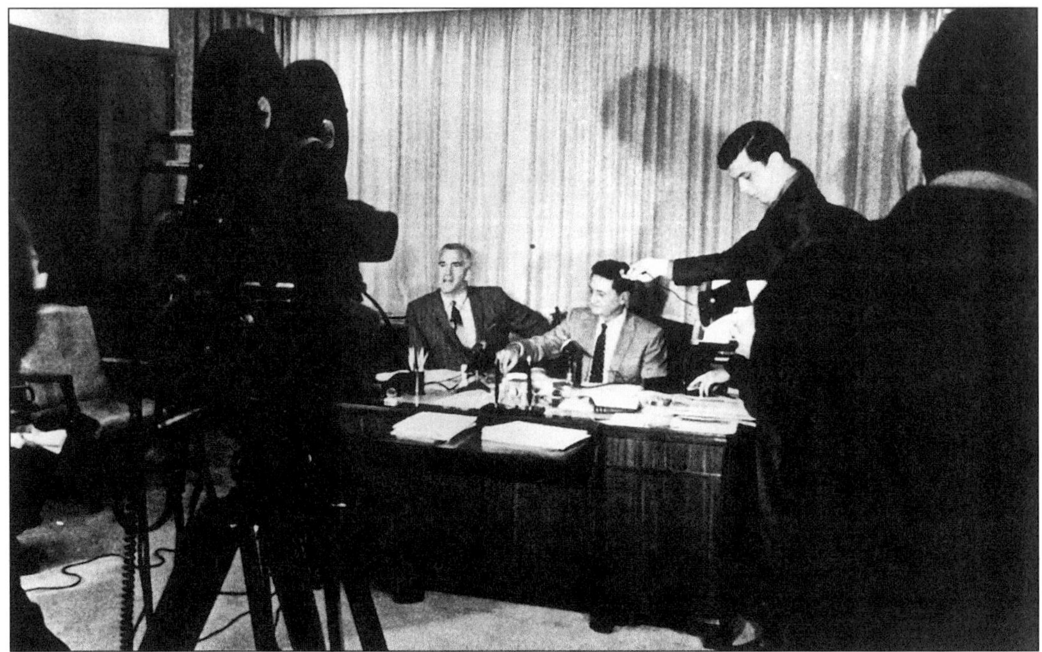

At a press conference, President O'Connell—with outgoing Coach Ray Graves on the left—named Doug Dickey head coach in 1970. Dickey, the school's 15th head coach, lasted nine years (1970–1978) and compiled a 58-43-2 record. He had also played quarterback for the Gators (1952–1953). (Courtesy University Archives, Dept. of Special Collections, George A. Smathers Libraries, Univ. of Florida.)

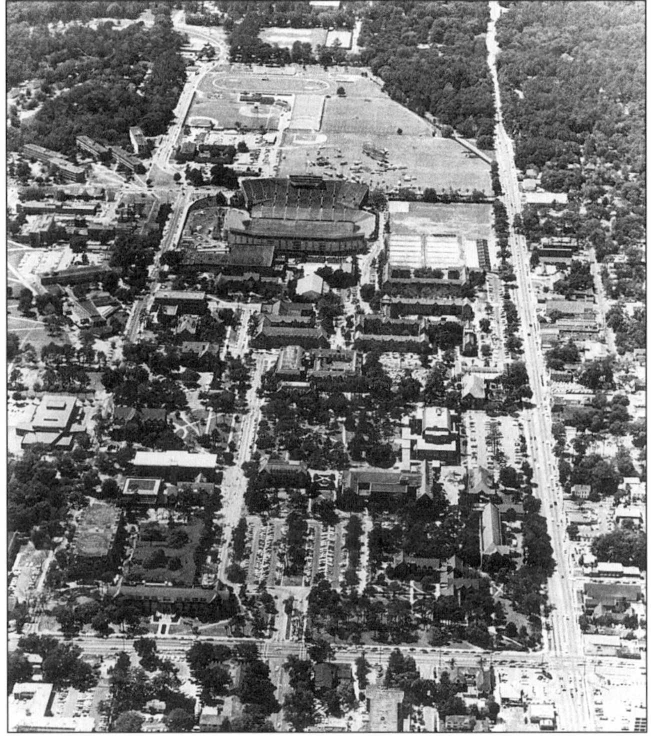

The UF campus was becoming one of the most beautiful in the Southeast because of its well-designed buildings and many trees. (Courtesy University Archives, Dept. of Special Collections, George A. Smathers Libraries, Univ. of Florida.)

Defensive end Jack Youngblood, who lettered at UF for three years (1968–1970) and is on the school's Defensive Team of the Century, is in the College Football Hall of Fame, was first-team All-American in his senior year (1970), and later starred with the Los Angeles Rams (1971–1984). He was twice named NFL Defensive Player of the Year, was a six-time All-Pro selection, and a seven-time Pro Bowler. (Courtesy UF News & Public Affairs.)

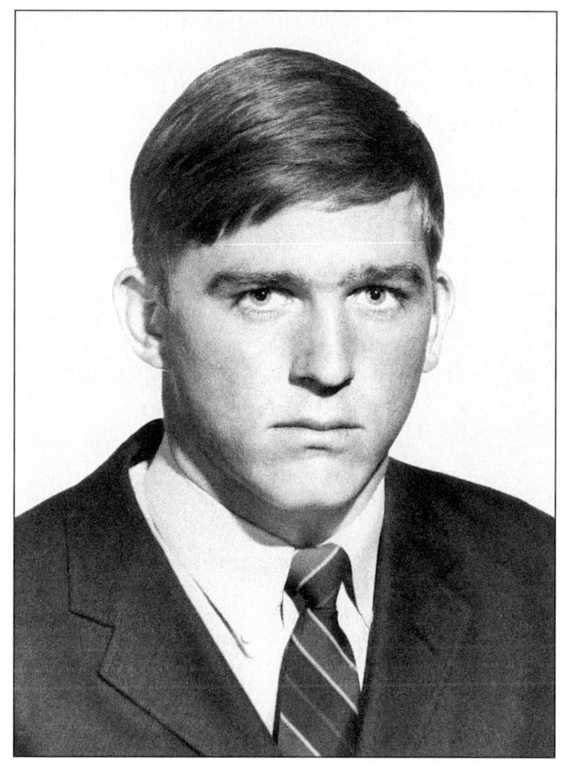

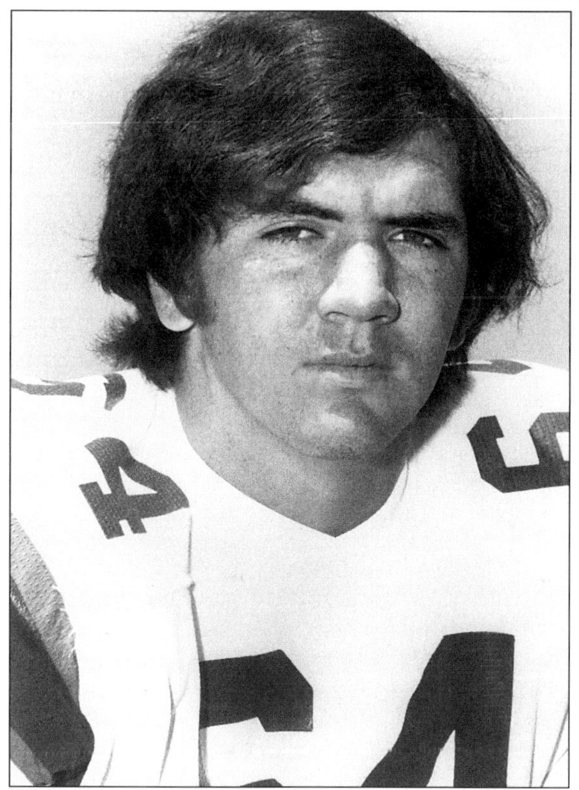

Guard Burton Lawless, who lettered for three years (1972–1974) and is on UF's Team of the Century, became a first-team All-American (1974). His senior team averaged 272 rushing yards a game, the second-best, single-season total in school history. In the NFL, he played for the Cowboys (1975–1979), Lions (1980), and Dolphins (1981). (Courtesy UF News & Public Affairs.)

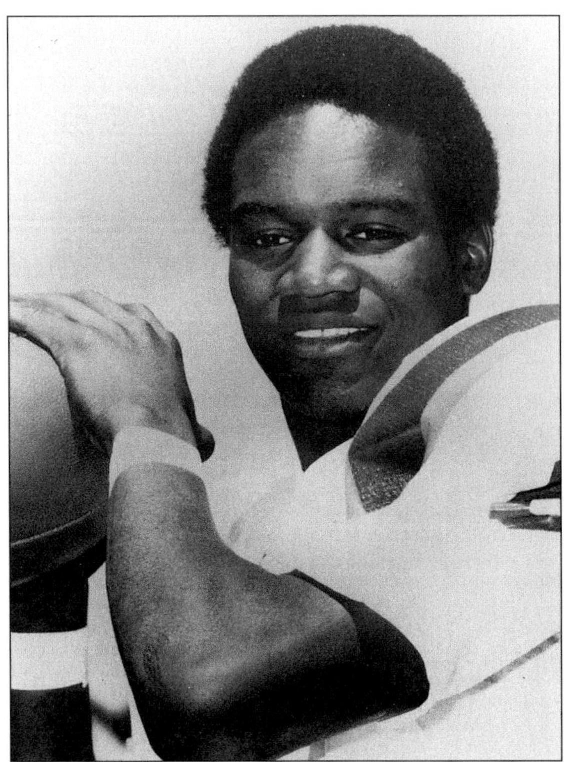

Don Gaffney, the first African American to start at quarterback at UF, played for three years.(1973–1975). In 1973 he was the starting quarterback of the first Gator team to win a game at Cliff Hare Stadium in Auburn. The Gators also defeated Georgia, FSU, and Miami all in the same month, a very rare feat. (Courtesy UF News & Public Affairs.)

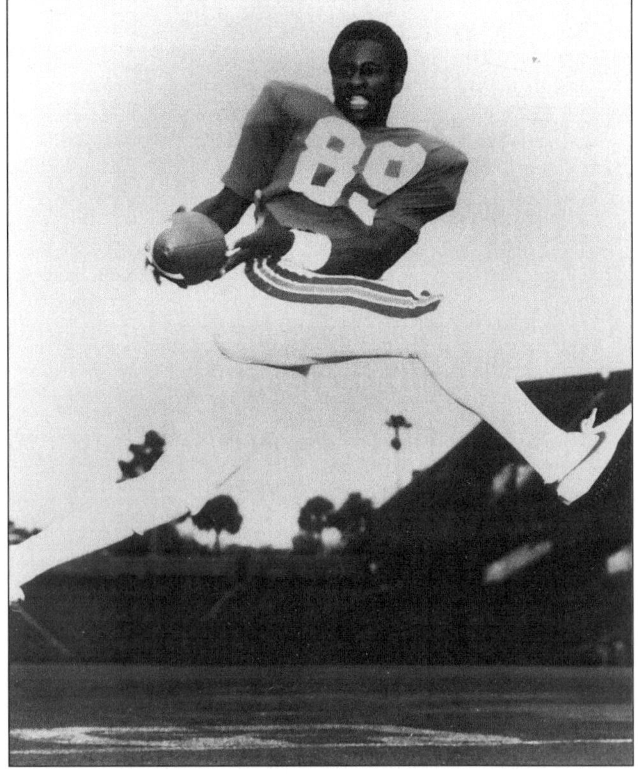

Wes Chandler, who is on UF's Team of the Century as a wide receiver, led the team in receptions in three years (1974–1976). He was a first-team All-American for two years (1976, 1977), holds the school record for yards per reception (21.3 on 92 catches), and is tenth in receiving yards (1,963). He later played in the NFL for the Saints (1978–1981), Chargers (1982–1987), and 49ers (1988). (Courtesy UF News & Public Affairs.)

Typical of the many fine assistant coaches at UF over the years was Jim Niblack, who worked with Doug Dickey as an assistant and coached in the World Football League, the University of Kentucky, and the Arena League. He also coached Gainesville High School to a state championship in 1980. (Courtesy UF News & Public Affairs.)

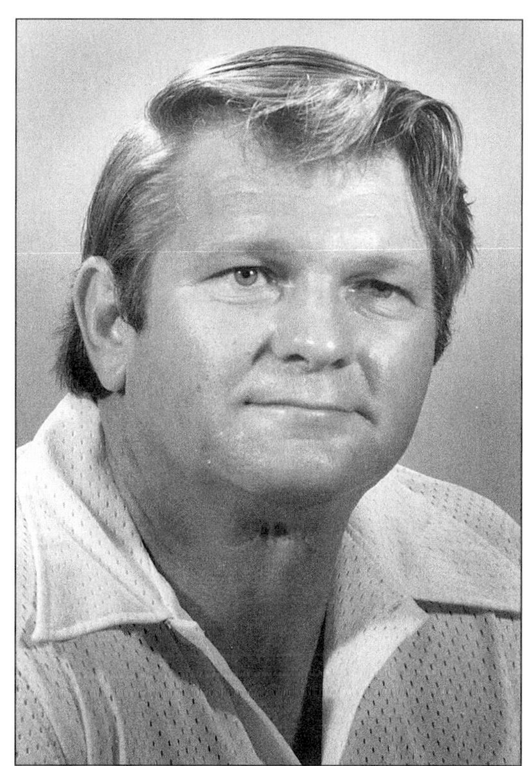

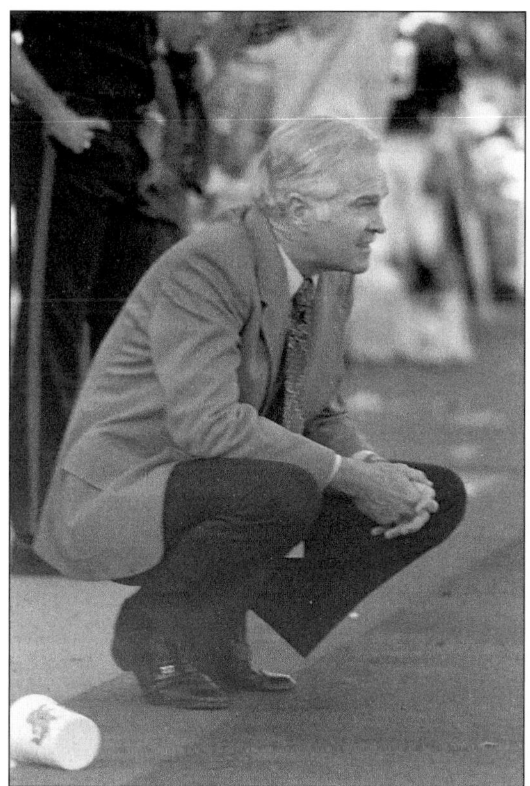

President Robert Marston would often watch the game from the sidelines, as he did here in 1977, mingling with the players and coaches and offering congratulations or commiserations. (Courtesy UF News & Public Affairs: John Woodhead.)

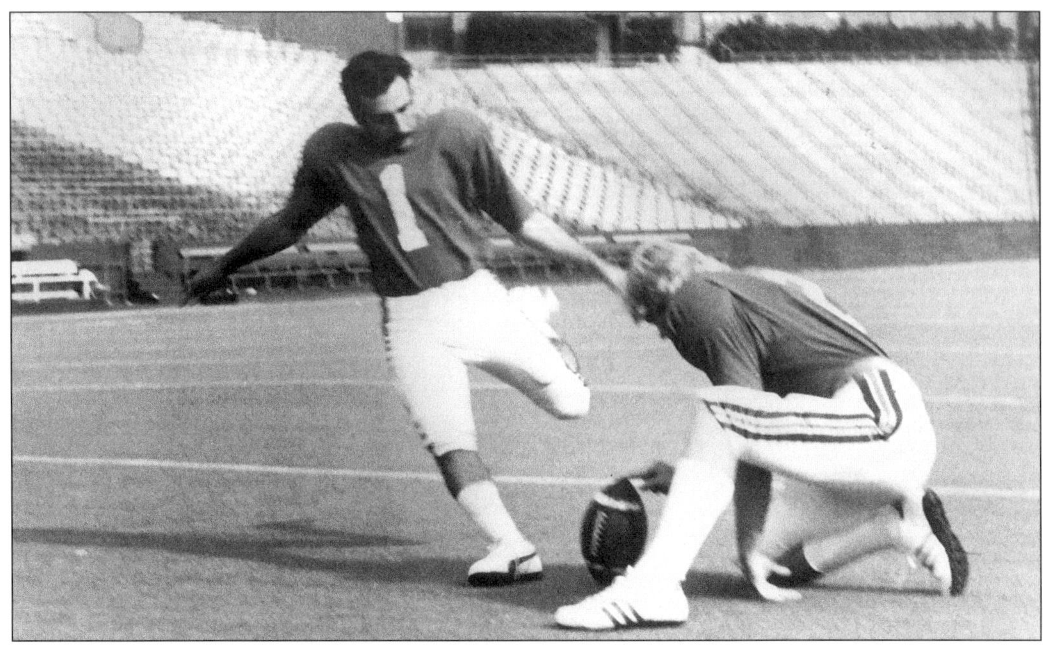

Berj Yepremian (#1), shown here with Alan Williams (#2) in 1977, is second in the record books for point-after-touchdown percentage accuracy for a minimum of 50 kicks (56 of 57), behind Brian Clark (1979–1981), who hit 62 of 62. Yepremian's four field goals in a 1978 game was surpassed once by Brian Clark (five in 1980) and twice by Bobby Raymond (six in both 1983 and 1984). (Courtesy UF News & Public Affairs.)

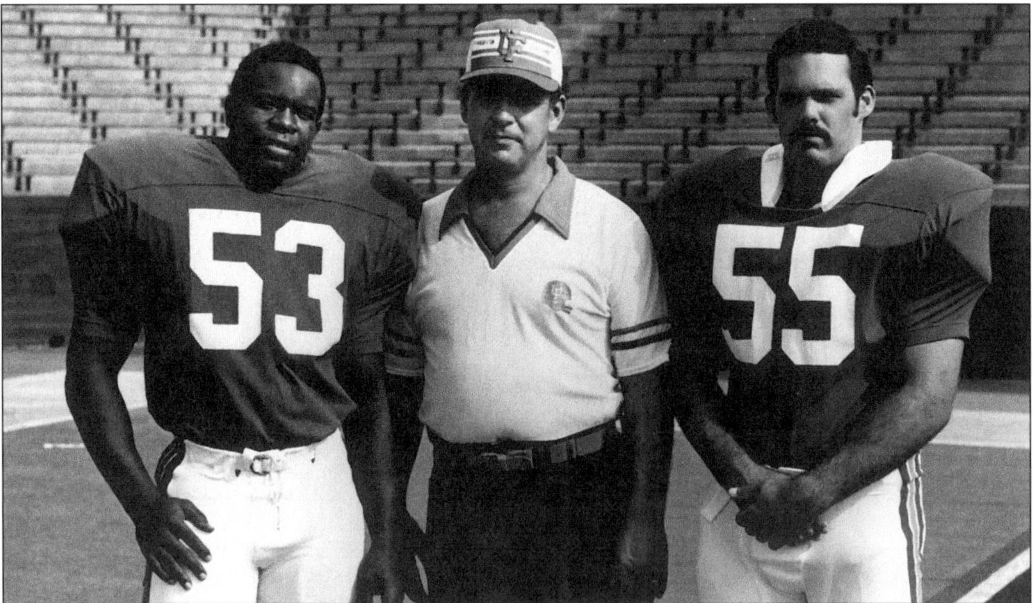

Charles Williams (#53) and Scot Brantley (#55), shown here in 1977 with defensive coach Doug Knotts, were two of the players who anchored a strong UF defense. One of those players, David Galloway, was first-team All-American tackle (1981) before playing for the St. Louis Cardinals (1982–1987), Phoenix Cardinals (1988–1989), and Denver Broncos (1990) in the NFL. (Courtesy UF News & Public Affairs.)

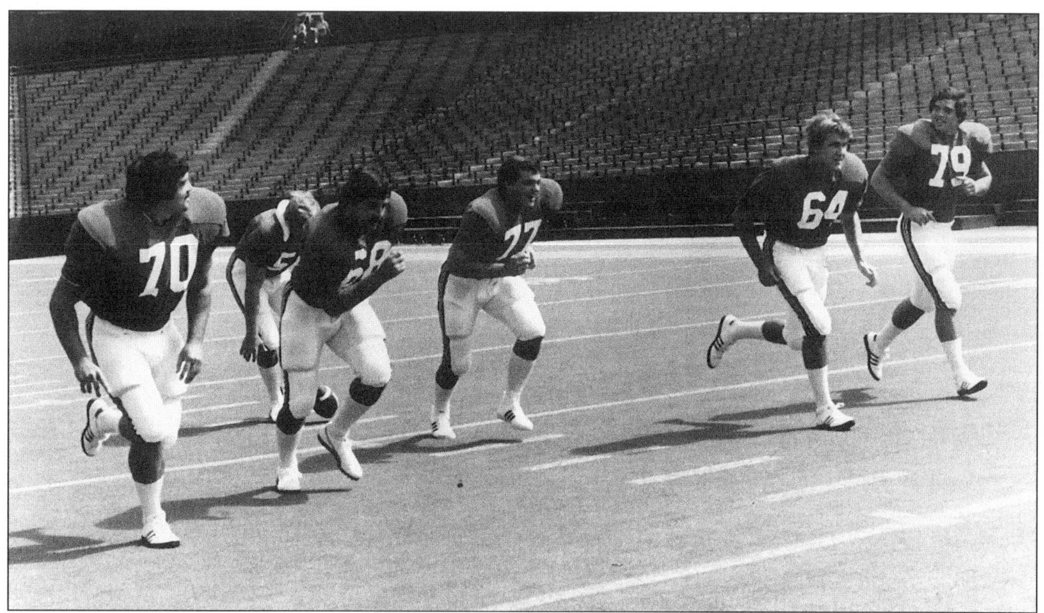

Dennis Forrester (on the far left), Steve Kiefer, Mark Totten, Bill Bennek, and David Forrester made up the offensive line in 1977. The Forrester twins, who lettered for three years (1975–1977), were two of many brother combinations who played for the Gators. (Courtesy UF News & Public Affairs.)

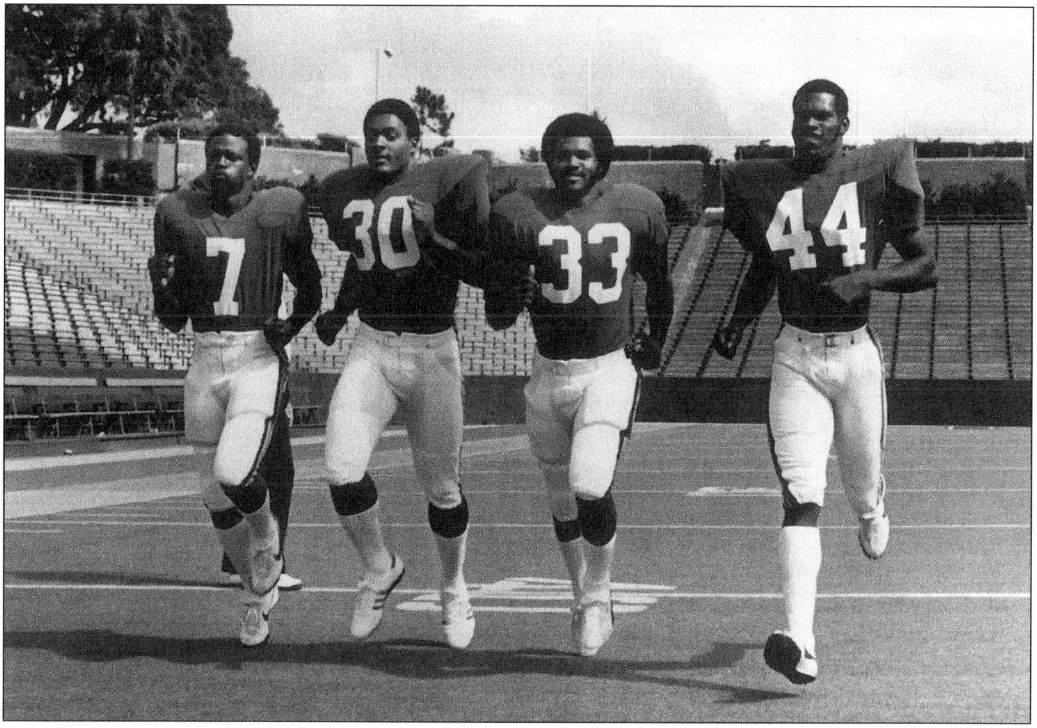

The 1977 Gator backfield consisted of (from left to right) quarterback Terry LeCount, fullback Earl Carr, halfback Tony Green, and halfback Willie Wilder. LeCount, Carr, and Green went on to play in the National Football League. (Courtesy UF News & Public Affairs.)

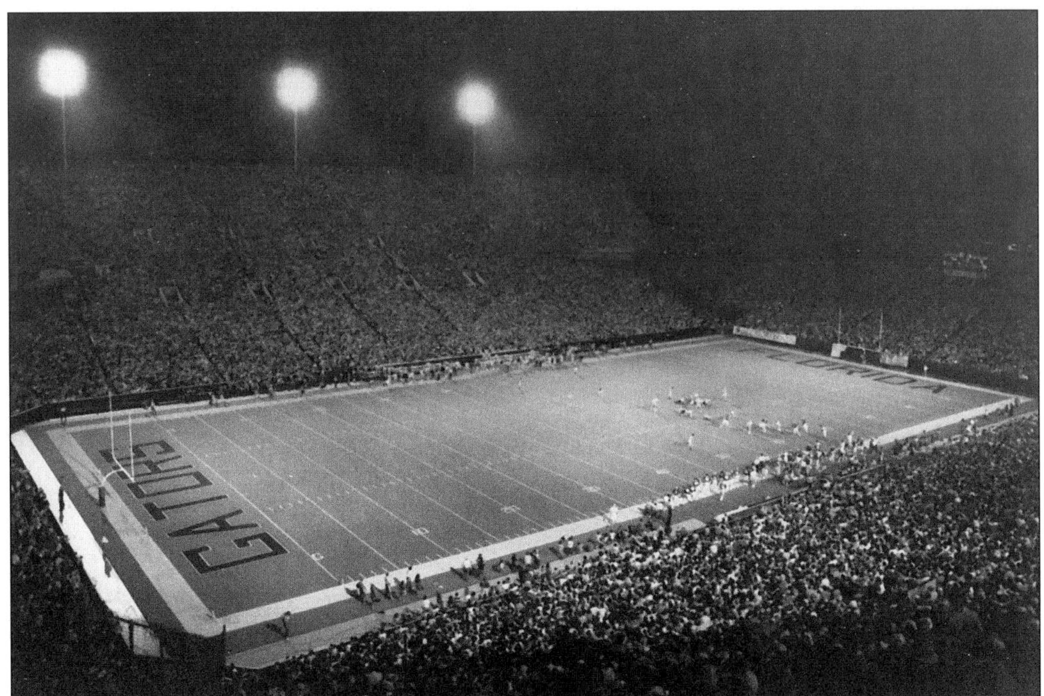

Night games at Florida Field, for example this one against Pittsburgh, provided relief to the players and fans from the high Florida humidity. The first night game at Florida Field, against the Citadel in 1950, proved popular with the fans. (Courtesy UF News & Public Affairs: Herb Press.)

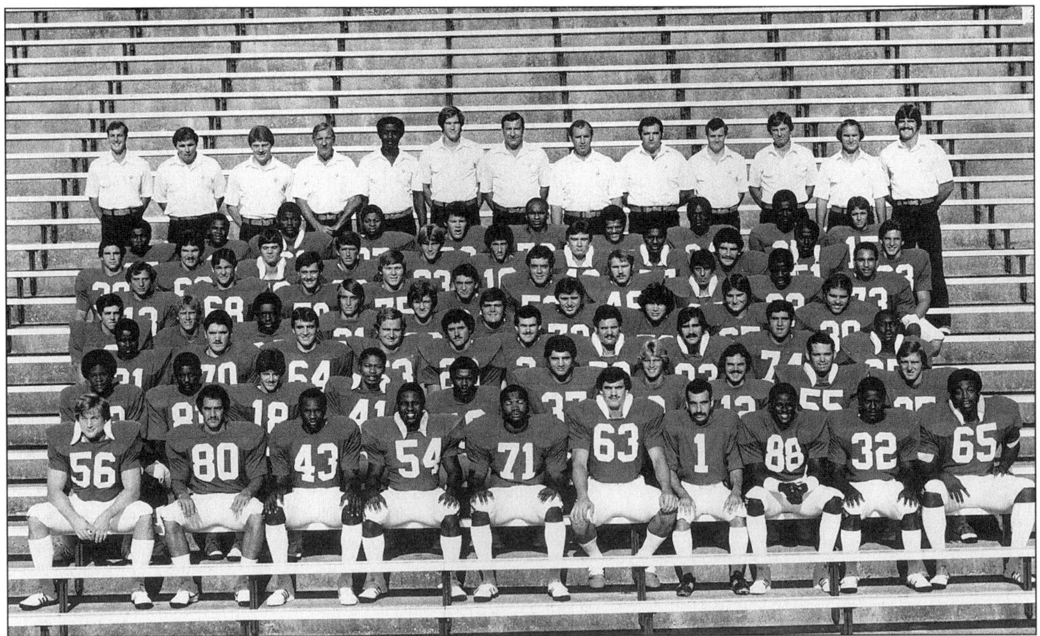

The 1978 Gator team had as its quarterback coach, Steve Spurrier (top row, third from the right), in his first coaching position. He would go on to coach at Georgia Tech (1979), Duke (1980–1982), the Tampa Bay Bandits (1983–1985), and Duke again (1987–1989). (Courtesy UF News & Public Affairs.)

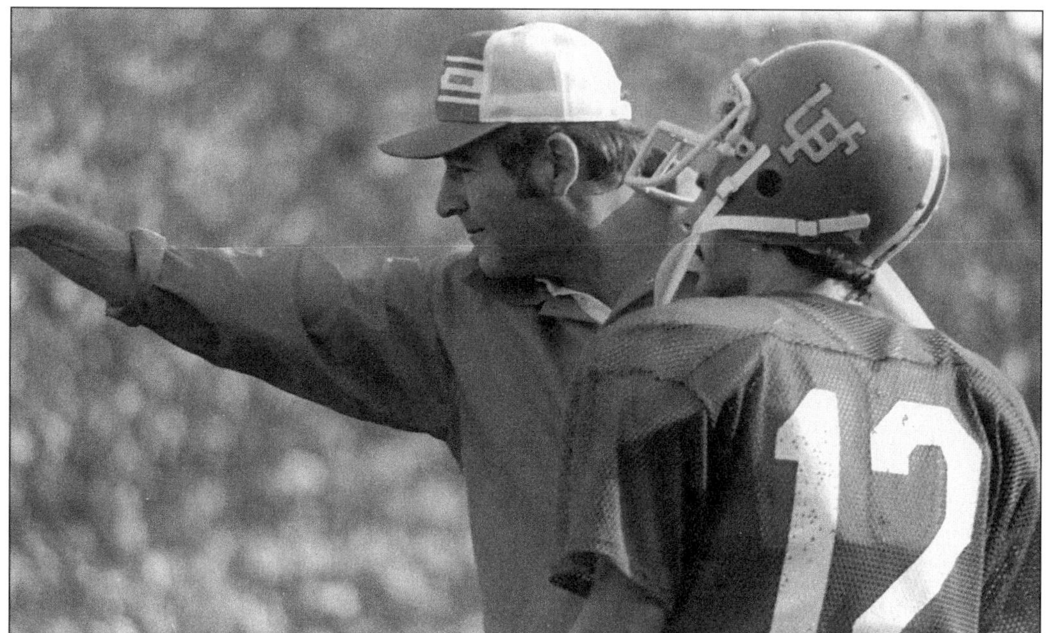

Coach Dickey is shown here with quarterback John Brantley (#12) in 1978. Brantley, a baseball player and brother of linebacker Scot Brantley, was a two-sport athlete, as were many such football-baseball players, for example Rodney Brewer, Reche Caldwell, Doug Johnson, Jamie McAndrew, Herbert Perry, and Aaron Walker. (Courtesy UF News & Public Affairs: John Woodhead.)

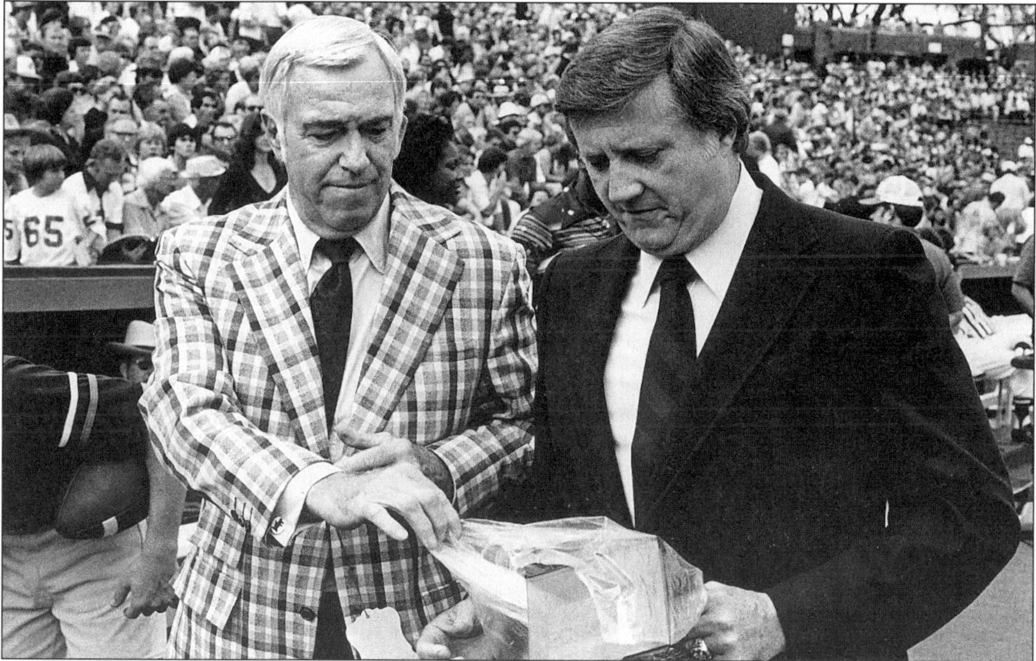

Ray Graves and George Steinbrenner (on the right) were at Florida Field in 1978. The owner of the New York Yankees was a strong Gator supporter and funded improvements to the school's athletic facilities. (Courtesy UF News & Public Affairs: John Woodhead.)

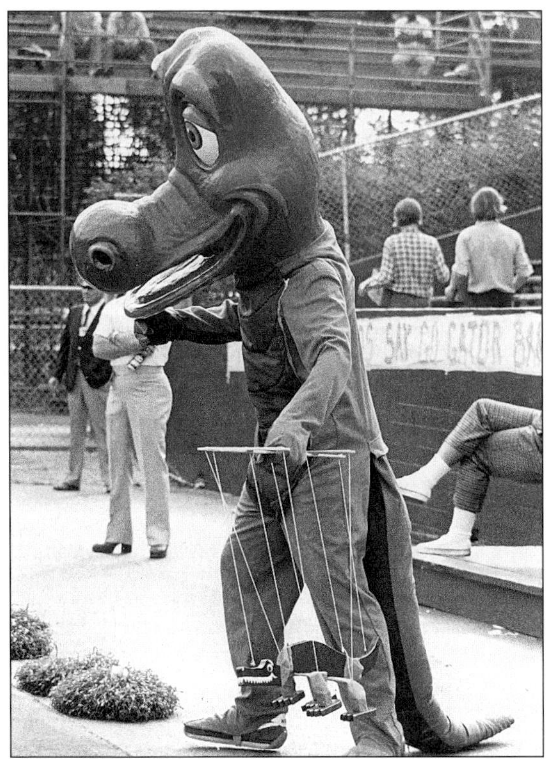

The Gator mascot was evolving into a not-so-fierce reptile. The gator costume, designed at Walt Disney World for about $5,000, was such that temperatures inside the outfit could reach up to 120°. The Gator mascot, which does not talk, has to mime a lot. (Courtesy UF News & Public Affairs: John Woodhead.)

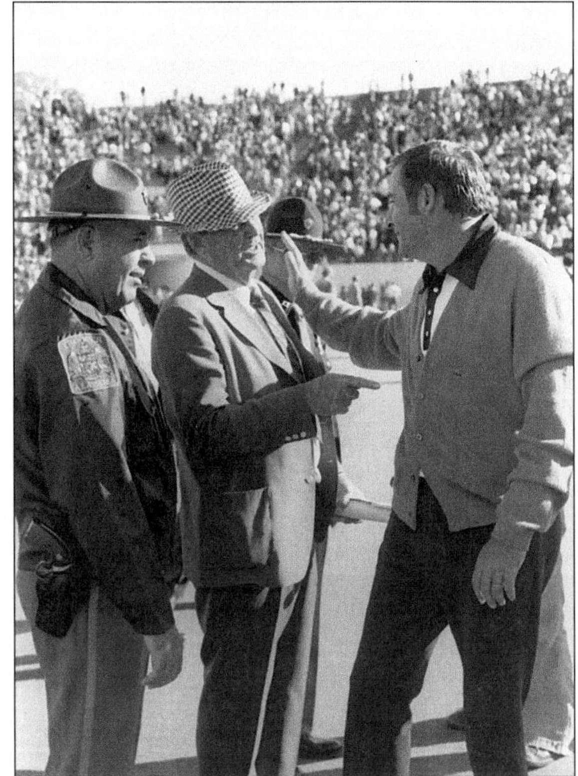

Alabama Coach "Bear" Bryant and UF Coach Dickey talked after a game at Florida Field. One of Bryant's protégés, Charley Pell, would soon become the next Gator head coach. (Courtesy UF News & Public Affairs: John Woodhead.)

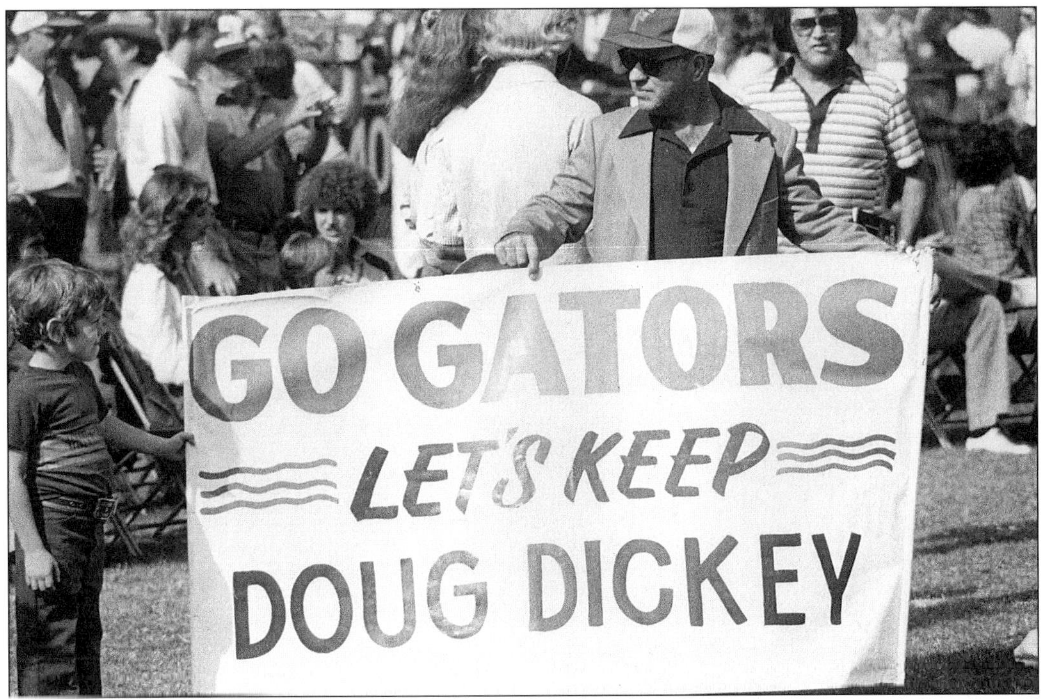

This sign-holder was definitely in the minority as alumni and fans clamored for the removal of the disappointing head coach. Dickey returned to the University of Tennessee (UT) to become the athletic director there and help the UF-UT rivalry become one of the best in the 1990s. (Courtesy UF News & Public Affairs: John Woodhead.)

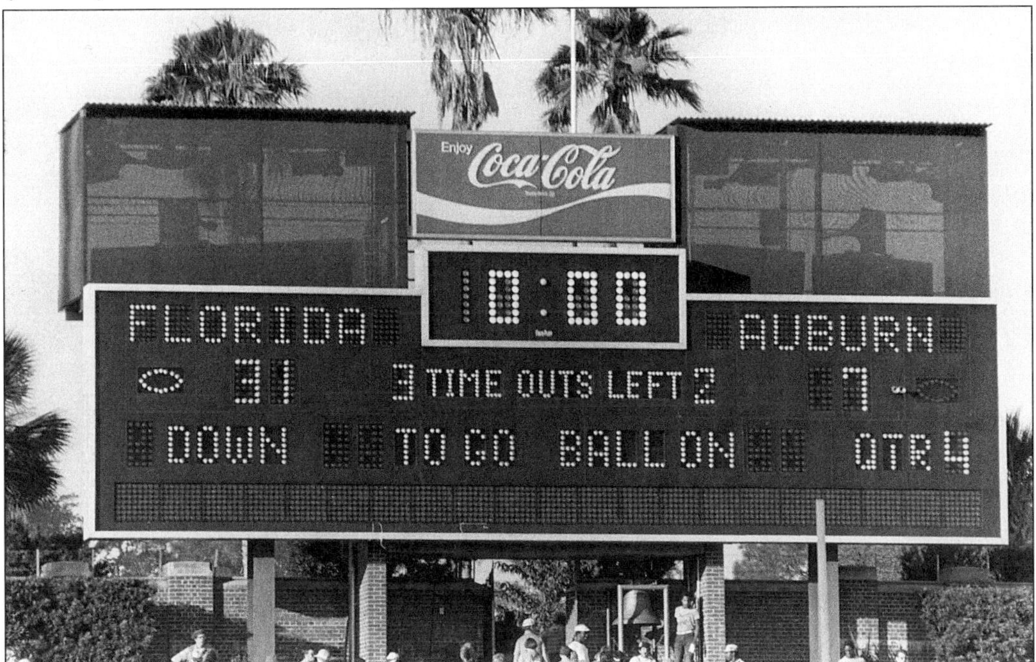

The scoreboard at the north end-zone was becoming bigger and more informational. (Courtesy UF News & Public Affairs.)

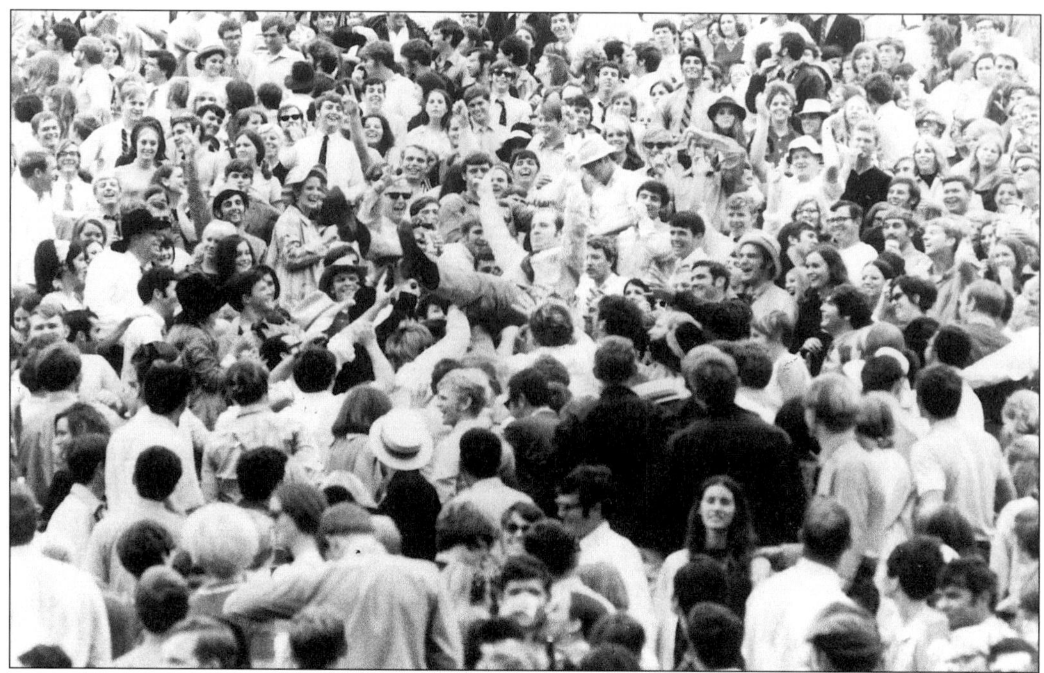

Passing up a fan in the stands became a favorite activity on the student side of the stands in the 1970s. (Courtesy UF News & Public Affairs.)

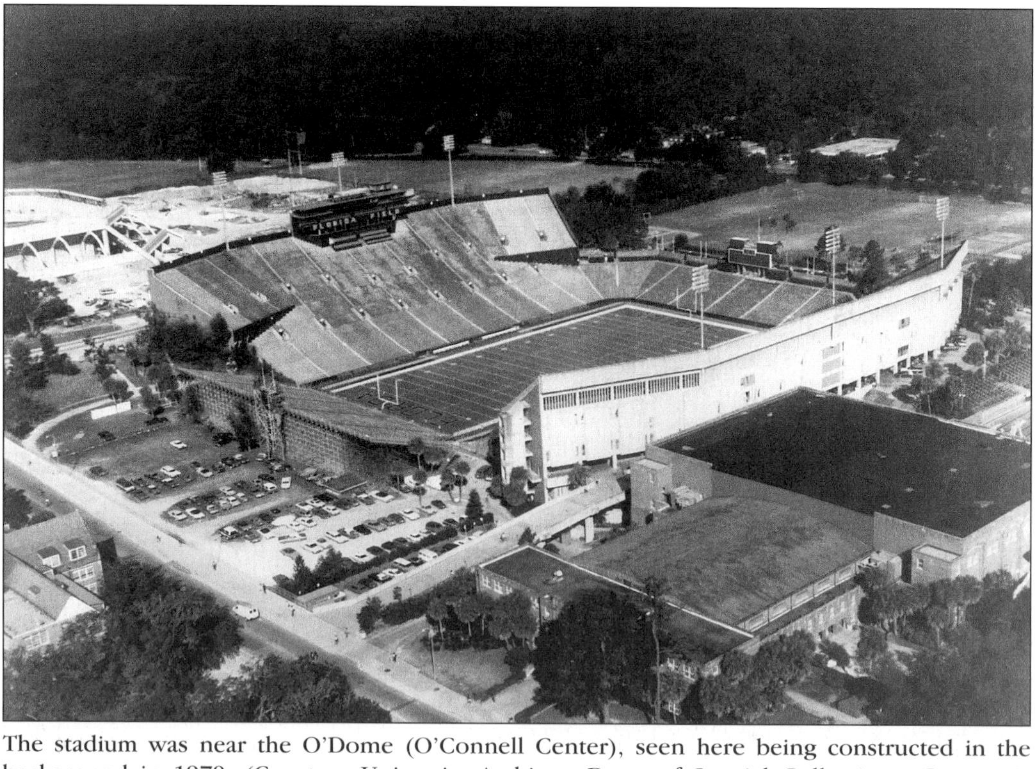

The stadium was near the O'Dome (O'Connell Center), seen here being constructed in the background in 1979. (Courtesy University Archives, Dept. of Special Collections, George A. Smathers Libraries, Univ. of Florida.)

Eight

1979–1989: Coaches Pell, Hall, and Darnell

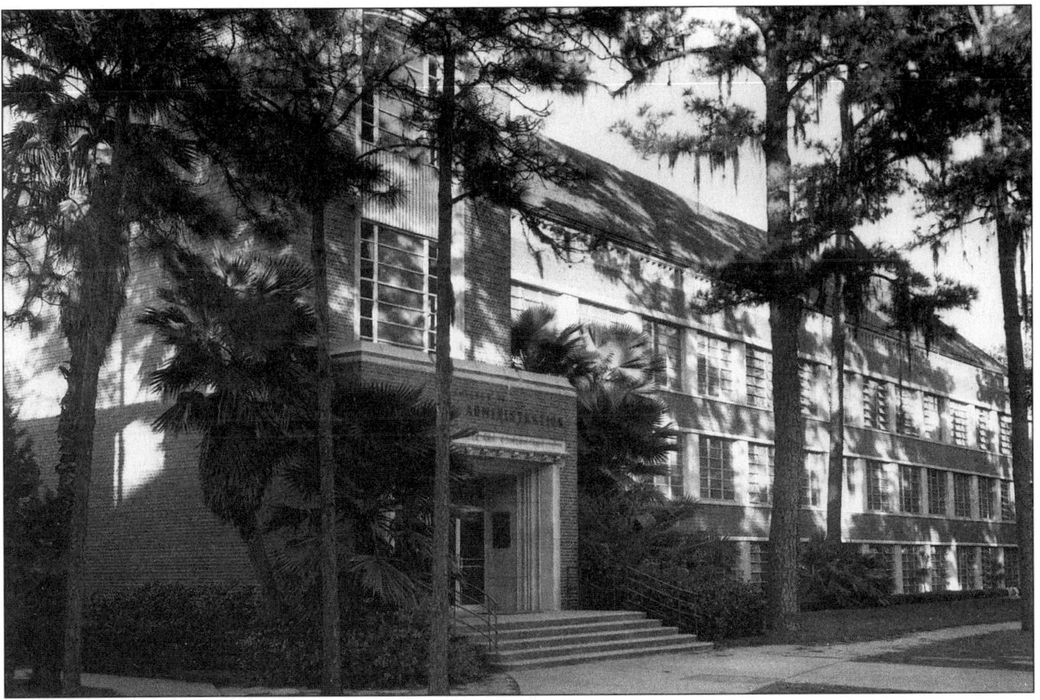

The College of Business Administration was one of the most popular places for Gator football players to prepare for careers after football. (Courtesy Florida State Archives.)

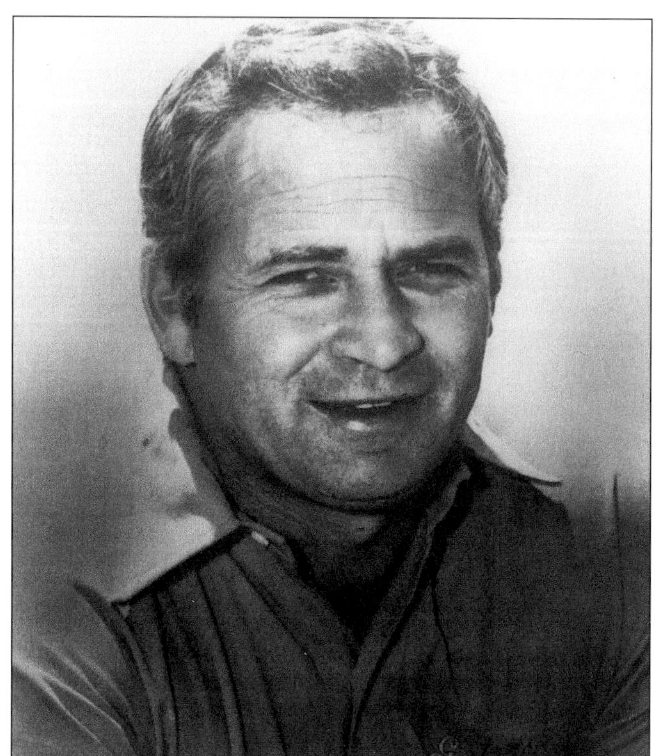

Coach Charley Pell became the school's 16th head coach and compiled a 33-26-3 record in his five-and-a-half seasons (1979–1984). After a terrible first year (0-10-1), the Gators won eight games in 1980 for the biggest turnaround in NCAA history up to that point. (Courtesy UF News & Public Affairs.)

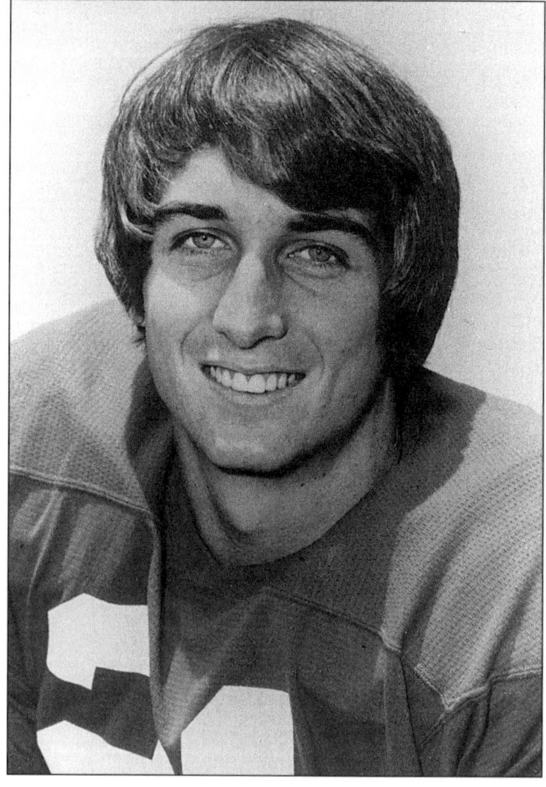

Wide receiver Cris Collinsworth lettered for four years (1977–1980) and tied the NCAA record for the longest collegiate touchdown passing play when his 1977 scoring pass to Derrick Gaffney went for 99 yards. He was a first-team All-American (1980), then played for the Bengals (1981–1988) in the NFL, and became a TV broadcaster. (Courtesy UF News & Public Affairs: Herb Press.)

Scot Brantley, who lettered at UF for four years (1976–1979) and was named to UF's Team of the Century as a linebacker, is second on UF's career-tackles list (467 tackles). After finishing a pro career with the Tampa Bay Buccaneers (1980–1987), he later became a broadcaster for UF games. (Courtesy UF News & Public Affairs: Herb Press.)

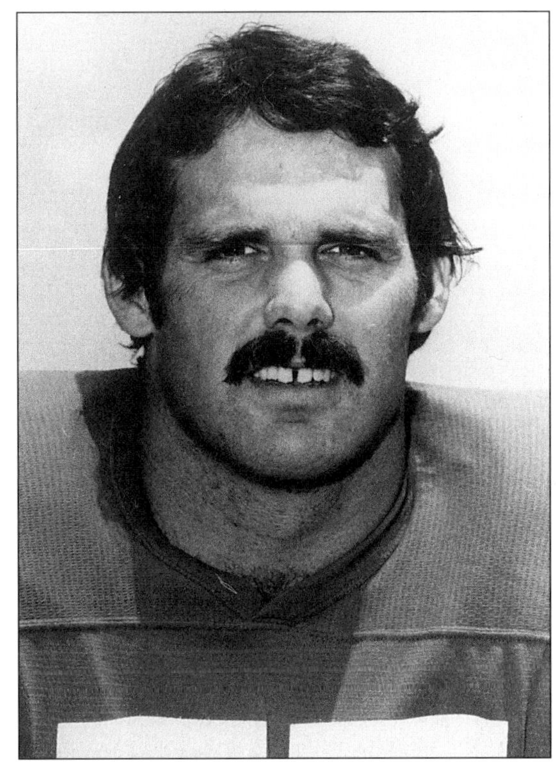

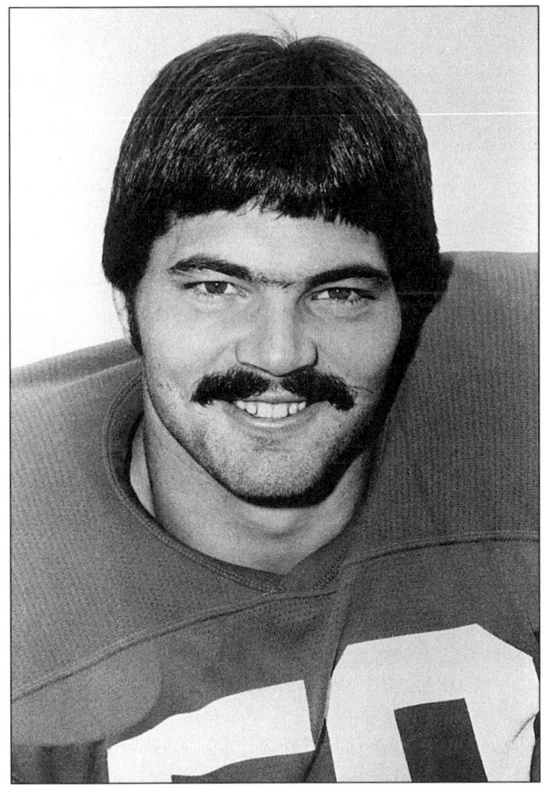

Yancey Sutton, a football letterman for the Gators (1978–1980), played for two coaches: Dickey and Pell. Sutton did not let his deafness interfere with his game and later became a professional golfer. (Courtesy UF News & Public Affairs: Herb Press.)

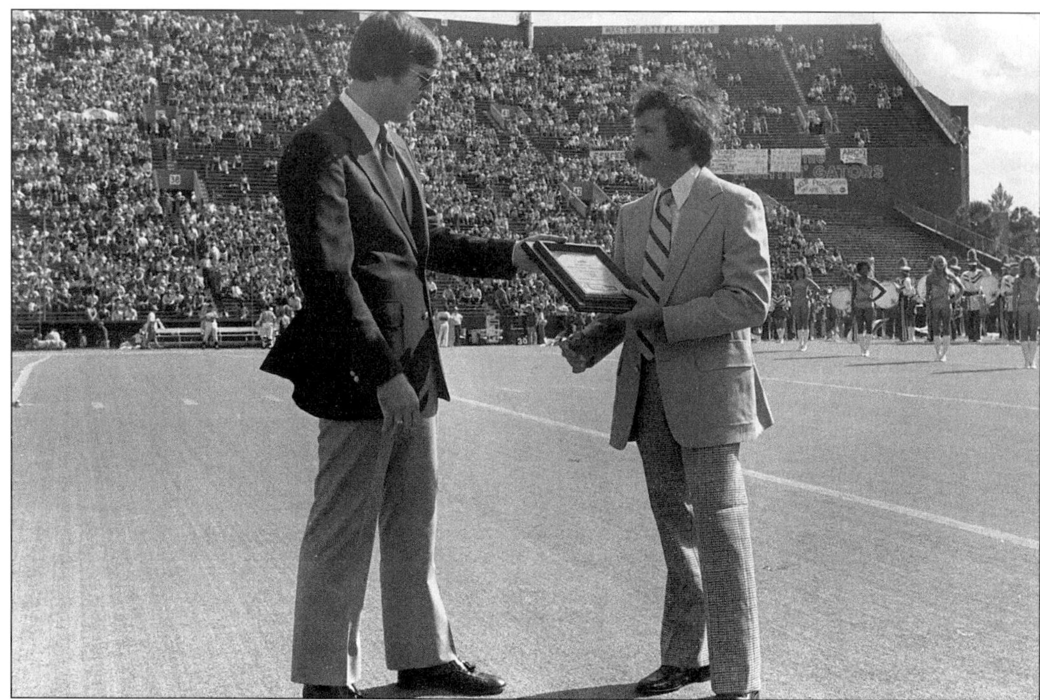

Athletic Director Bill Carr (on the left), shown here making a presentation to the swimming coach at a halftime in 1979, had been a football letterman for the Gators (1964–1966) and a first-team All-American center (1966). (Courtesy UF News & Public Affairs: Marshall Prine.)

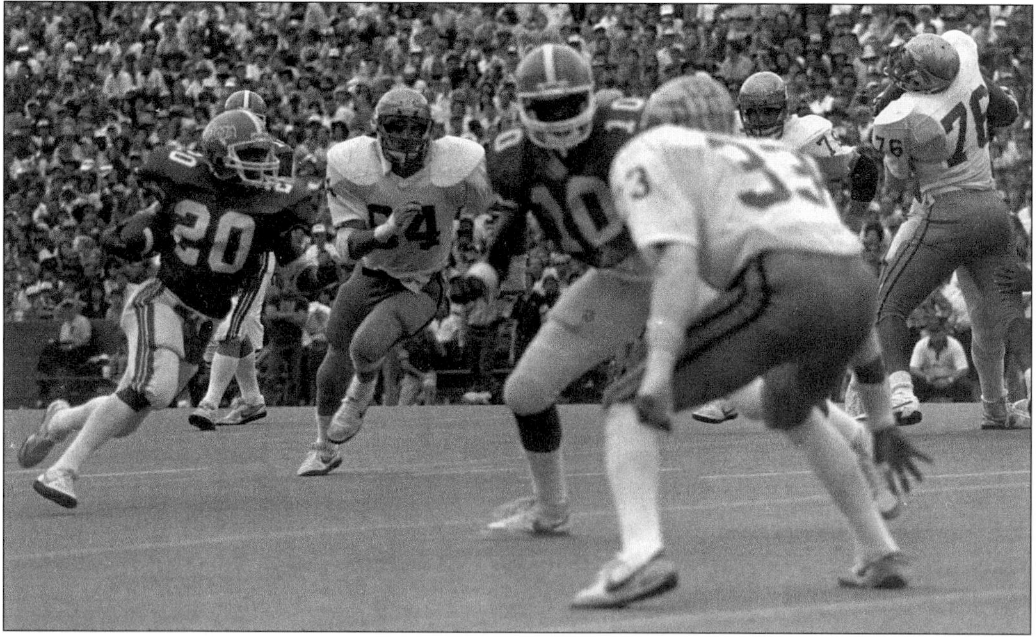

UF's Tyrone Young (#10) blocks for Steve Miller (#20), while FSU's Tommy Young (#54) and James Harris (#33) close in during a 1981 game. After struggling as a quarterback, the 6-foot-6-inch Young excelled as a pass receiver during his four years as a Gator (1979–1982). (Courtesy UF News & Public Affairs: Marshall Prine.)

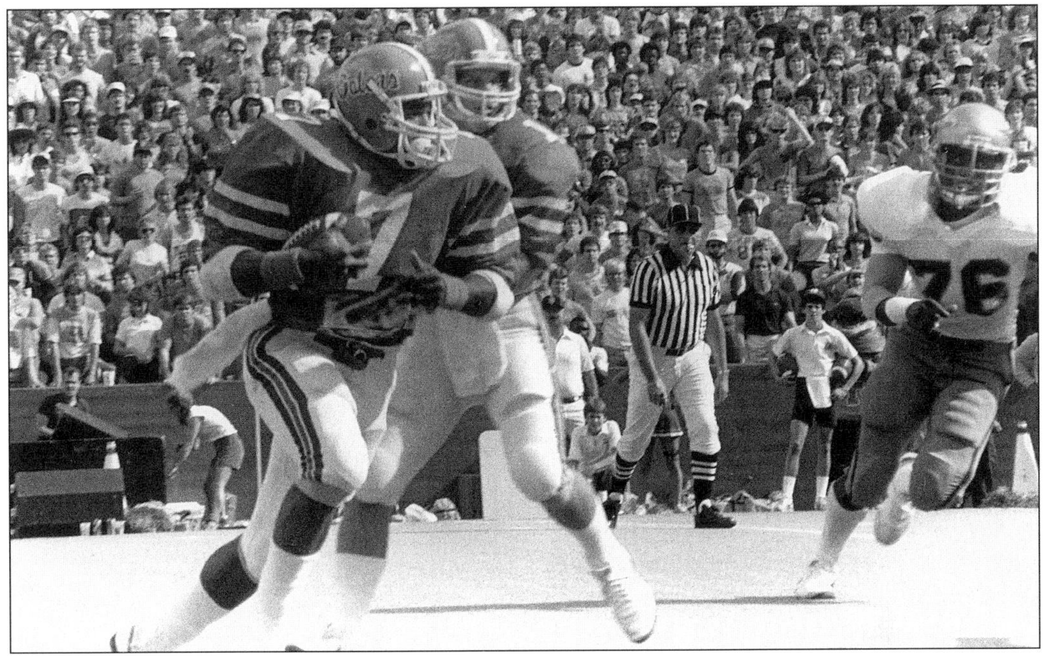

Lorenzo Hampton (#7) provided more strength in the running game during his years as a letterman (1981–1984). His 1,993 rushing yards puts him 12th on the career-yardage list for the Gators. He went into the NFL as a first-round draft choice to play for the Miami Dolphins (1985–1989). (Courtesy UF News & Public Affairs: Chris Runk.)

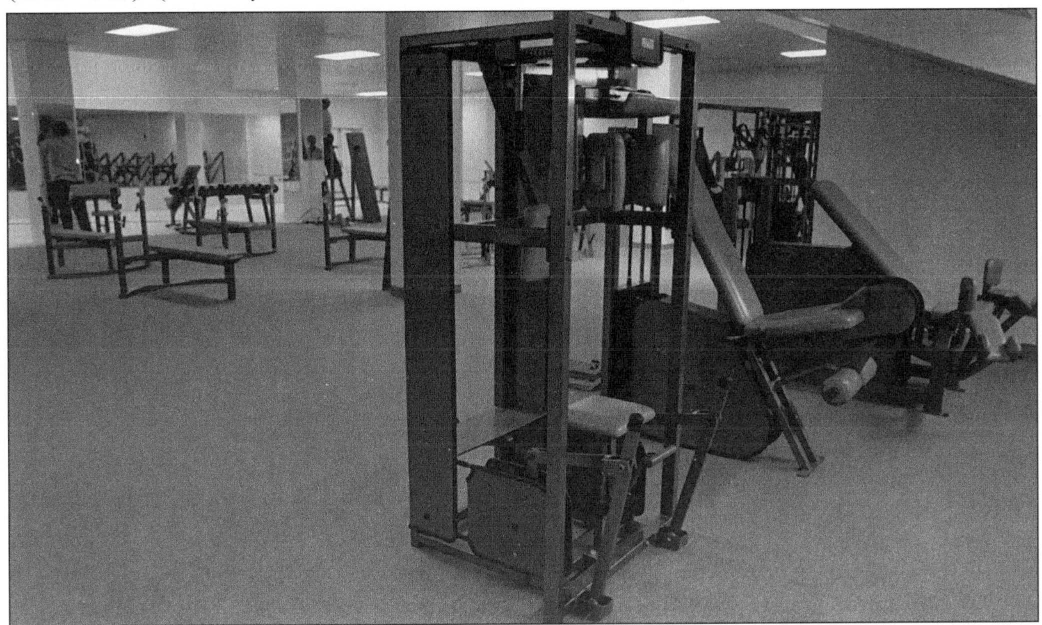

A new weight room in 1982 enabled the Gators to achieve the strength they had been lacking and helped them compete with Division-I teams on a more equal footing. The Strength and Conditioning coach then, Rich Tuten, who worked at UF in two stints (1979–1988, 1993–1994), went on to work for the Denver Broncos in the NFL. (Courtesy UF News & Public Affairs: Herb Press.)

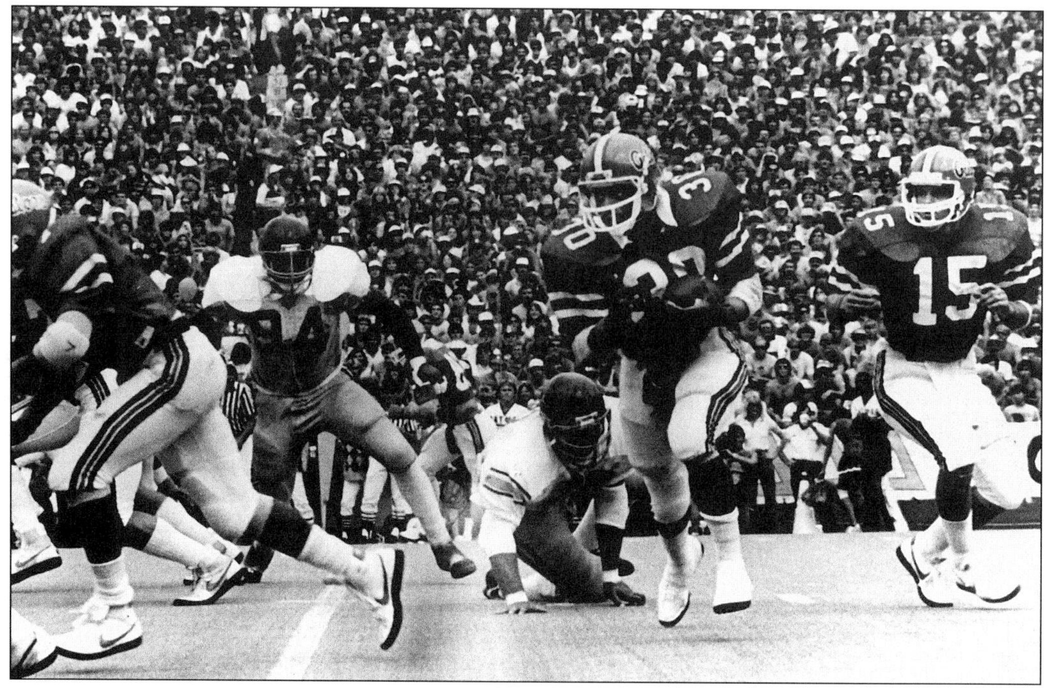

Quarterback Wayne Peace (#15) hands off to James Jones (#30) in the 1982 University of Southern California game. UF defeated USC in that nationally televised game, 17-9. That season, Peace's 70.3 percent completion rate broke the NCAA single-season record. He and the team's other quarterback, Bob Hewko, led the team to an 8-4 record. (Courtesy UF News & Public Affairs: Herb Press.)

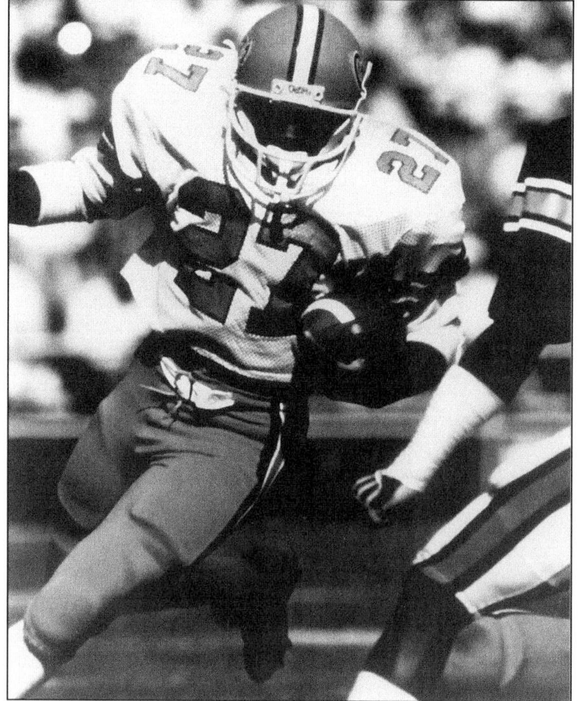

Neal Anderson starred as a running back for the Gators (1982–1985) and led them in rushing for three seasons (1983–1985). He became only the second Gator to rush for more than 1,000 yards (1,034 in 1985) and is now third on the career yardage list with 3,234 yards, behind Errict Rhett and Emmitt Smith. (Courtesy UF News & Public Affairs: Herb Press.)

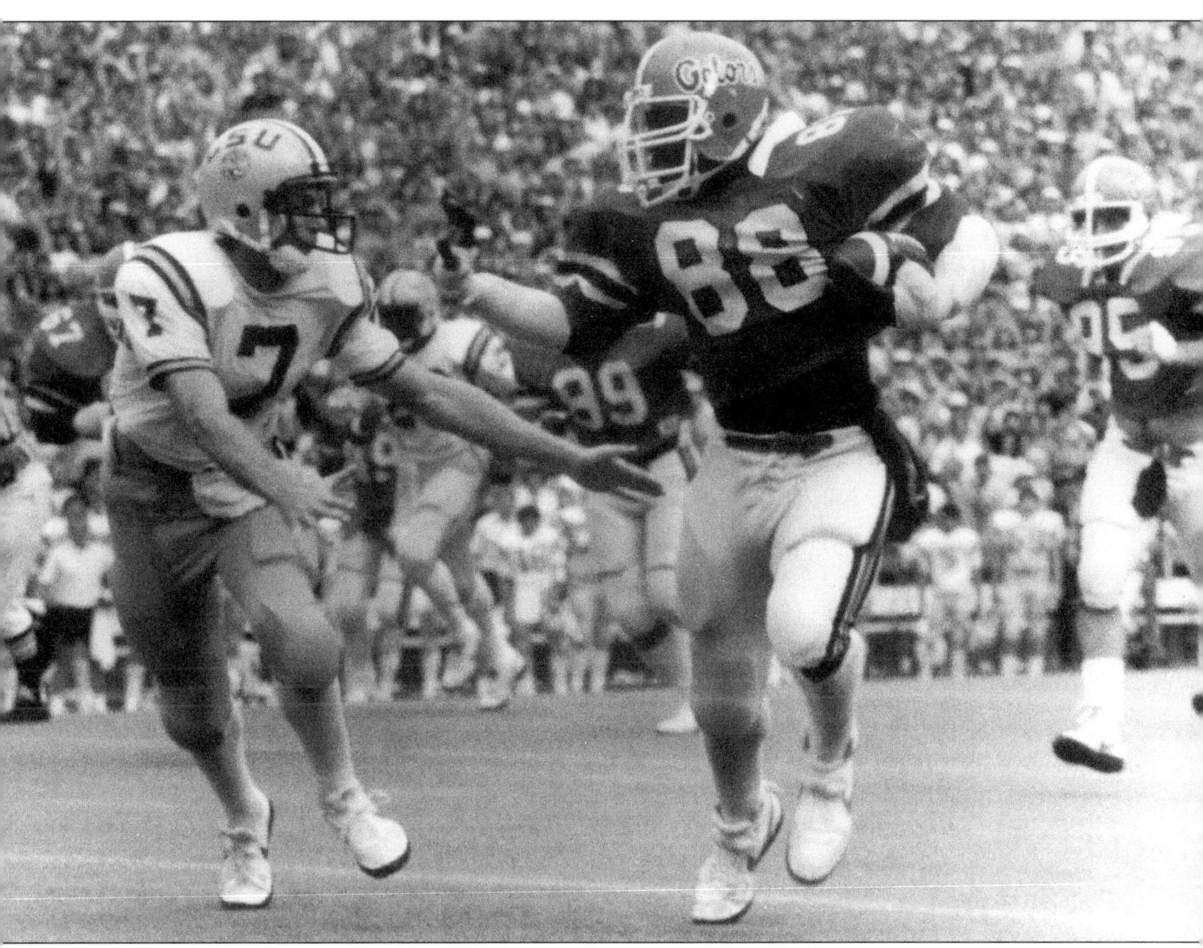

Wilber Marshall (#88), shown here returning an interception in the 1982 LSU game, was a finalist for (although he did not win) the Lombardi Award (presented to the nation's top linebacker/lineman) for two years (1982,1983) and was chosen the National Defensive Player of the Year by ABC in 1983. He was named to UF's Team of the Century as a linebacker and the school's best defensive player ever. As a four-year letterman (1980–1983), he is UF's career leader in tackles-for-loss (58), was a two-time All-American (1982,1983), and had 343 tackles, including 23 sacks. He went on to play for five different NFL teams (1984–1995): Chicago Bears, 1984–1987; Washington Redskins, 1988–1992; Houston Oilers, 1993; Arizona Cardinals, 1994; and New York Jets, 1995. (Courtesy UF News & Public Affairs.)

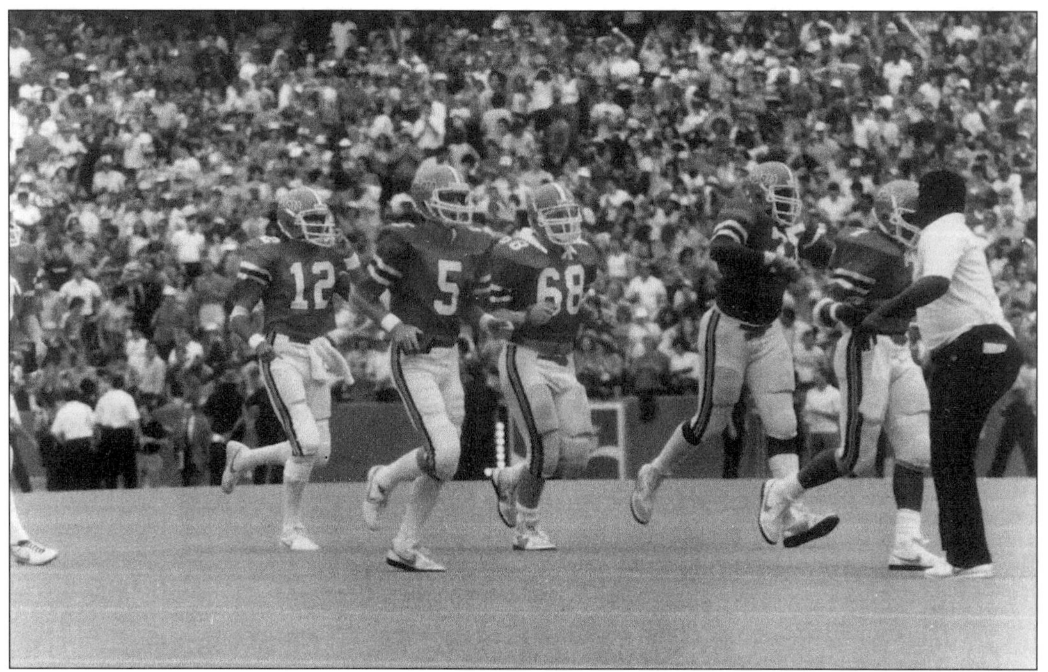

Quarterback Bob Hewko (#12), place-kicker Jim Gainey (#5), offensive guard John Hunt (#68), offensive tackle Lomas Brown (#75), and running back Lorenzo Hampton (#7) were part of the 1982 team that set a school record for total offense (4,450 yards) and a then-national record for passing-completion percentage (68.8 percent). (Courtesy UF News & Public Affairs.)

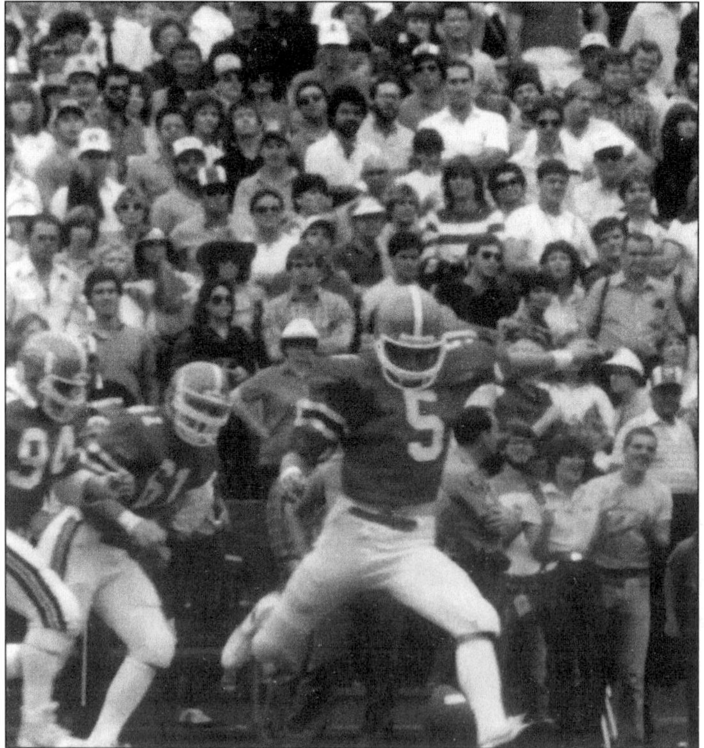

Jim Gainey (#5) kicks off in a 1982 game, followed by linebackers John Landry (#94) and Pepper Downie (#61). That season, the addition of about 18,000 new seats to Florida Field brought the seating capacity to 73,000 and helped UF finish tenth in football attendance that year with an average over 72,000. (Courtesy UF News & Public Affairs.)

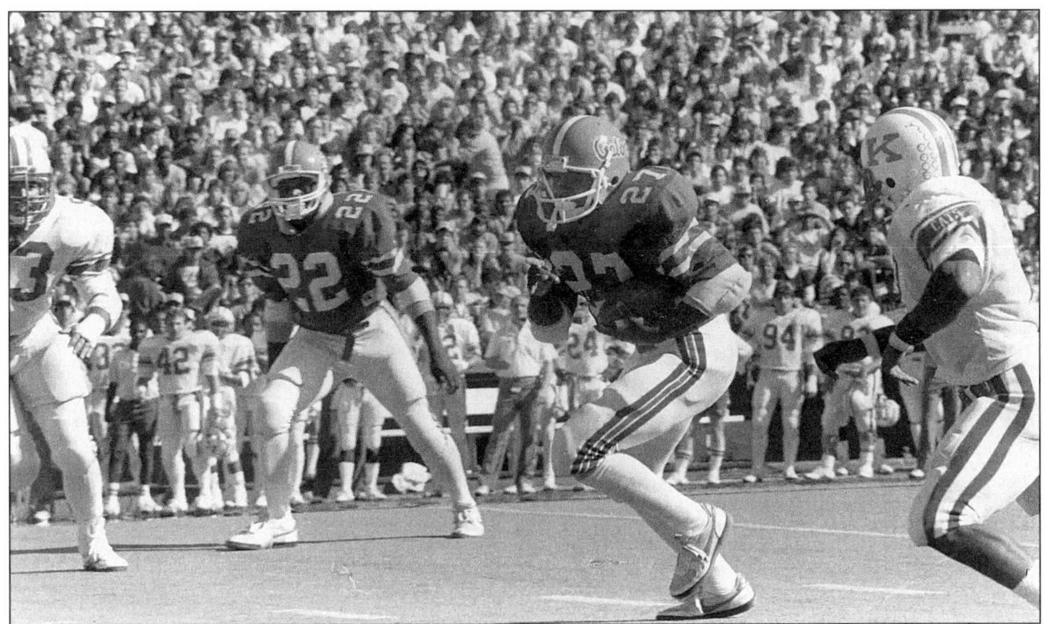

John L. Williams (#22) and Neal Anderson (#27) gave the Gators a potent running attack for four years (1982–1985). Williams, sixth on the career-yardage rushing list with 2,409 yards, later played for the Seahawks (1986–1993) and Steelers (1994–1995) in the NFL. Anderson played for the Bears in the NFL (1986–1993), retiring in 1993 as the team's second-leading career rusher behind Walter Payton. (Courtesy UF News & Public Affairs: Chris Runk.)

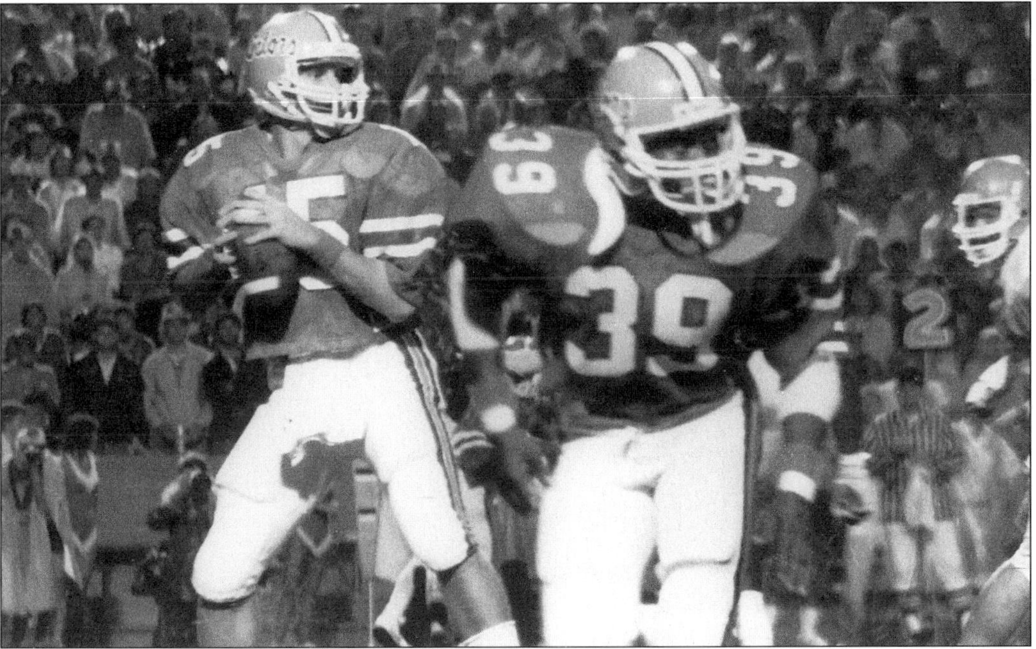

Quarterback Wayne Peace, shown here with fullback Joe Henderson (#39) in 1983, set the UF record of career completions when he hit 61.6 percent (610 of 991) in his 1980–1983 UF career. He later played professional football for the Tampa Bay Bandits of the United States Football League. (Courtesy UF News & Public Affairs: Neil C. Berger.)

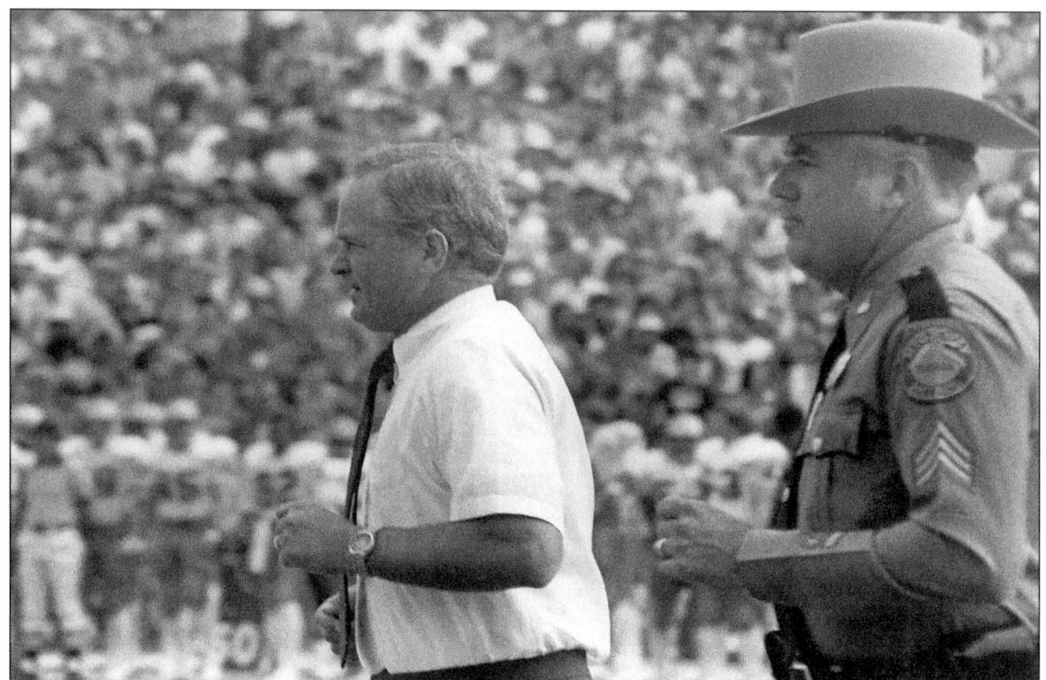

Coach Pell led the 1983 Gator team to a number-six ranking in the nation with a 9-2-1 record, the highest ranking of any UF team up to that point and the school's first top-10 finish. They beat eventual national champion Miami, 28-3, early in the season, and finished the season by defeating Iowa in the Gator Bowl, 14-6. (Courtesy UF News & Public Affairs: Chris Runk.)

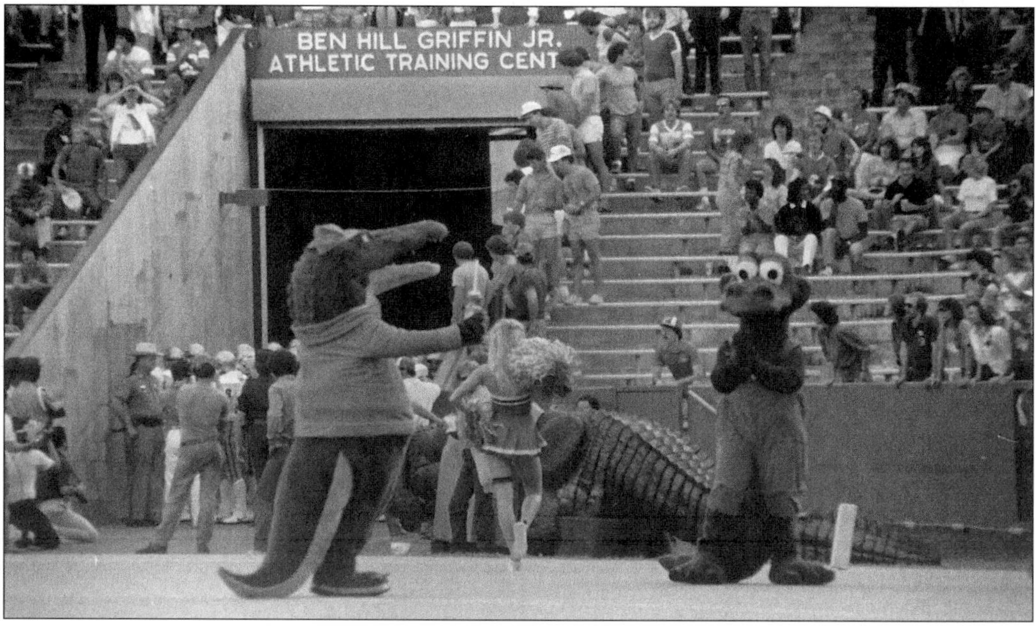

Albert and Alberta in 1983 are seen in front of a movie alligator prop. Although schools like Allegheny College, San Francisco State University, San Jacinto College, and Green River Community College have used the gator as a mascot, no other school has become so identified with the alligator as UF. (Courtesy UF News & Public Affairs: Chris Runk.)

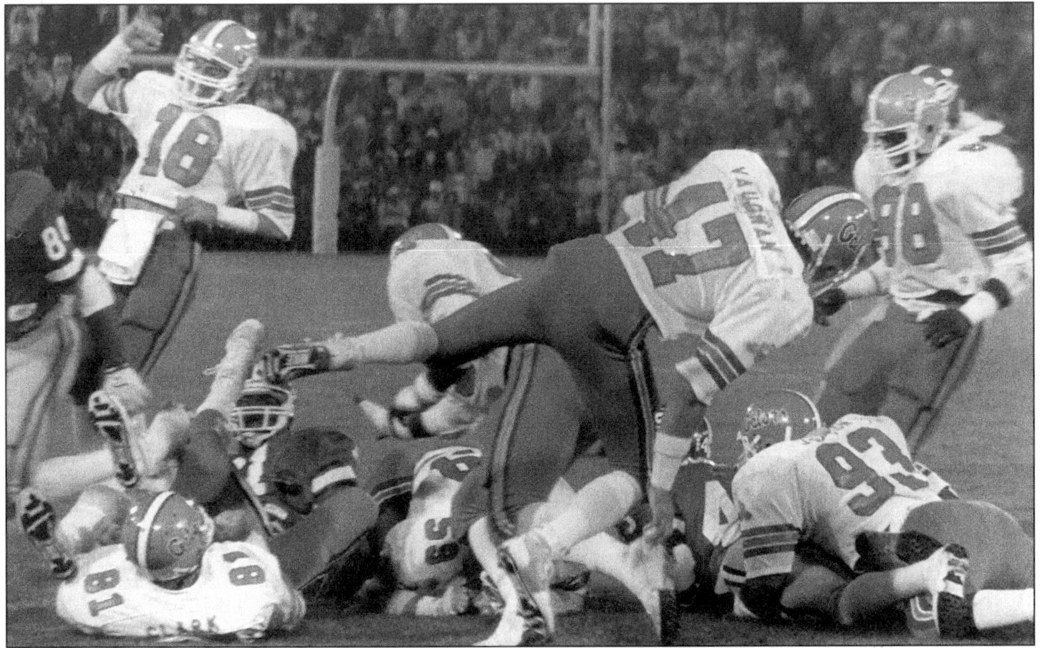

Tony Lilly (#18), Randy Clark (#81), Mark Korff (#59), Bruce Vaughan (#47), Alonzo Johnson (#93), and Wilber Marshall (#88) were part of the 1983 defensive squad that held the opposition to an average of just 13 points a game. Lilly, Clark, Johnson, and Marshall went on to play in the NFL. (Courtesy UF News & Public Affairs: Neil C. Berger.)

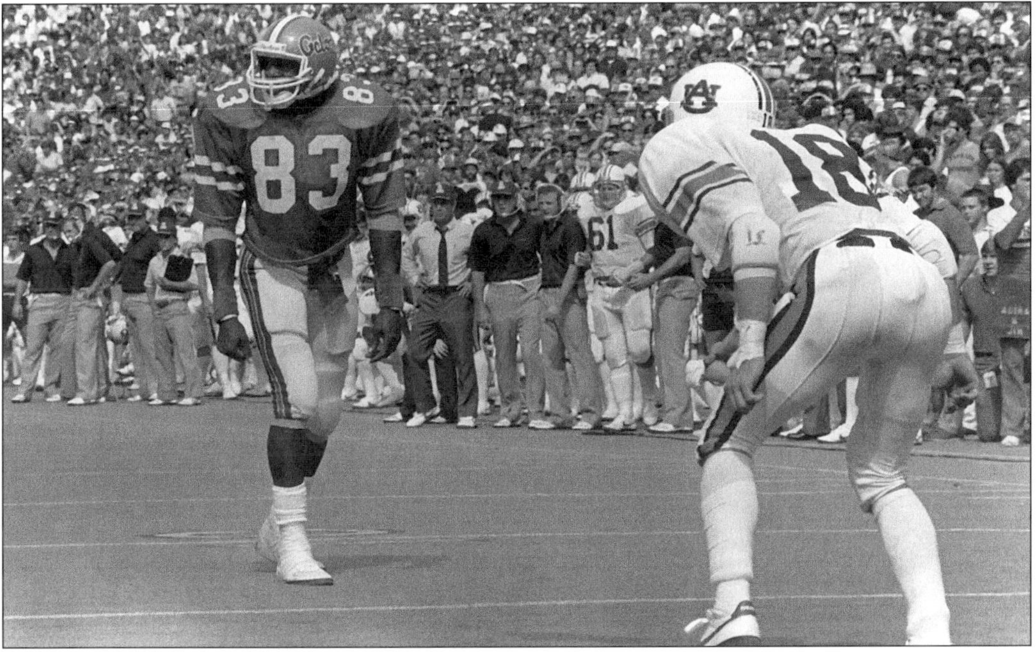

Dwayne Dixon (#83) lettered at UF (1980–1983), went on to play in the NFL (1984–1985, 1987) and Arena Football League (1987–1991), before becoming a coach of wide receivers at UF (1990–present). Among his accomplishments is his winning the Arena Football League's top award, the "Iron Man," two times. (Courtesy UF News & Public Affairs.)

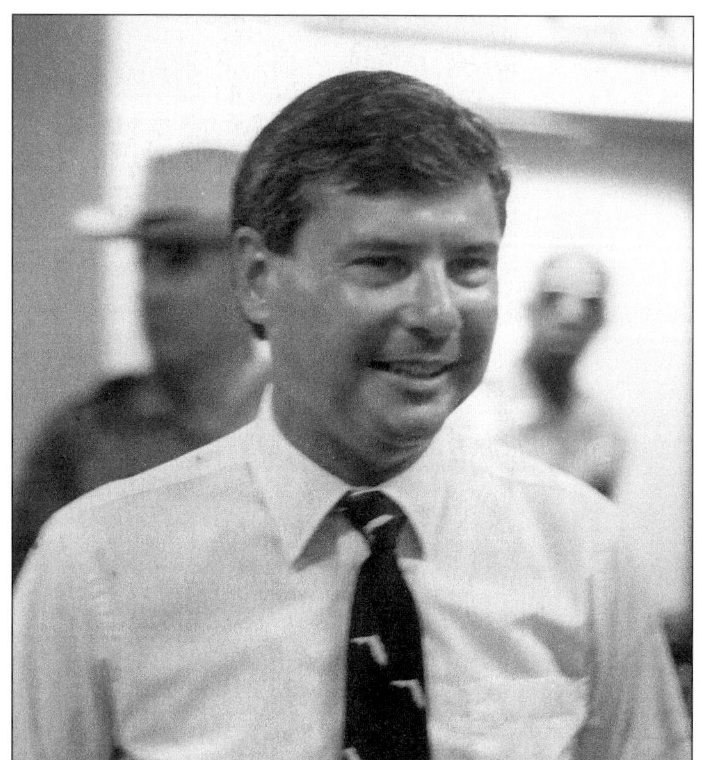

Governor, later Senator Bob Graham, was always a strong supporter of Gator sports. He earned his bachelor's degree in 1959 from UF, where he was a Phi Beta Kappa, a member of Florida Blue Key, and president of the Honor Court. (Courtesy UF News & Public Affairs.)

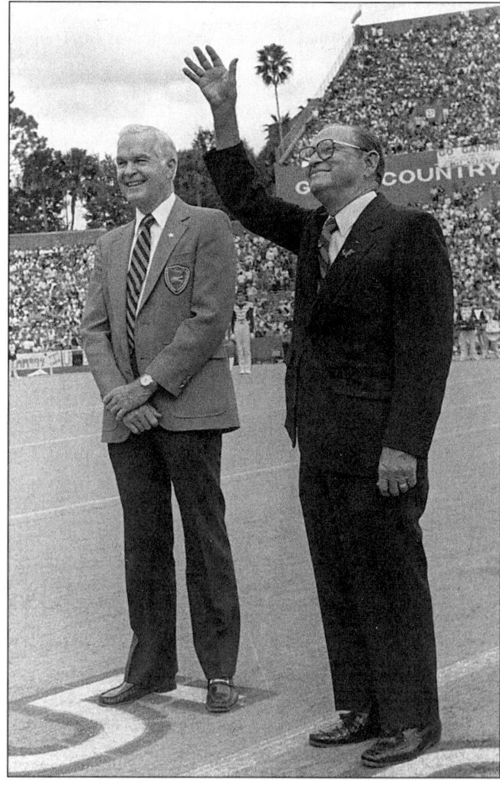

President Bob Marston and Provost Bob Bryan, shown here on Florida Field, were two popular UF administrators who supported UF athletics, both men's and women's teams. The school's success in athletics consistently ranked it in the top ten in terms of championships in all sports. (Courtesy UF News & Public Affairs.)

After serving as the Gators' offensive coordinator for four years (1980–1983), Mike Shanahan went on to become a coach of the Denver Broncos, eventually leading them to back-to-back wins in the Super Bowl (1998,1999). During his four years at UF, Gator teams went to four bowl games, two of which they won. (Courtesy UF News & Public Affairs: Herb Press.)

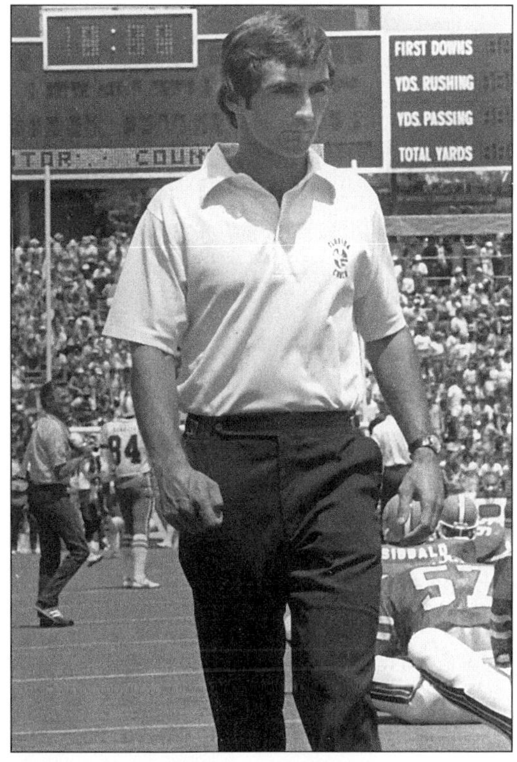

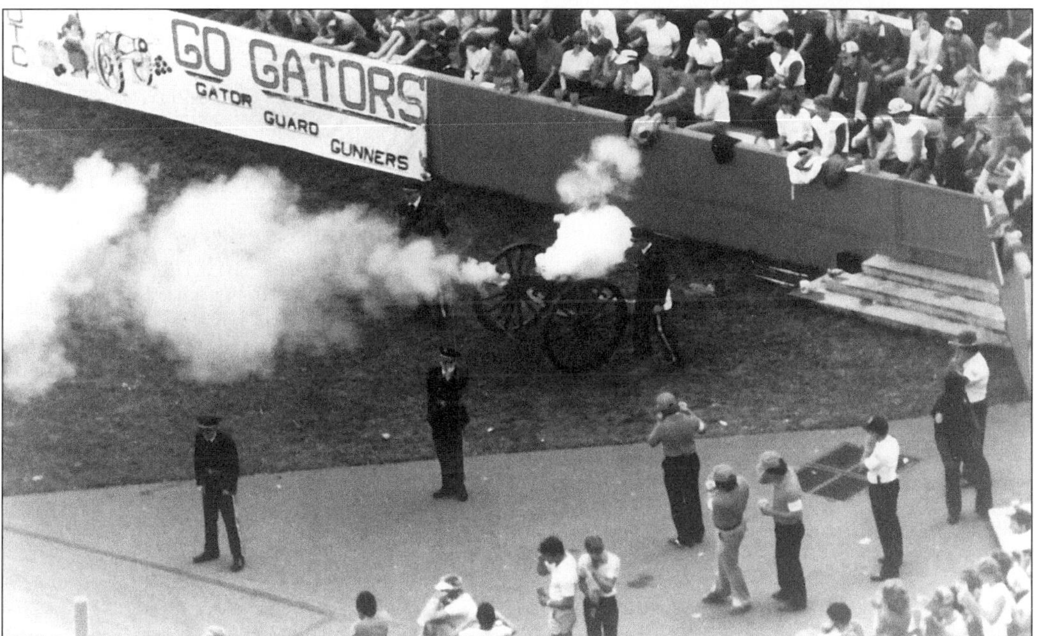

The Gator Guard Gunners fired a cannon whenever the team scored in 1984. The team's third-place finish at the end of the season (with its 9-1-1 record) was the highest up to that point. The *New York Times* and *The Sporting News* named the team national champions, but the SEC did not allow the team to play in a bowl game after a long NCAA investigation found 59 infractions in the program. (Courtesy UF News & Public Affairs.)

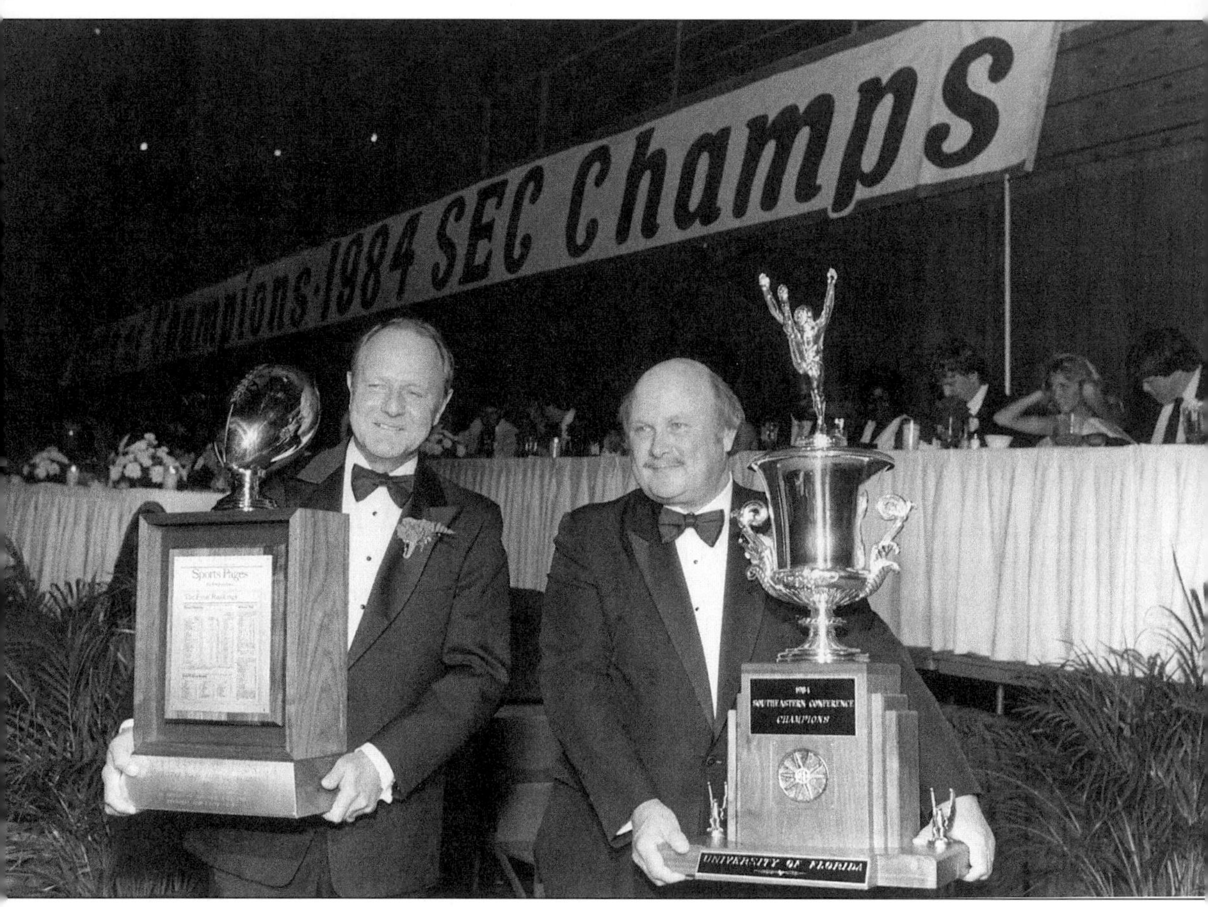

UF President Marshall Criser and Head Coach Galen Hall hold the New York Times National Championship Trophy and the 1984 SEC Championship Trophy that the team won. The SEC trophy was presented in December, but the title was vacated in late May by the conference. The *New York Times* has its computer version of the national champion based on a variety of factors. Hall had a 40-18-1 record in his five-and-a-half seasons (1984–1989) but was replaced in 1989 by Gary Darnell, who would compile a 3-4 record in part of one season. (Courtesy UF News & Public Affairs: Bruce Fine.)

UF's Kerwin Bell, who quarterbacked the Gators for four years (1984–1987), had a passing efficiency that was ranked best in NCAA history for a freshman quarterback (1984). (Courtesy University Archives, Dept. of Special Collections, George A. Smathers Libraries, Univ. of Florida.)

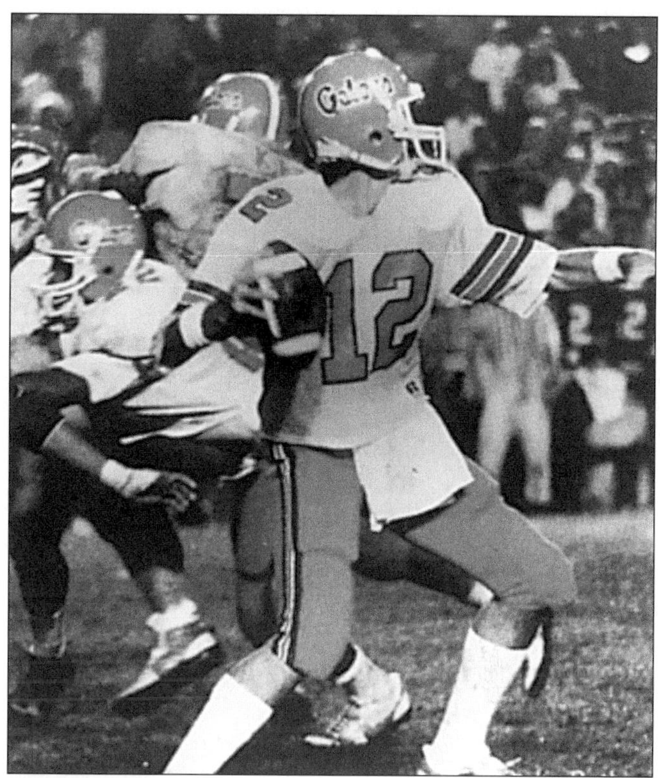

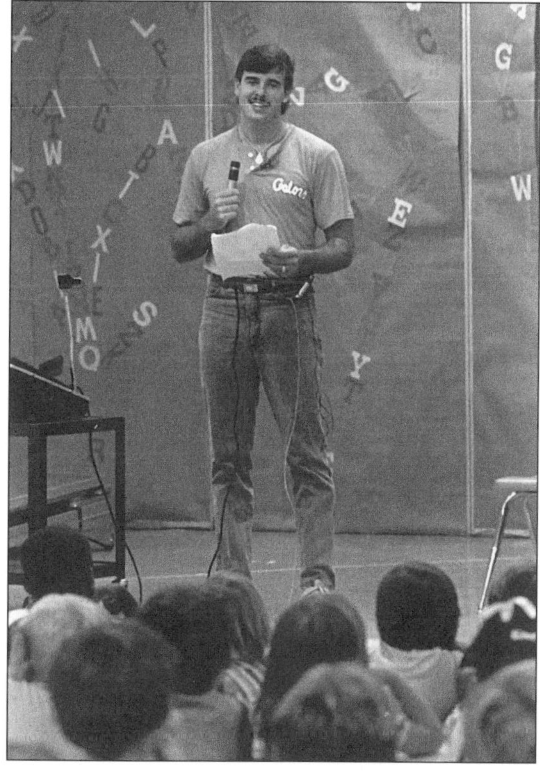

Gator athletes like Kerwin Bell often make presentations at local schools to encourage students to do well in academics. Student-athletes have contributed many hours of community service to Gainesville and the surrounding area as they have served as role models and public speakers for many nonprofit organizations. (Courtesy UF News & Public Affairs: Walter Coker.)

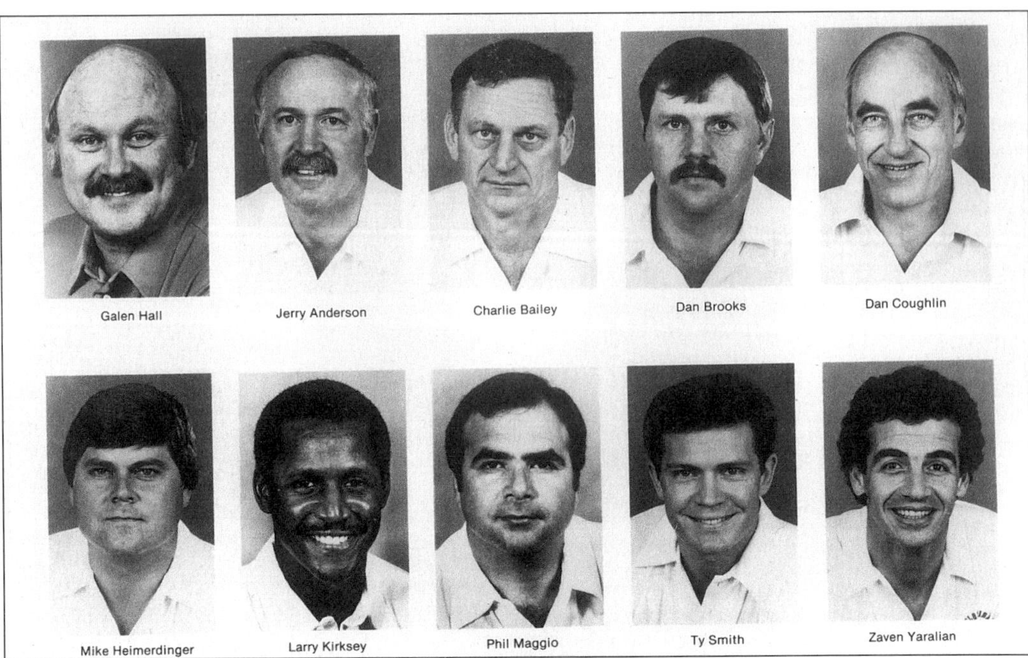

The 1985 coaching staff was led by Head Coach Galen Hall, who took over from Charley Pell as the school's 17th head coach after his team beat Kentucky for the school's first-ever first-place finish in the SEC. (Courtesy UF News & Public Affairs.)

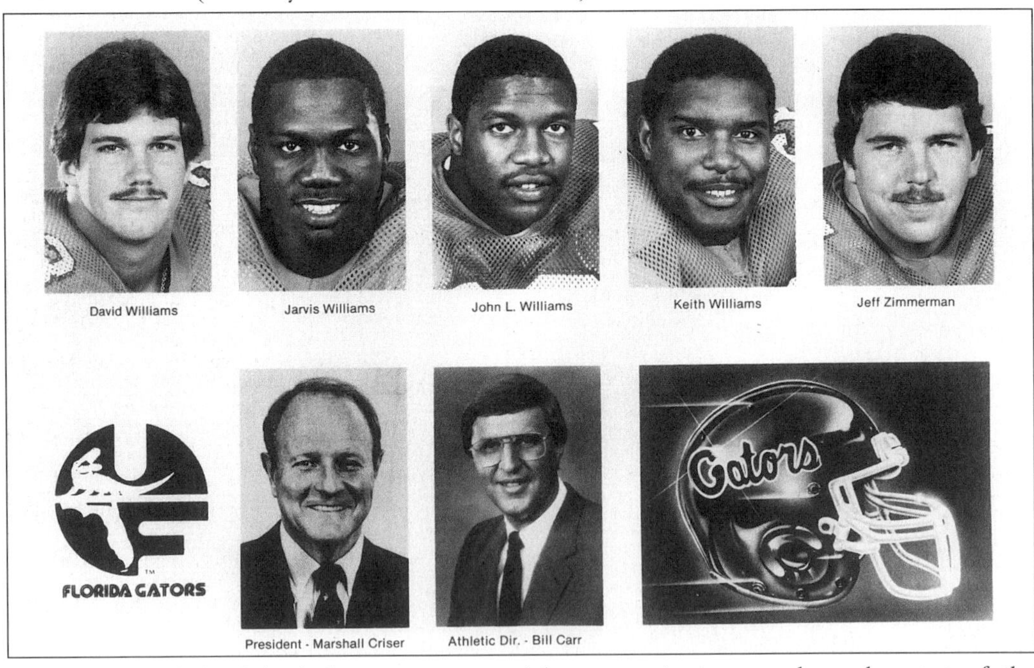

These players helped lead the team to an eight-game winning streak at the start of the 1985 season and a number-one ranking for the first time in school history. That winning streak extended the team's unbeaten mark to 18 consecutive games. The team finished with a second-straight 9-1-1 record and a number-five ranking in the AP list. (Courtesy UF News & Public Affairs.)

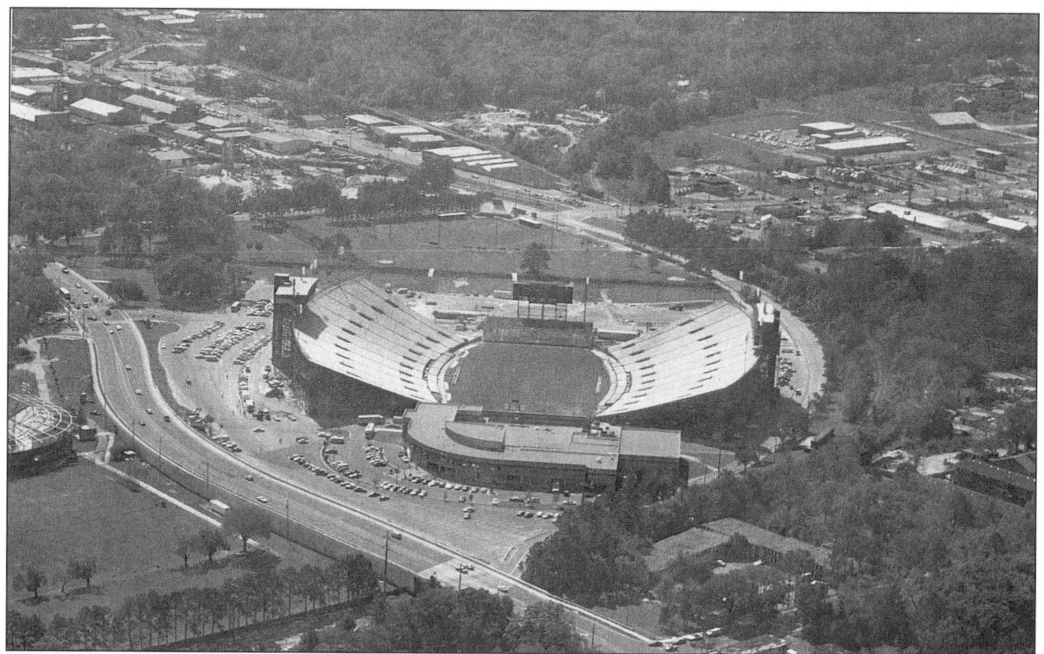

FSU's Campbell Stadium in Tallahassee was the scene of some great UF-FSU games. Many of the players on the two teams had been teammates or opponents in high school and would later become teammates or opponents in the NFL. (Courtesy Florida State Archives.)

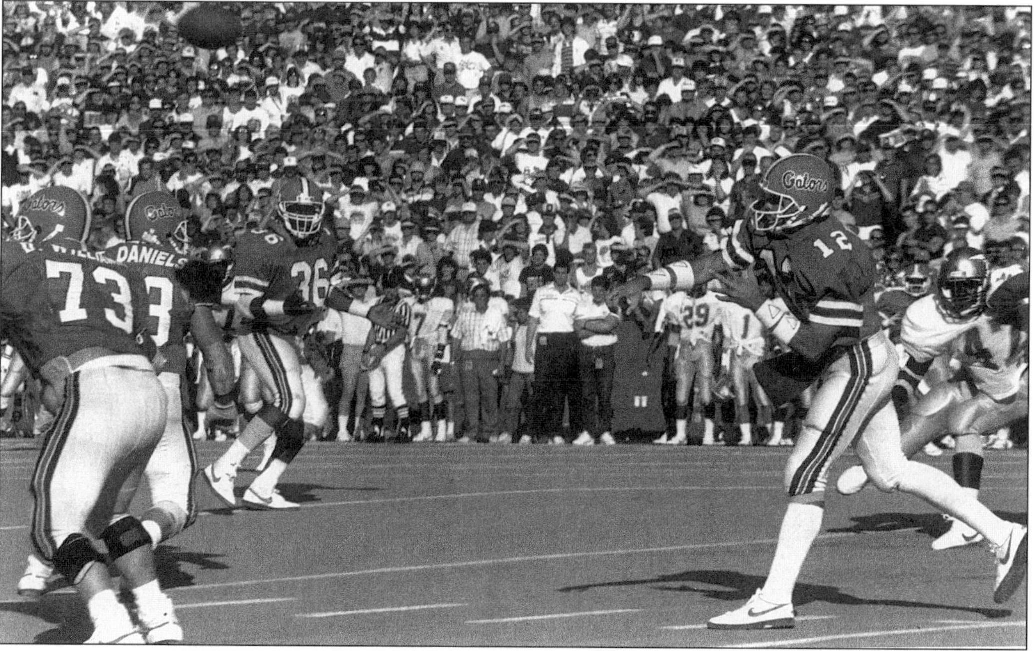

Kerwin Bell's pass protection in 1987 was helped by David Williams (#73), Tracy Daniels (#63), and Anthony Williams (#36). Offensive tackle David Williams, who lettered for four years (1985–1988) and was named to UF's Team of the Century in 1999, started in every game in his UF career (46), after which he played in the NFL for the Oilers (1989–1995) and Jets (1996–1997). (Courtesy UF News & Public Affairs: Neil C. Berger.)

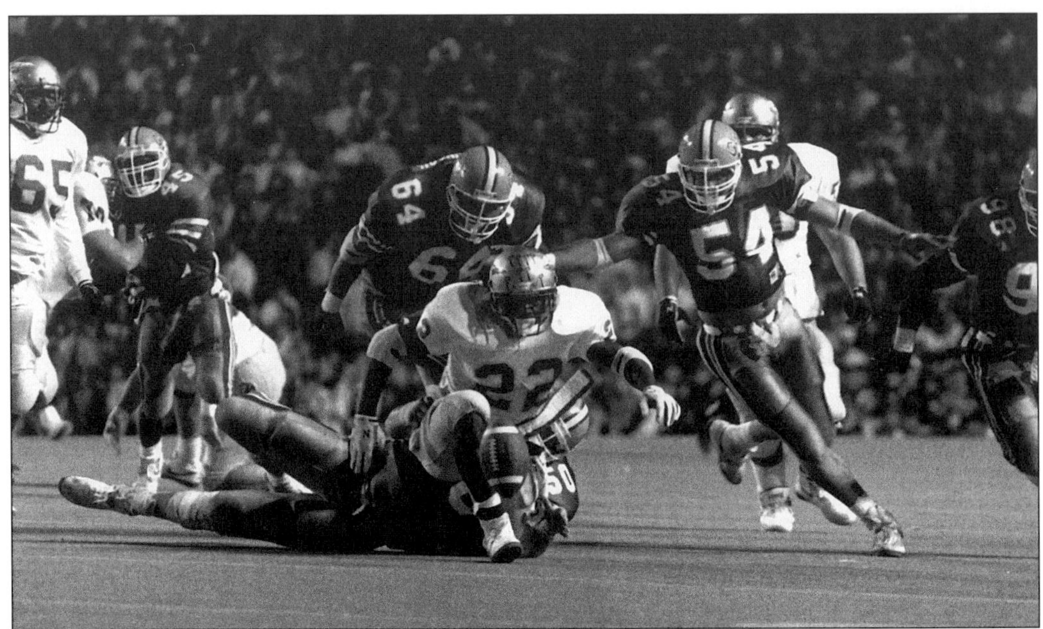

UF's Mark Murray (#54) and Phillip Johnson (#64), and FSU's Edgar Bennett (#22), chase a loose ball in their annual showdown in 1989. Despite a poor 7-5 record that year, including a loss to Washington in the Freedom Bowl, and a change of coaches after five games (Gary Darnell replaced Galen Hall), one bright spot was running back Emmitt Smith. (Courtesy UF News & Public Affairs: Walter Coker.)

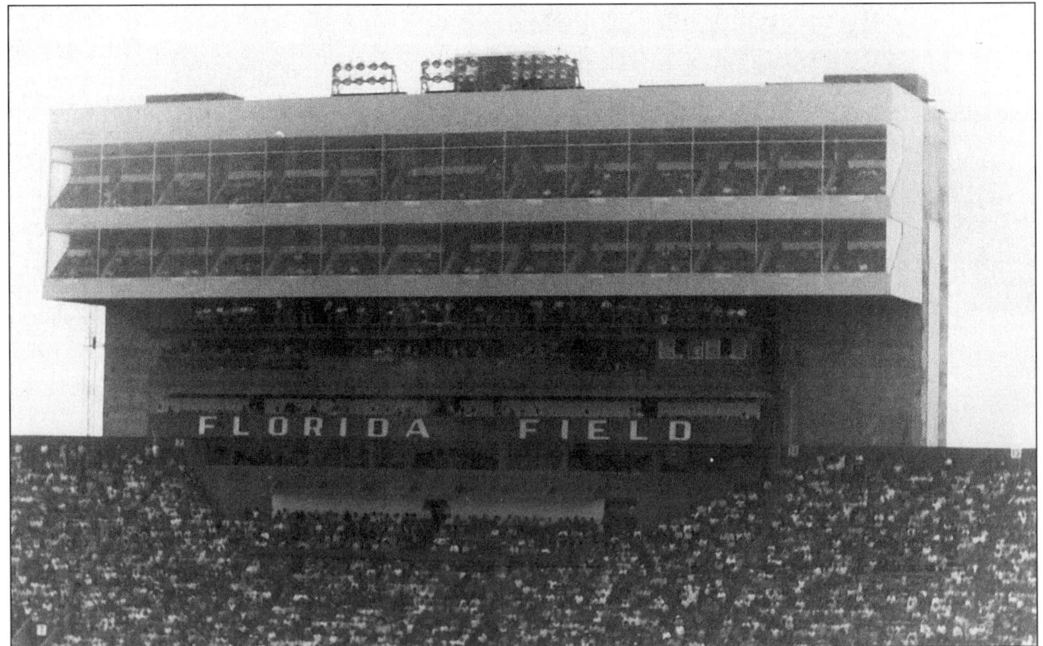

Skyboxes provided a good source of income to the athletic program. The football field was expanded several times, and in 1989 it was renamed for citrus magnate Ben Hill Griffin Jr. after he helped contribute to a $17-million expansion. (Courtesy University Archives, Dept. of Special Collections, George A. Smathers Libraries, Univ. of Florida.)

Nine

1990–1999: Coach Spurrier

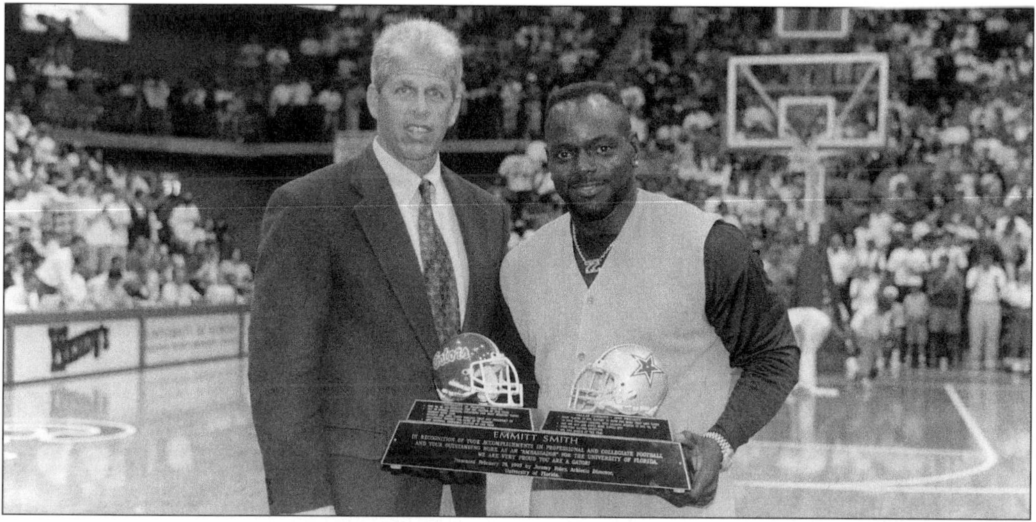

Two important figures in UF's sports programs are athletic director Jeremy Foley and running back Emmitt Smith. Smith, who lettered at Florida for three years (1987–1989) and is on UF's Team of the Century, set a then-school record in his freshman year: 1,341 yards and 13 touchdowns on 229 carries, which helped him finish ninth in the Heisman voting that year and marked a transition to the successful decade of Steve Spurrier. In his first start, an away-game against Alabama, he rushed for a then school record 224 yards on 39 carries as the Gators won, 23-14. In 1988 he set school records for rushing yardage in one season (1,599), carries (284), rushing touchdowns (14), and rushing yards in one game (316 against New Mexico). The SEC named him Player of the Year, and he finished seventh in the Heisman voting. After setting 58 school records, he left for the NFL after his junior season and starred for the Dallas Cowboys (1990–), becoming the first back in league history to rush for 1,400 yards in five consecutive seasons (1991–1995). (Courtesy UF News & Public Affairs: Walter Coker.)

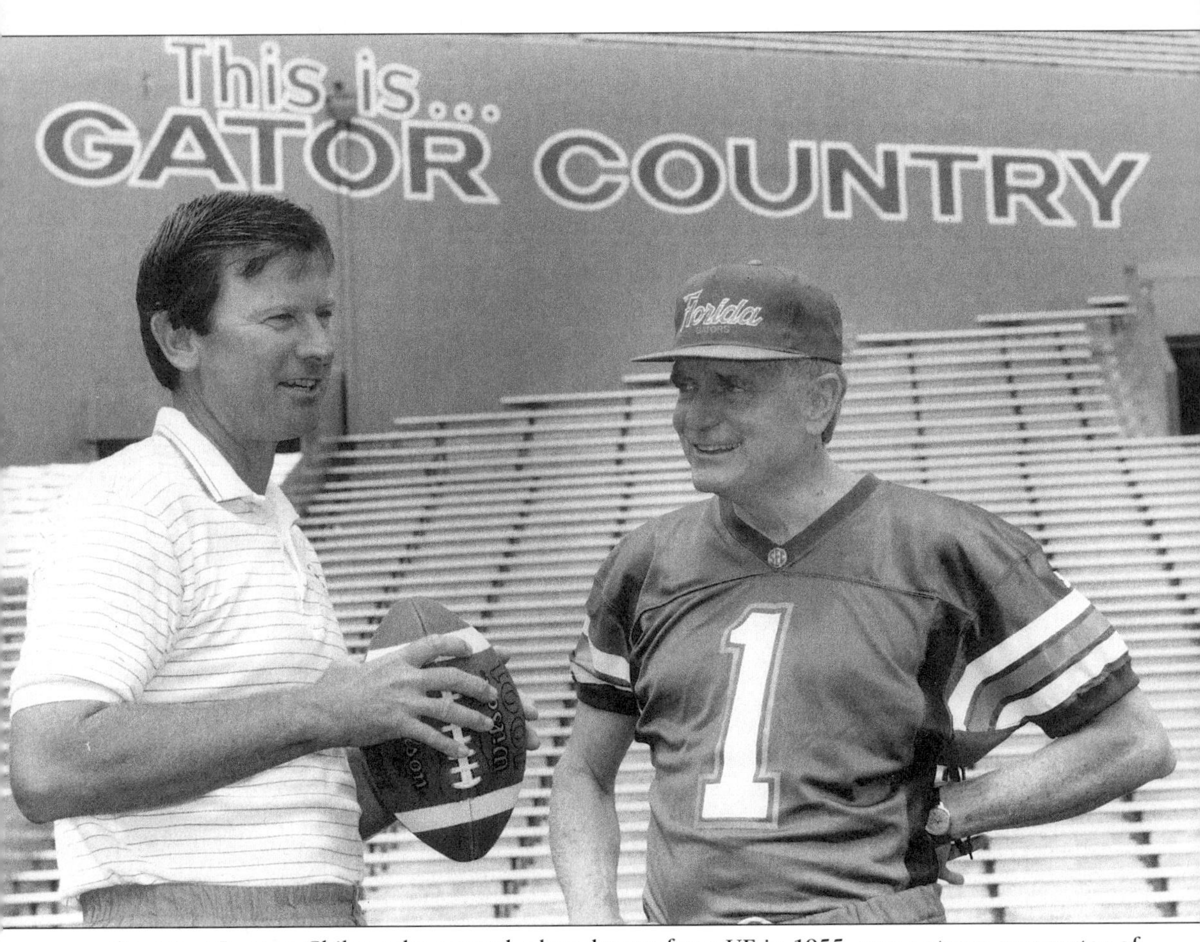

Governor Lawton Chiles, who earned a law degree from UF in 1955, was a strong supporter of football at both UF and FSU. The late governor is shown on the right here, talking with Coach Spurrier. (Courtesy UF News & Public Affairs.)

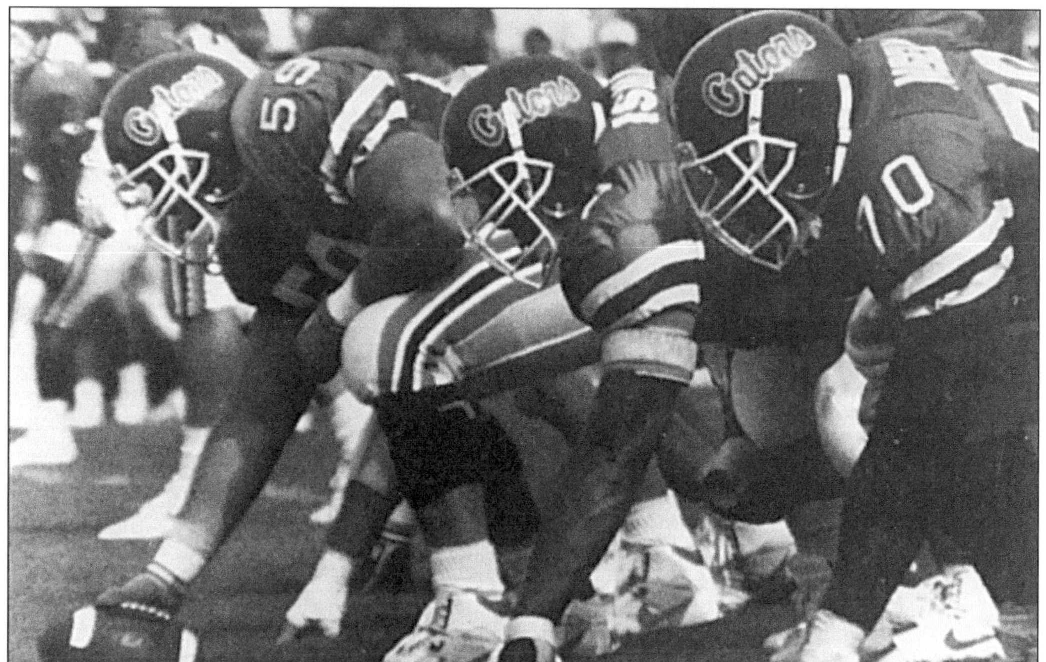

All-SEC center Cal Dixon (#59), guard Hesham Ismail (#77), and tackle Glenn Neely (#70) line up on the offensive side of the ball in 1990. (Courtesy University Archives, Dept. of Special Collections, George A. Smathers Libraries, Univ. of Florida.)

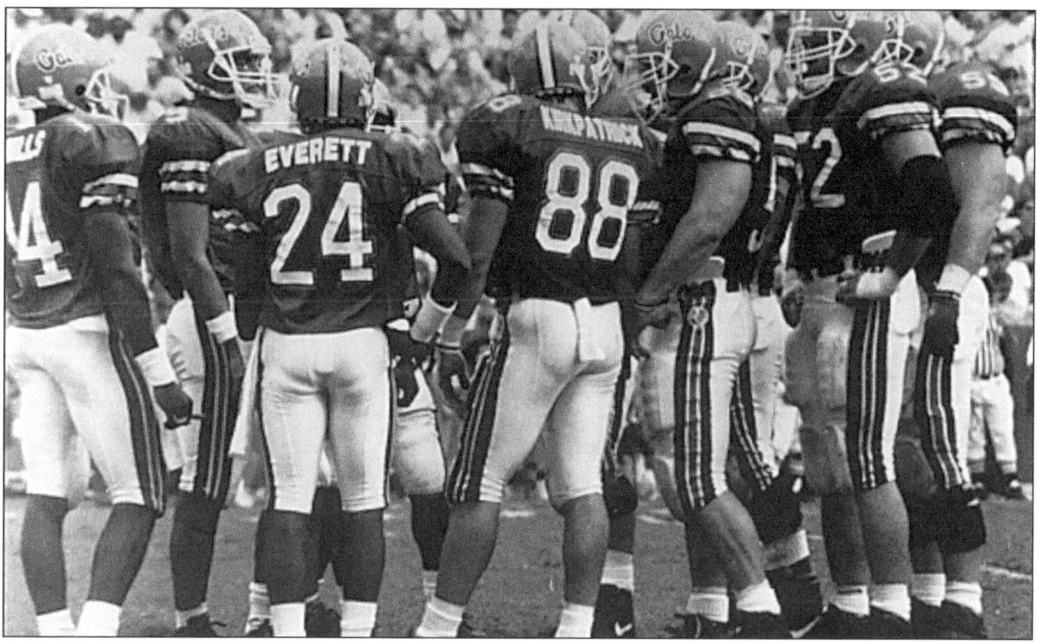

UF's offense, including Ernie Mills (#14), Tre Everett (#24), Kirk Kirkpatrick (#88), and Chris Bromley (#52), listen to quarterback Shane Matthews (#9, second from the left). Matthews was named the SEC Player of the Year twice (1990, 1991) and was fifth in the Heisman voting in 1991, the highest for a Gator behind winners Steve Spurrier and Danny Wuerffel. (Courtesy UF News & Public Affairs.)

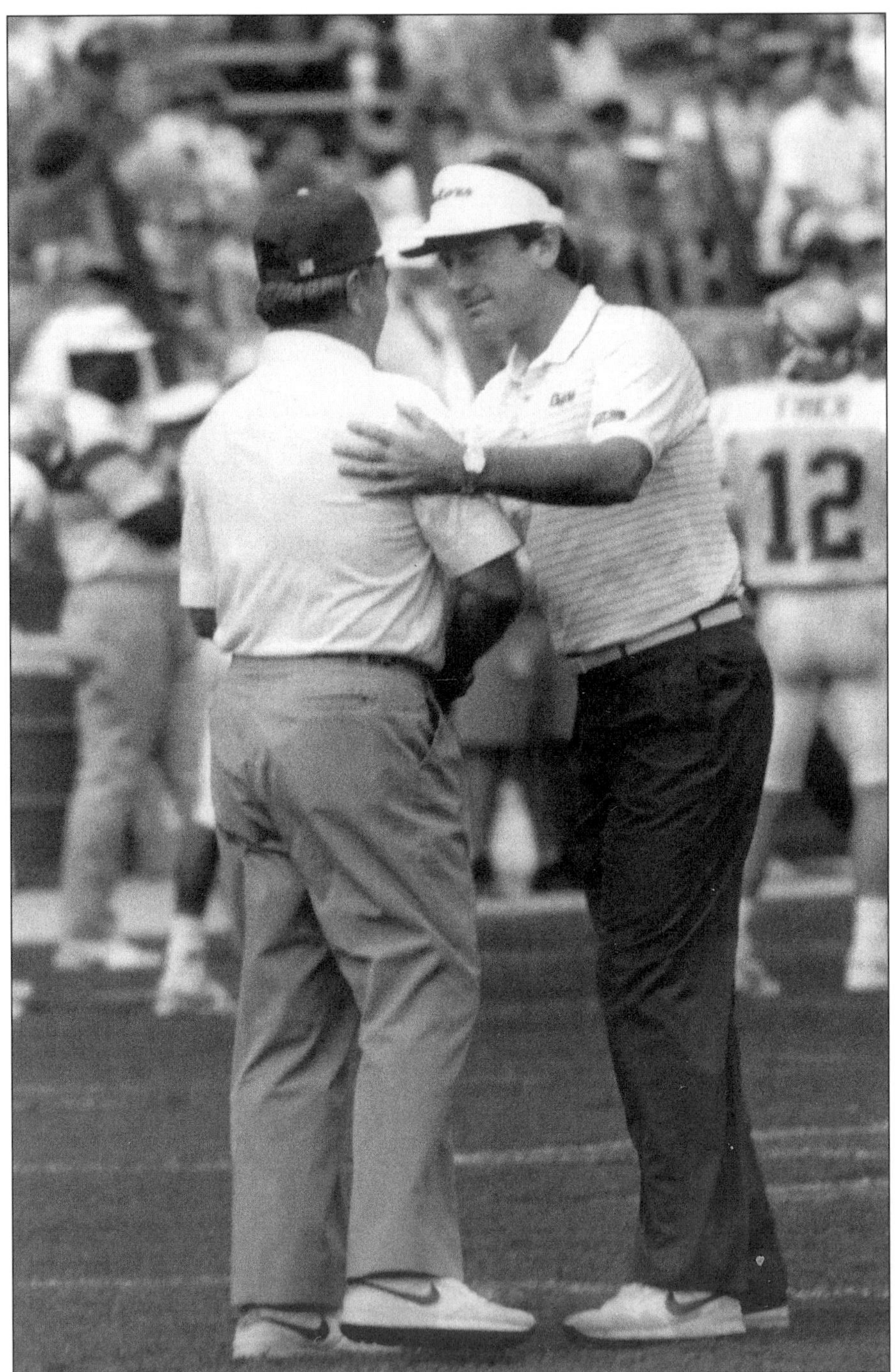

Coaches Bobby Bowden of FSU and Steve Spurrier of UF have coached their teams to exciting matches. Spurrier became the school's 19th head coach and compiled an amazing record of 102-21-1 in the 1990s. The game with FSU was always a tough one for Spurrier's Gators, which complied a 4-7-1 record against the Seminoles in the 1990s, including a 52-20 victory over them in the Sugar Bowl for the 1996 national championship. (Courtesy UF News & Public Affairs: Buddy Long.)

Wide receiver Willie Jackson Jr., who lettered for three years (1991–1993), was the son of Willie B. Jackson, who also lettered for three years (1970–1972), and was the first African-American player on the UF squad. Willie Jr. went on to the NFL to play for the Cowboys (1994), Jaguars (1995–1997), and Bengals (1998–). (Courtesy UF News & Public Affairs.)

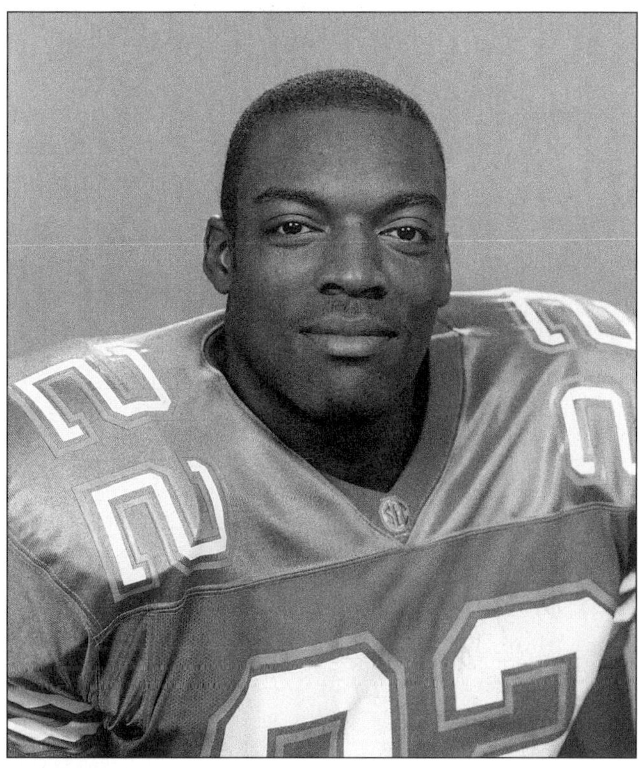

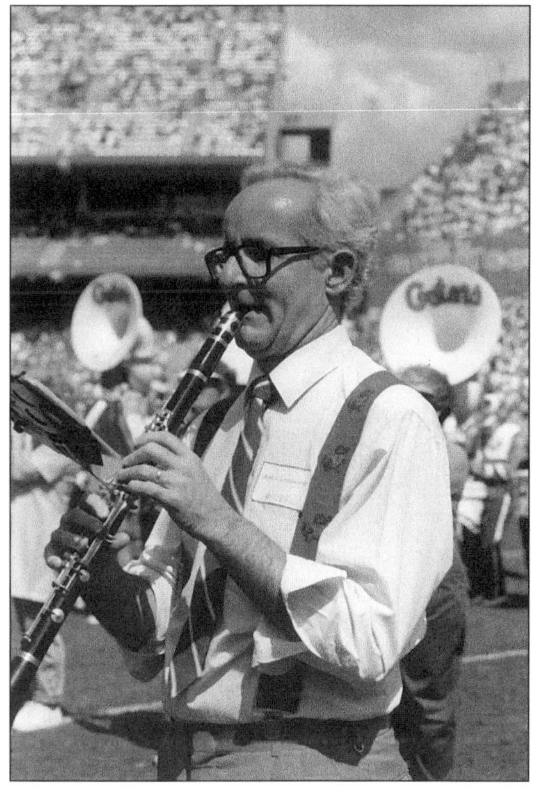

President John Lombardi enjoyed playing in the band. His Gator suspenders, distinctive glasses, and enthusiastic smile made him stand out in a crowd. He returned to full-time teaching and research in 1999. (Courtesy UF News & Public Affairs: Andy Windham.)

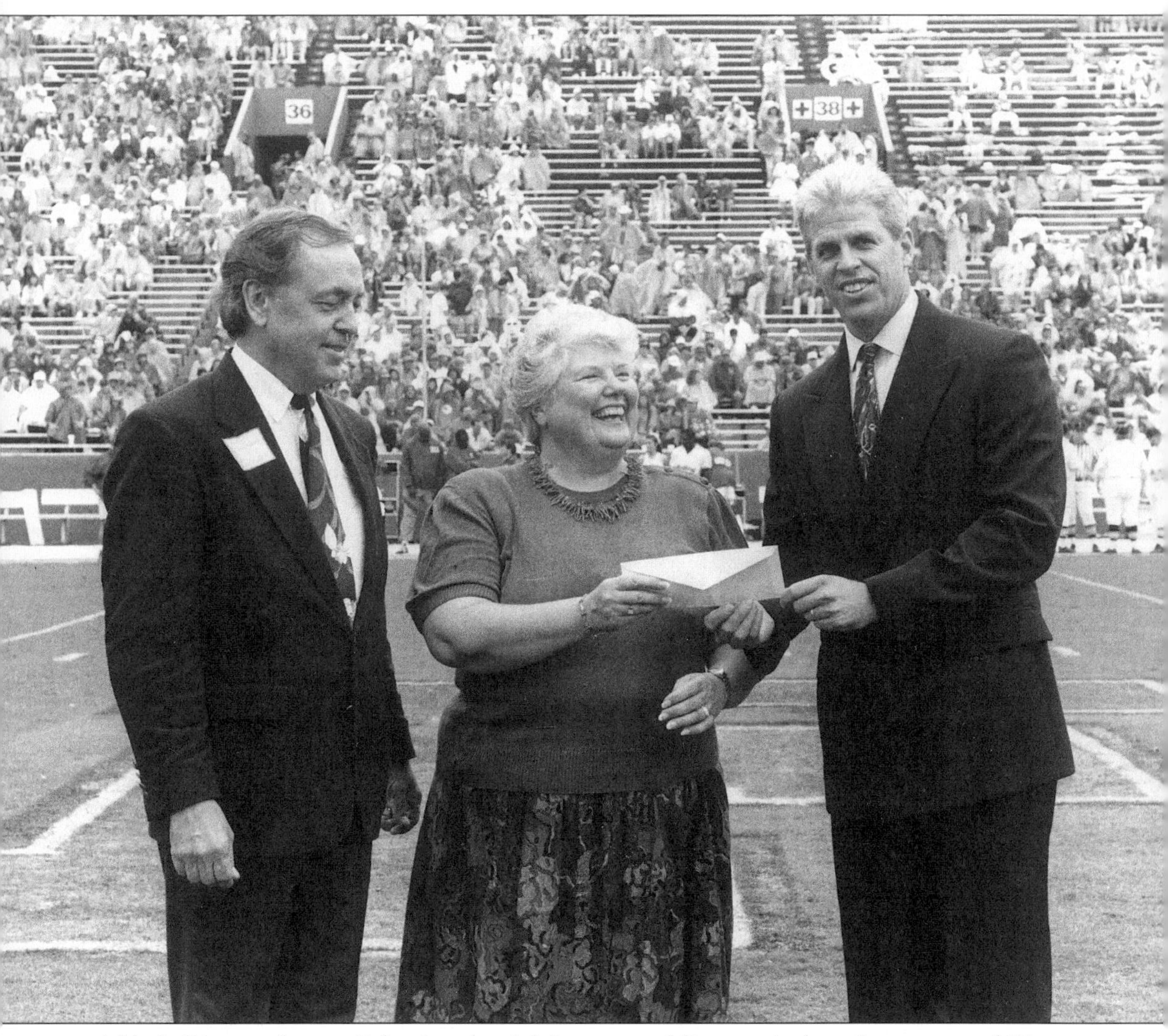

Athletic Director Jeremy Foley (on the right) presented Provost Andrew Sorenson and Director of Libraries Dale Canelas a check from the income generated by the team in a bowl game. The Gators averaged over nine TV appearances each year of the 1990s, a feat that brought in much income to the university and the athletic program. The Athletic Association provided the university library with many computers that all the students could use and helped fund the Academic Advising Building in the middle of campus, which provided counseling for all the students, including athletes. (Courtesy UF News & Public Affairs: Jeff Gage.)

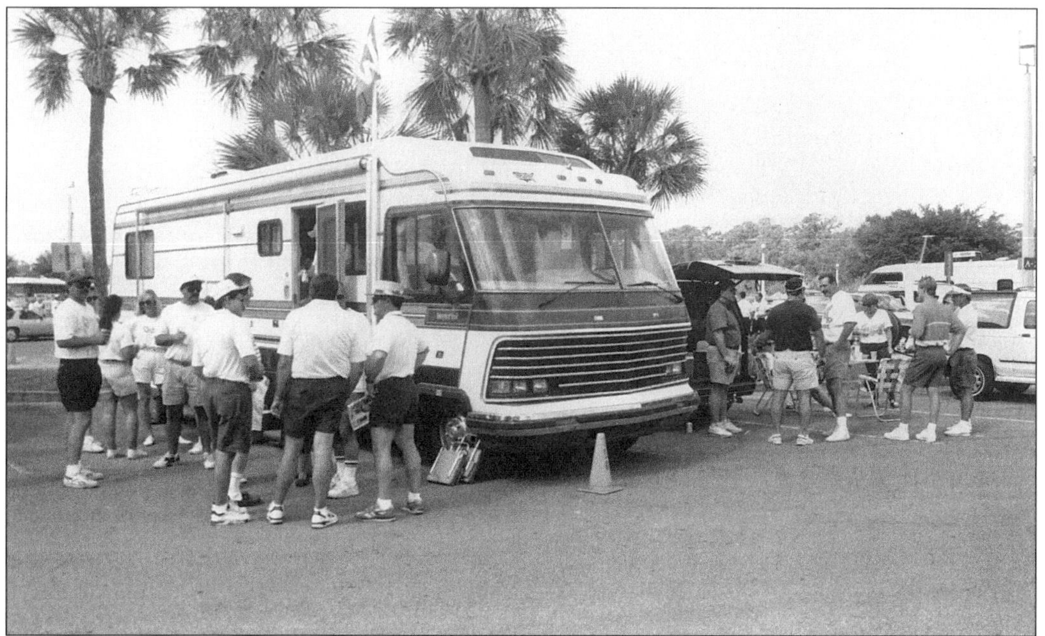

Tailgating became a popular pre-game ritual for Gator fans as they gathered in the same spot and discussed the upcoming game with longtime acquaintances. Other rituals were doing the wave throughout the whole stadium and joining the players after a home game in the singing of the school's alma mater. (Courtesy UF News & Public Affairs: Ray Carson.)

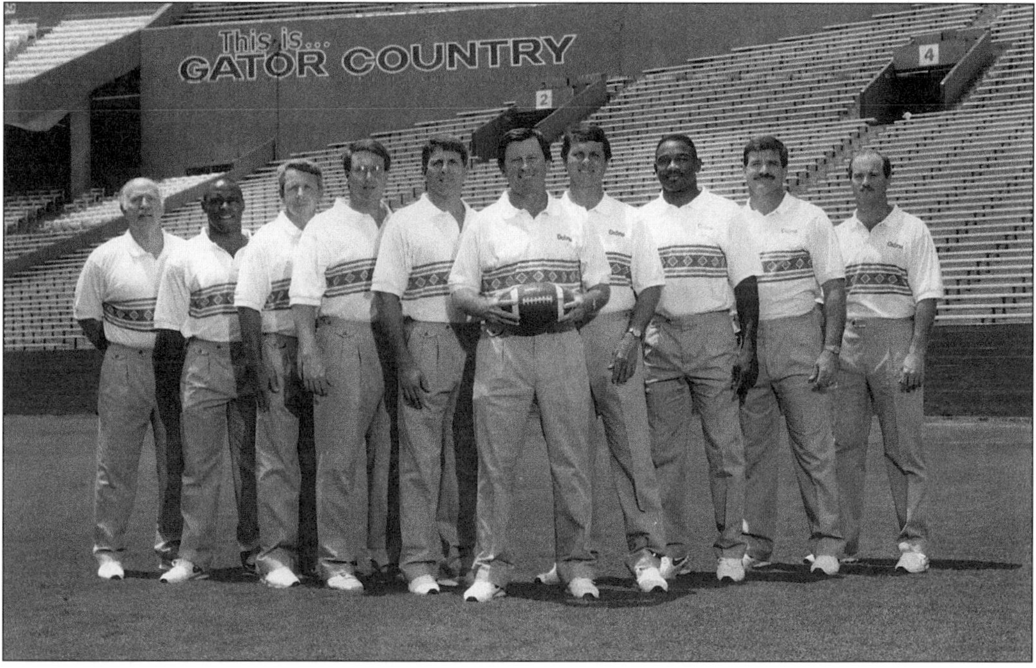

Coach Spurrier's 1993 coaching staff is pictured from left to right: Red Anderson, Charlie Strong, Jim Collins, Bob Sanders, Ron Zook, Steve Spurrier, John Reaves, Dwayne Dixon, Jimmy Ray Stephens, and Carl Franks. As the Gators' success increased, Spurrier's coaches became coaches elsewhere. (Courtesy UF News & Public Affairs.)

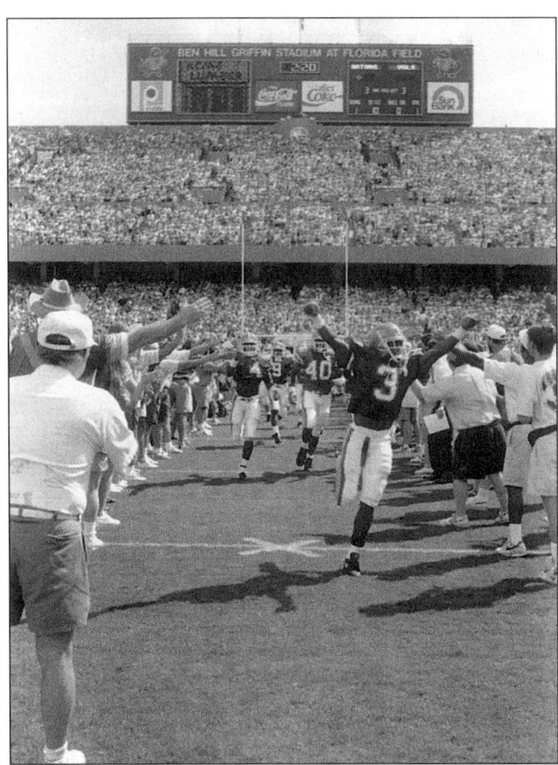

Cornerback Larry Kennedy (#3) led the team out from under the large scoreboard in 1993. Kennedy, who lettered for four years (1991–1994), was just one of many cornerbacks who have starred for the Gators. Others include Richard Fain, Steve Tannen, Fred Weary, and Jarvis Williams. (Courtesy UF News & Public Affairs: Ray Carson.)

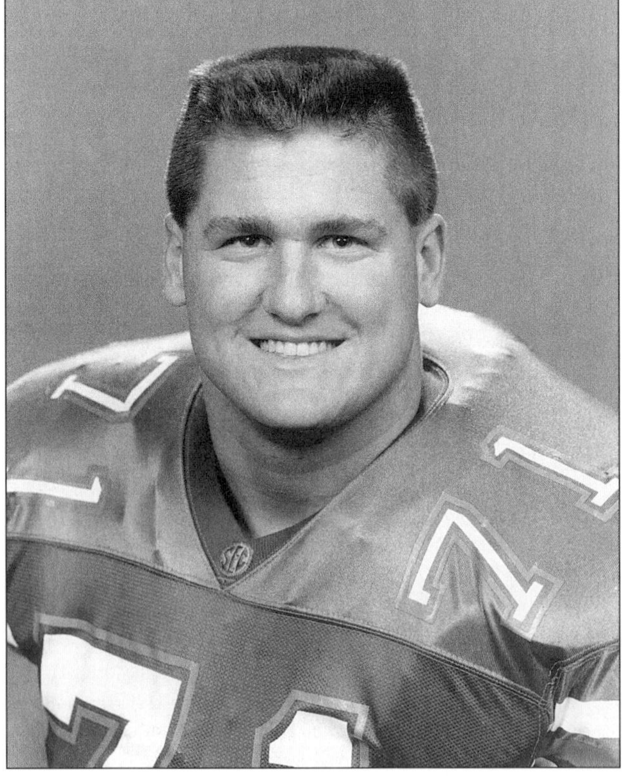

Center Jeff Mitchell, who lettered for four years (1993–1996) and was named to the UF Team of the Century, was a first-team All-SEC pick (1996) on a team that set a school and SEC record by scoring 559 points (44.6 points a game) during the regular season. He went on to the NFL to play center for the Baltimore Ravens (1997–). (Courtesy UF News & Public Affairs.)

Offensive guard Donnie Young, who also lettered for four years (1993–1996) and was named to the UF Team of the Century, was an All-SEC selection (1996), when he received the Jacobs Blocking Trophy as the league's best blocker and won the James W. Kynes Award, given annually to the offensive lineman who best exemplified the mental and physical toughness of Gator Great Jimmy Kynes. (Courtesy UF News & Public Affairs.)

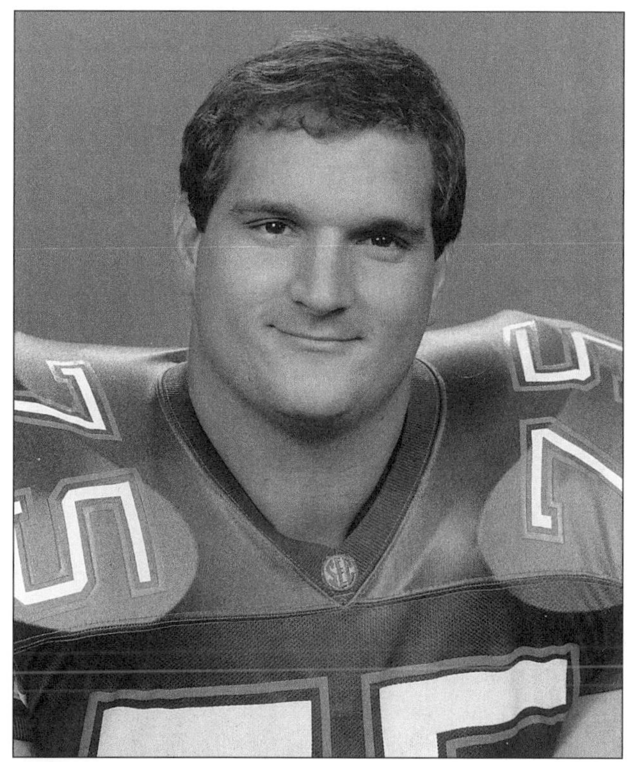

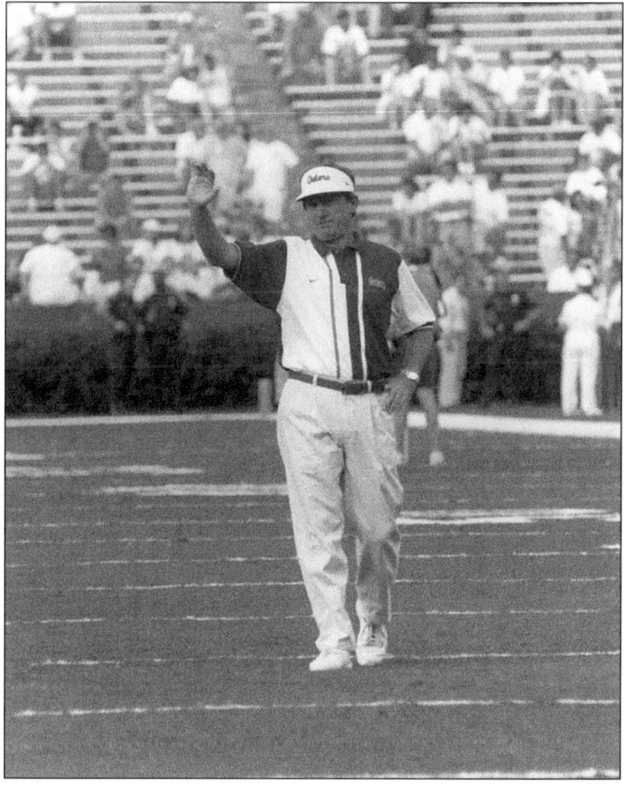

Before a game Spurrier was calm and relaxed, but his high intensity kicked in once the game began. His tremendous success at UF has led to consistently high expectations from Gator fans. (Courtesy UF News & Public Affairs: Jeff Gage.)

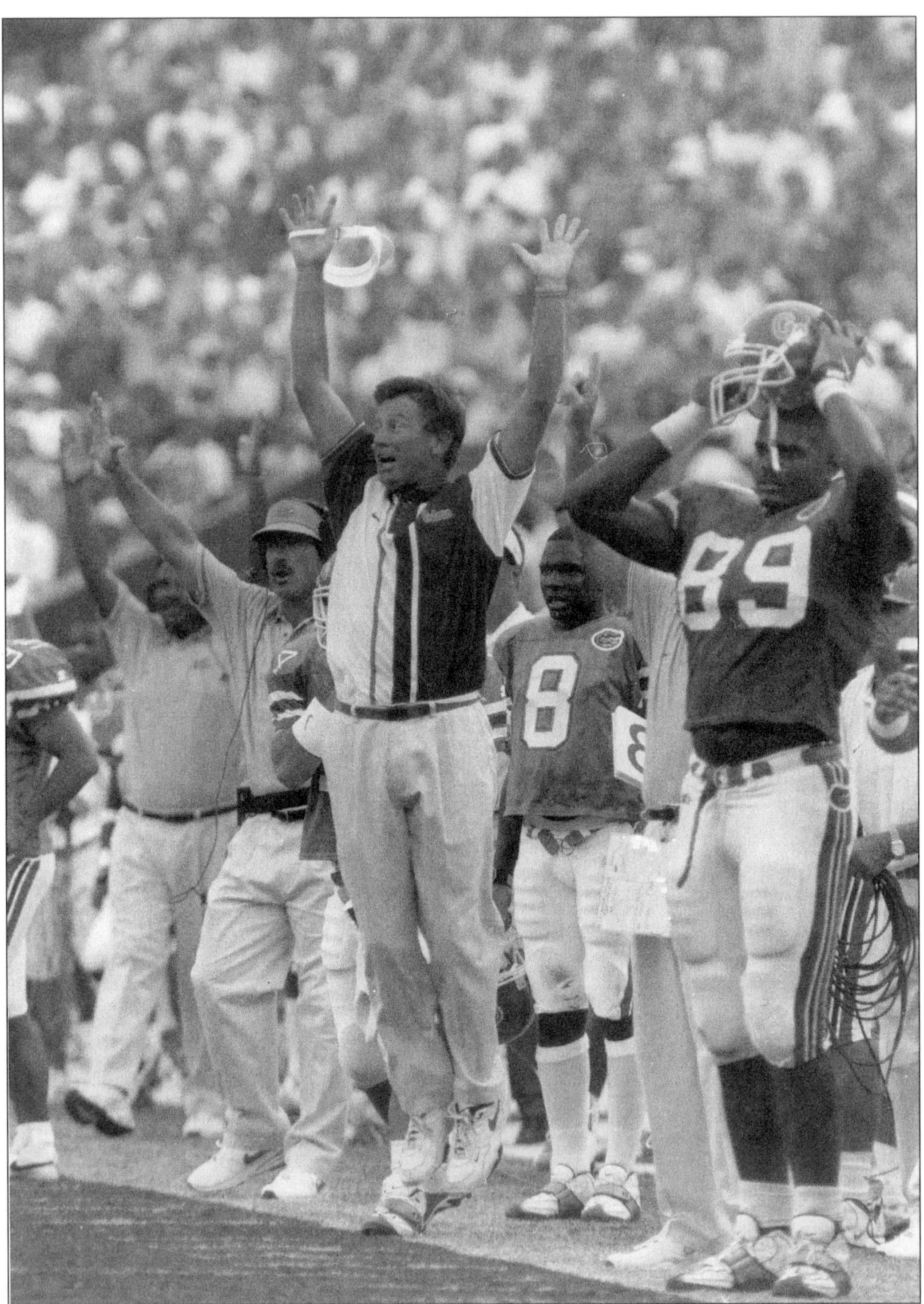

Unlike many more-sedate coaches, Steve Spurrier showed his emotions, whether after the Gators scored a touchdown or played poorly. More often than not, his fun-n-gun offense scored many points. (Courtesy UF News & Public Affairs: Jeff Gage.)

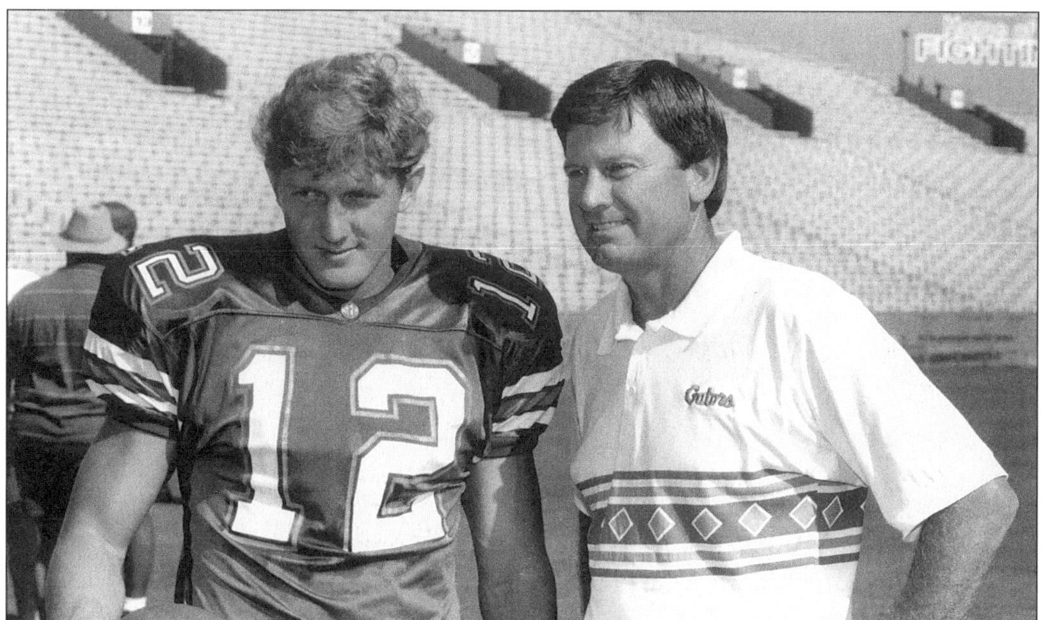

Quarterback Terry Dean, who lettered for four years (1991–1994), was on some unique Gator teams: the 1991 team, the first in school history to win ten games in a season and the first to win an outright SEC Title; the 1993 team, which won more games (11) in a season than any team in school history; and the 1994 team, which beat Georgia for a record fifth straight season. (Courtesy UF News & Public Affairs.)

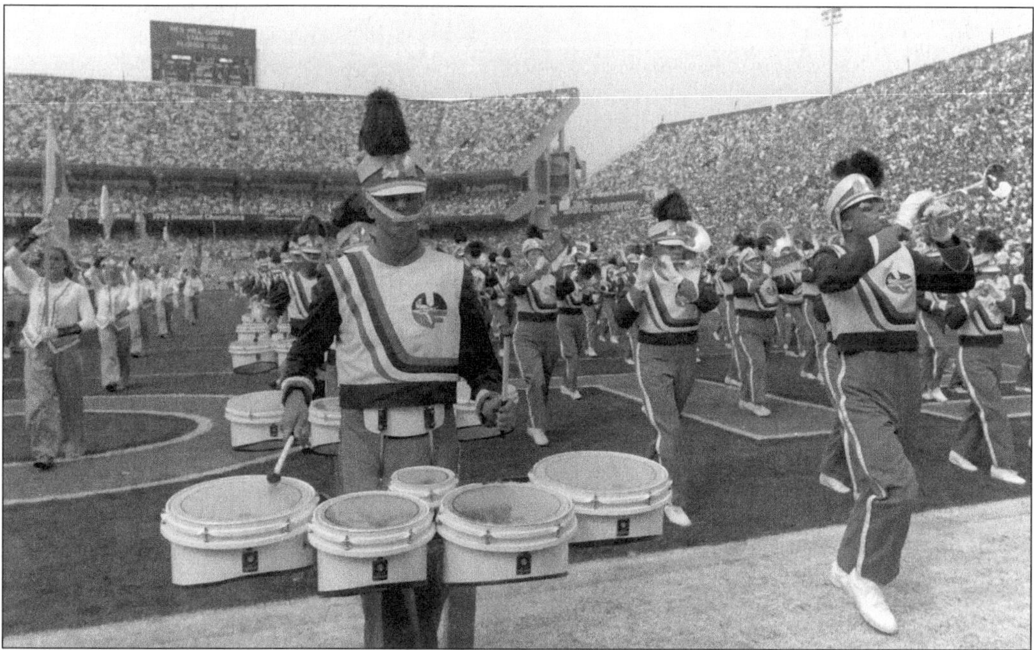

The Gator band played at halftime in the Swamp and often accompanied the team on away trips. The band would get the crowd excited by playing the theme from the movie *Jaws* and would accompany the singing of "We Are the Boys of Old Florida" before the start of the fourth quarter. (Courtesy UF News & Public Affairs: Jeff Gage.)

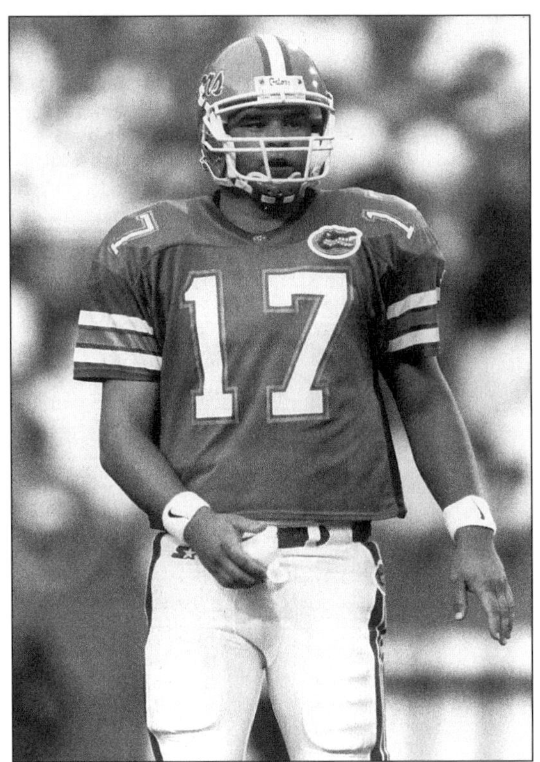

Quarterback Noah Brindise, who lettered for three years (1995–1997) and played backup quarterback to Wuerffel, was a two-time member of the SEC Academic Honor Roll and on the 1997 College Football Chronicle's Unsung Hero All-America Team. He later coached at Ursinius College before joining Coach Spurrier's staff in 1999 as an assistant working with the offense. (Courtesy UF News & Public Affairs: Jason.)

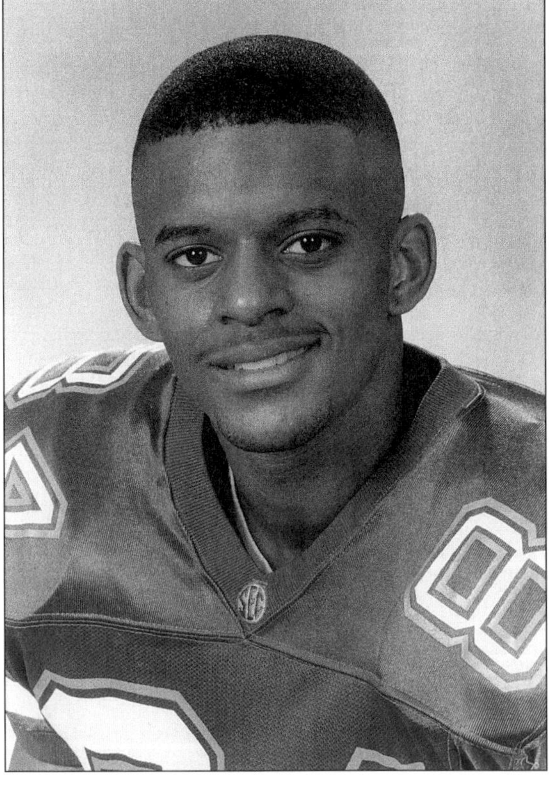

Ike Hilliard, who lettered for three years (1994–1996) before joining the New York Giants as a wide receiver, is second in career touchdown receptions at UF with 29. On those same Gator teams was another great receiver, Reidel Anthony, who caught an SEC-record 18 touchdown passes in 1996 before joining the Tampa Bay Buccaneers in the NFL. (Courtesy UF News & Public Affairs: Herb Press.)

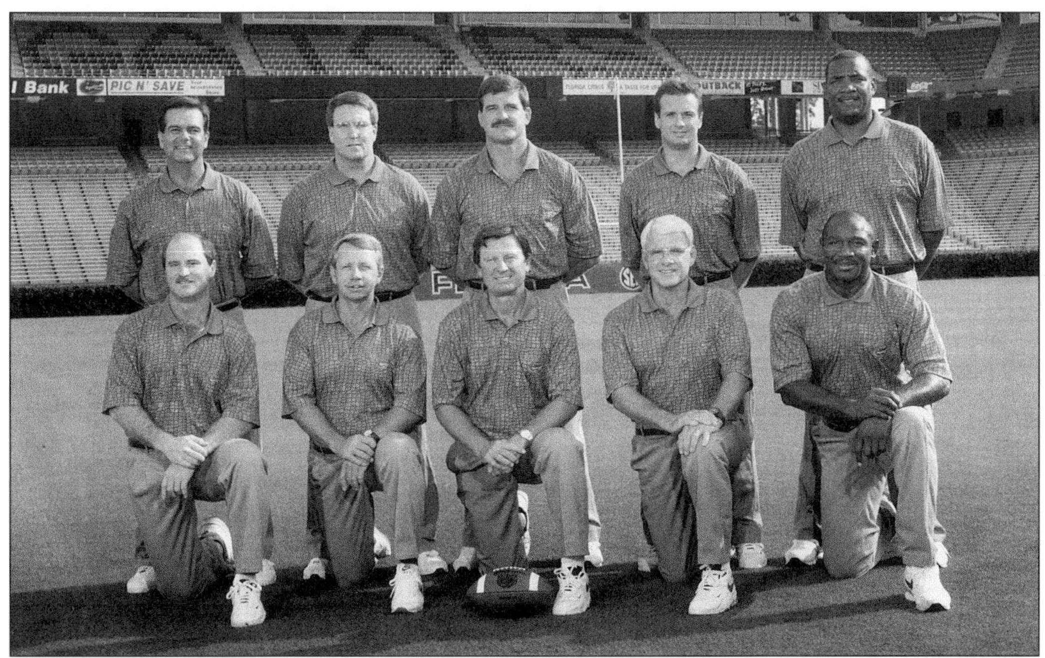

Steve Spurrier's 1996 football staff is pictured from left to right: (front row) Carl Franks, Jim Collins, Steve Spurrier, Barry Wilson, and Dwayne Dixon; (back row) Lawson Holland, Bob Sanders, Jimmy Ray Stephens, Bob Stoops, and Rod Broadway. (Courtesy UF News & Public Affairs: Jeff Gage.)

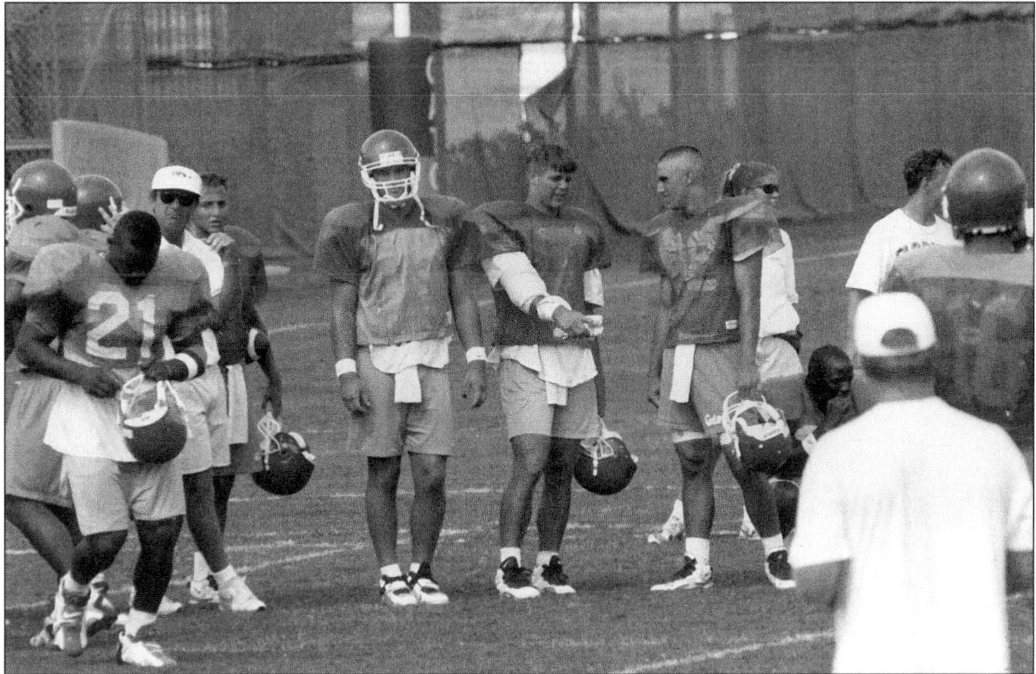

Danny Wuerffel talks to Doug Johnson (#12) at practice. Wuerffel was a two-time, first-team All American (1995,1996) and a two-time recipient of the O'Brien National Quarterback of the Year Award (1995, 1996). (Courtesy UF News & Public Affairs: Jeff Gage.)

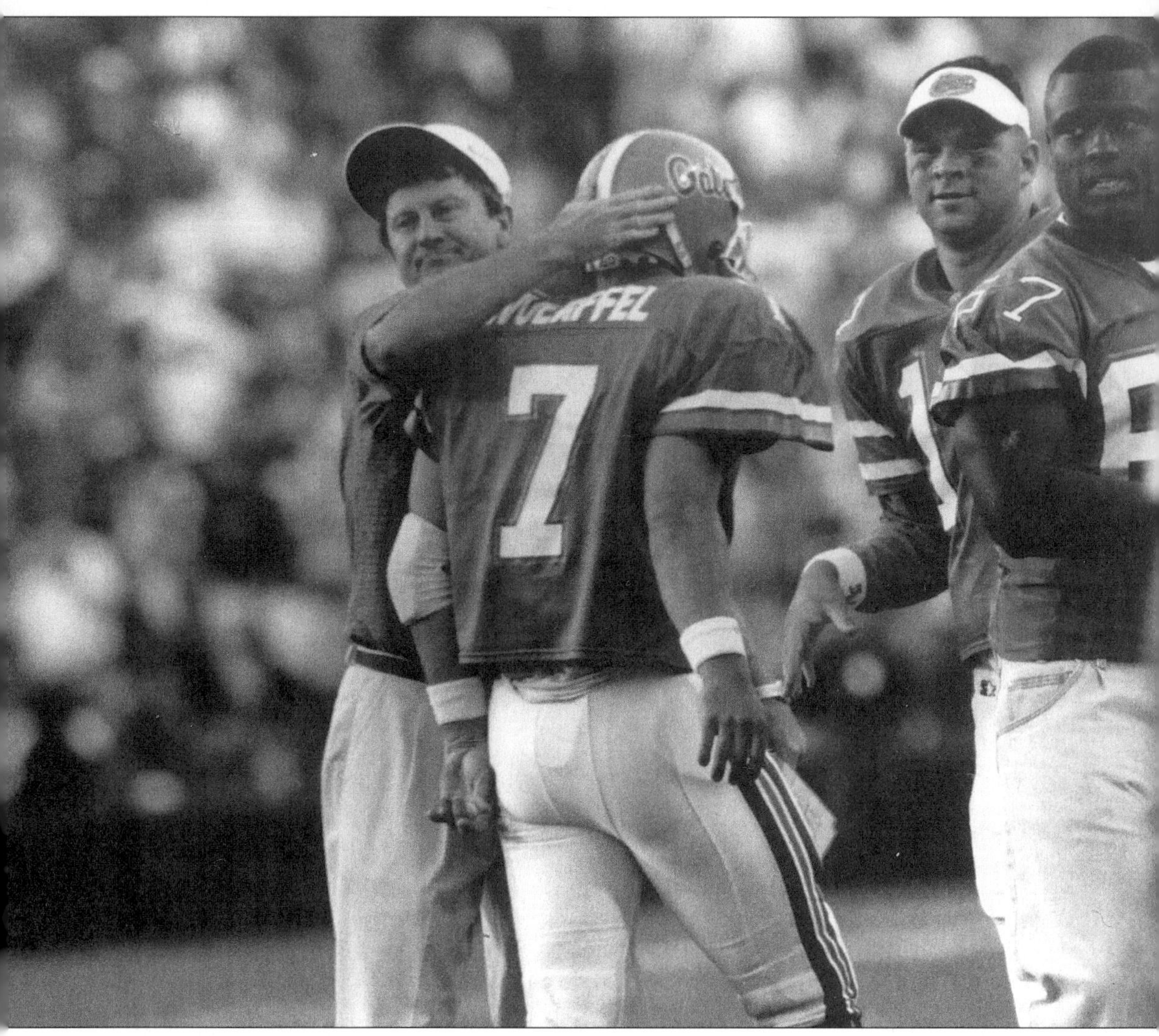

The two Heisman Trophy winners at UF were Steve Spurrier and Danny Wuerffel (#7), seen here in the 1996 championship season. Wuerffel's 39 TD passes that season were the best in UF and SEC history. In his UF career, he completed 708 of 1,170 passes for 10,875 yards (fifth-best in major-college history) and 114 touchdown passes (best in SEC history and second-best in major-college history). In 1999, Wuerffel was named UF's offensive player of the century for his four-year career (1993–1996). (Courtesy UF News & Public Affairs: Jeff Gage.)

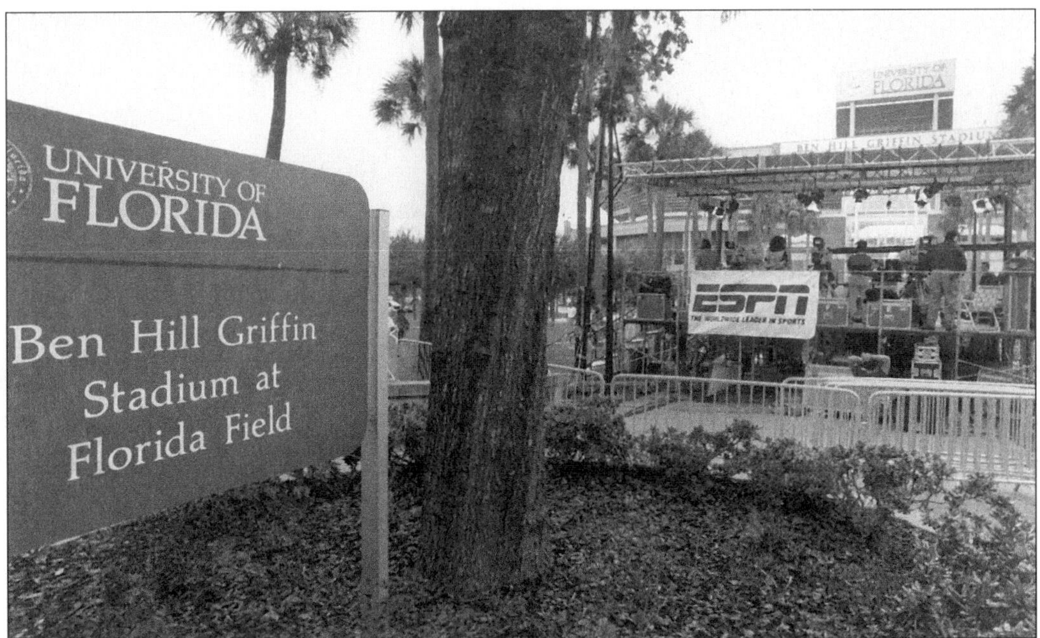

The increasing success of the Gators, as evidenced by an ESPN broadcast at Ben Hill Griffin Stadium, brought frequent exposure on national television. Such frequent TV appearances brought in much income to both the SEC and the University of Florida. (Courtesy UF News & Public Affairs.)

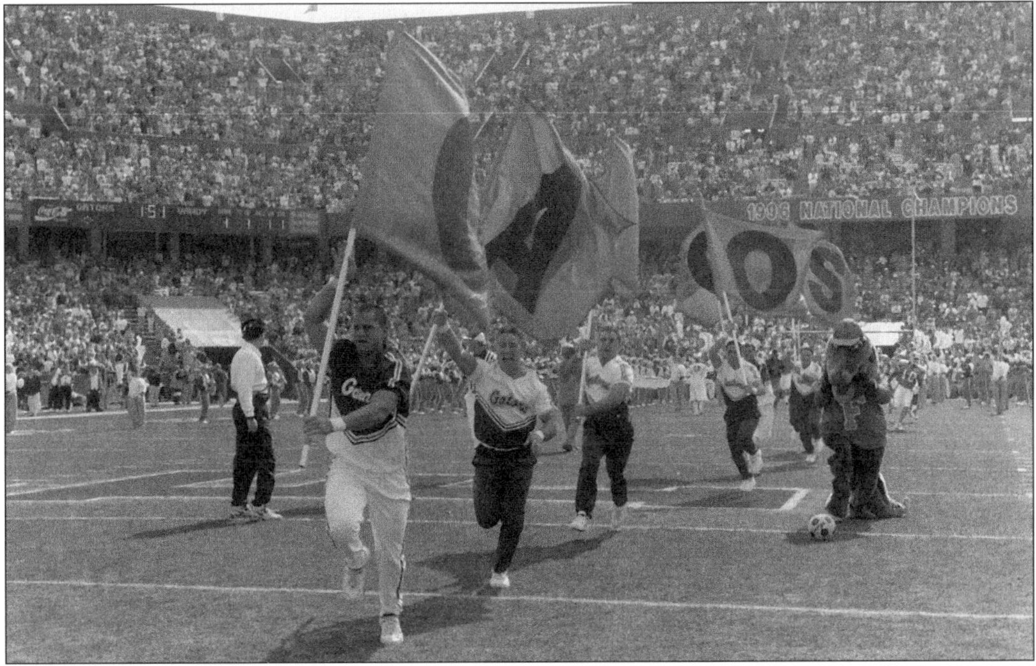

Cheerleaders and Albert the Alligator lead out the team to the friendly confines of the Swamp and its 85,000-plus inhabitants. The cheerleaders would lead fans in the "Jaws" cheer, when loyal Gators imitated a gator attack by bringing their hands together in a chomping motion. (Courtesy UF News & Public Affairs: Jeff Gage.)

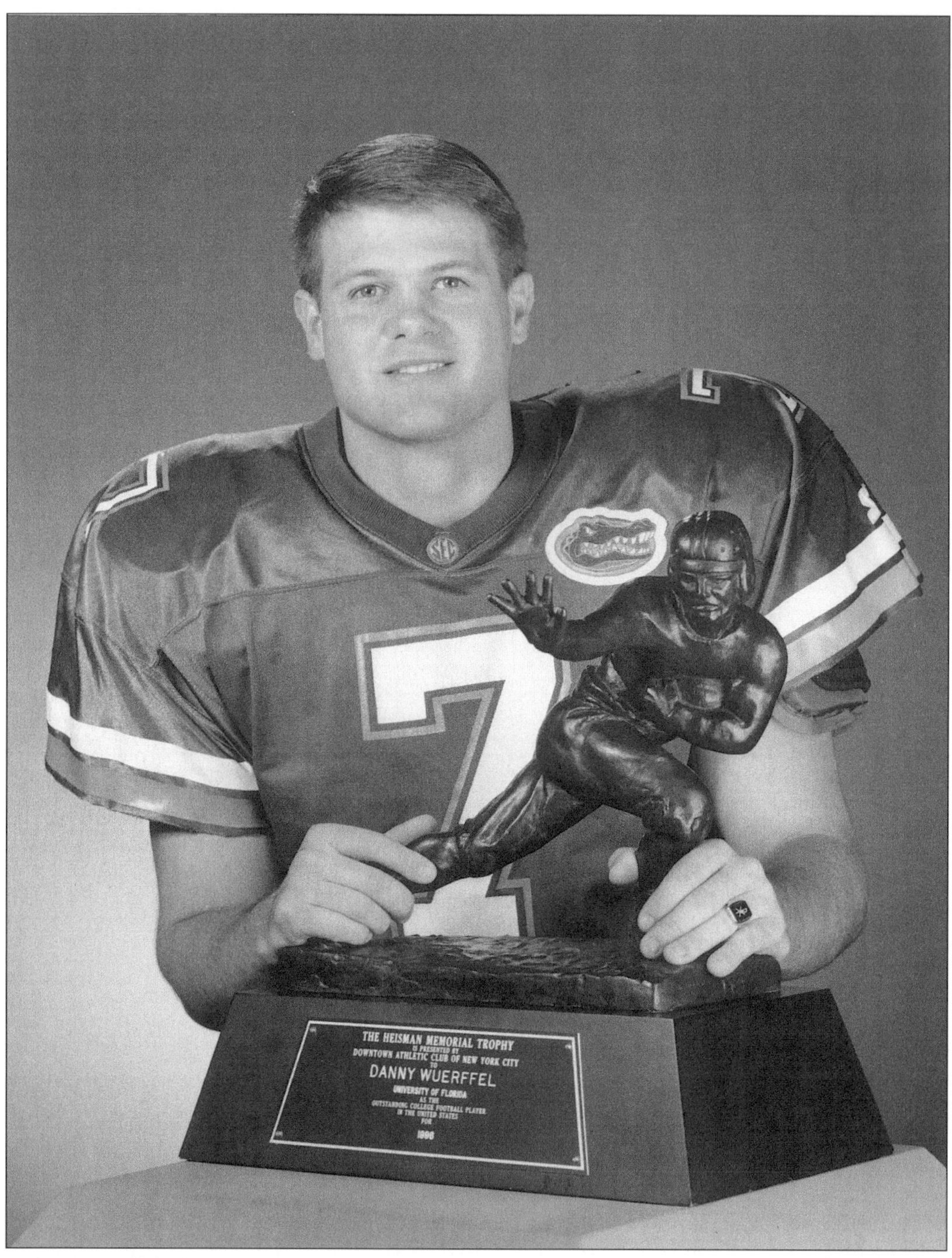

Danny Wuerffel, shown here with his Heisman Trophy, had a pass-efficiency rating that ranked first in NCAA history. He led the nation in touchdown passes in 1995 (35 TDs) and 1996 (39 TDs) and thus became one of only two quarterbacks in history to throw for 35 or more touchdowns in two successive seasons. He went on to play for the New Orleans Saints in the NFL. (Courtesy UF News & Public Affairs: Ray Carson.)

The trophies won in 1996 brought much-deserved recognition to the school's athletic programs and helped recruit more student-athletes who could continue the winning tradition at UF. (Courtesy UF News & Public Affairs: Ray Carson.)

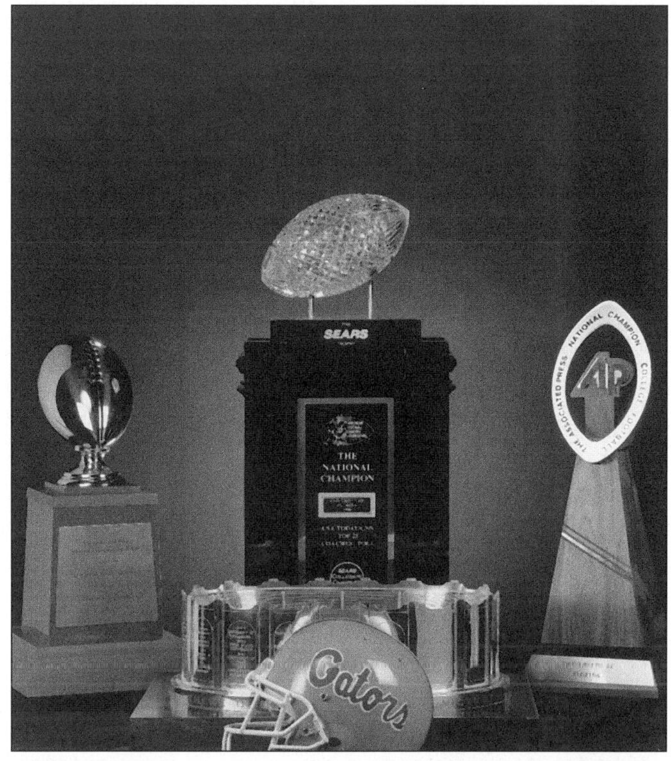

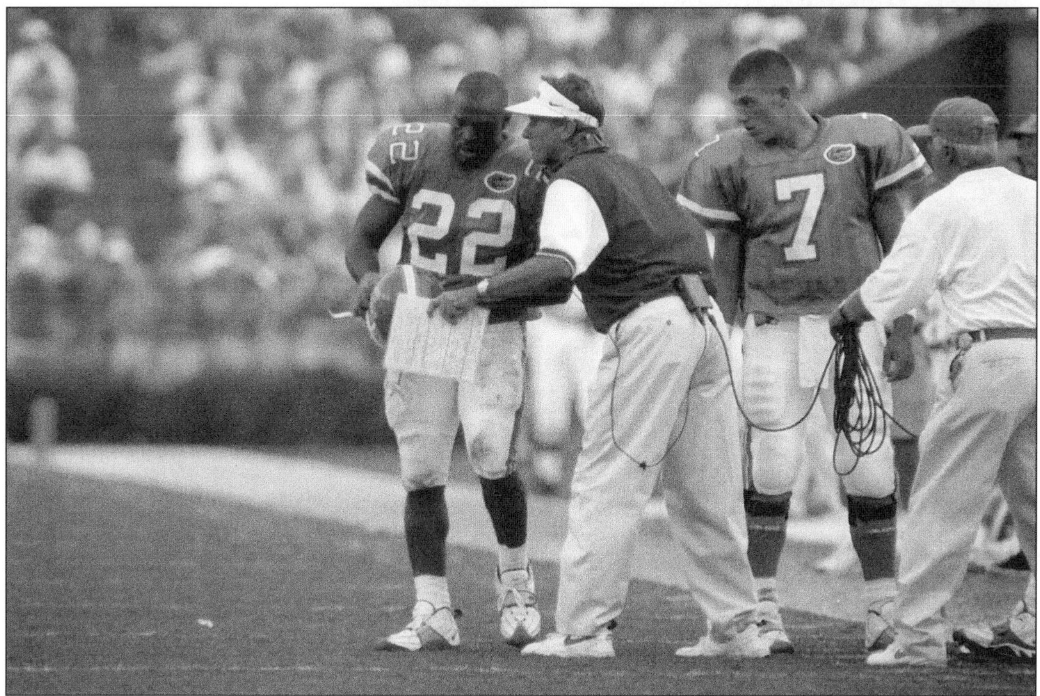

Tailback Terry Jackson (#22), seen here with Coach Spurrier and Jessie Palmer (#7), lettered for four years (1995–1998) and was one of the team's most exciting open-field runners with his speed and agility. (Courtesy UF News & Public Affairs: Jeff Gage.)

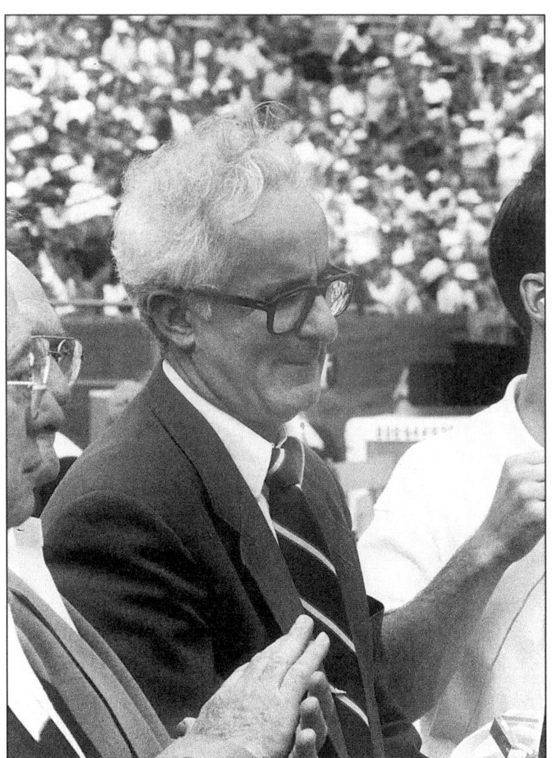

President John Lombardi, UF's ninth president (1990–1999), was a strong supporter of all the athletic programs at UF and also helped the university enter the prestigious Association of American Universities. (Courtesy UF News & Public Affairs.)

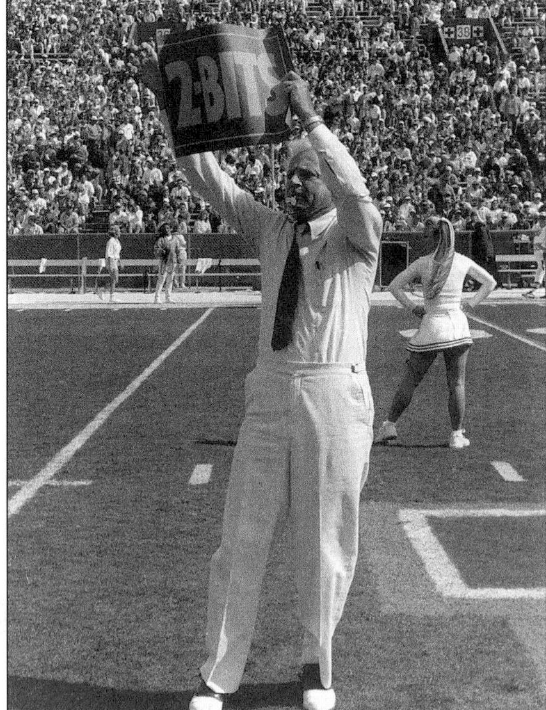

Mr. Two-Bits led cheers among the students and fans. After 50 years as the school's unofficial head cheerleader at Florida Field, George Edmondson, one of the many traditions associated with UF football, retired in 1998. (Courtesy UF News & Public Affairs: Jeff Gage.)

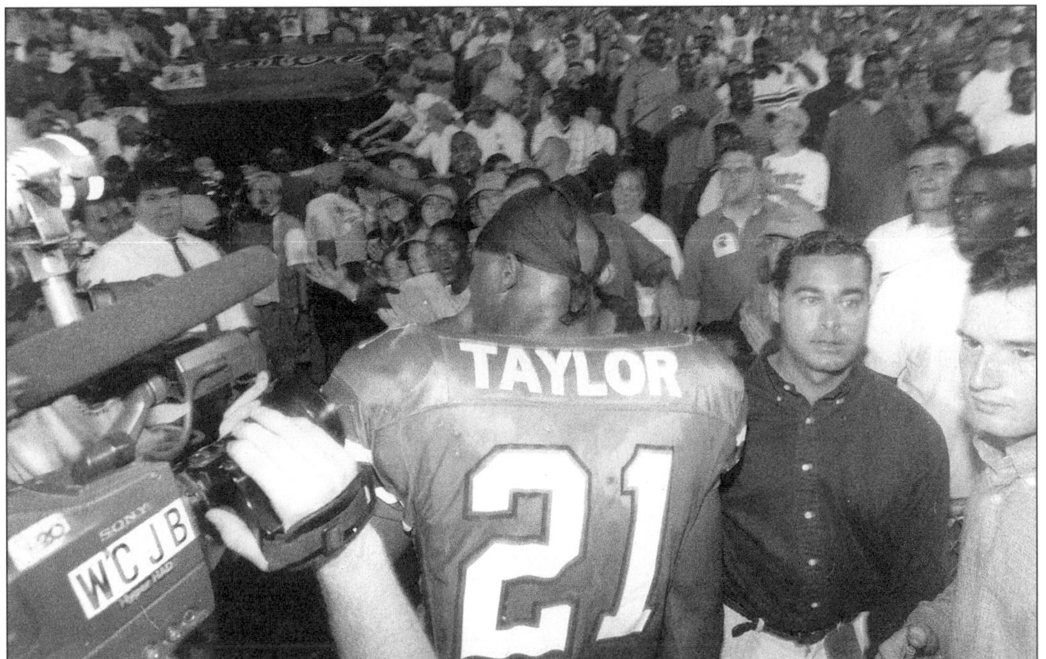

Running back Fred Taylor (#21) wound up fourth-best career rusher for the Gators, amassing 3,075 yards from 1994 through 1997. He would go on to the NFL's Jacksonville Jaguars. (Courtesy UF News & Public Affairs: Jeff Gage.)

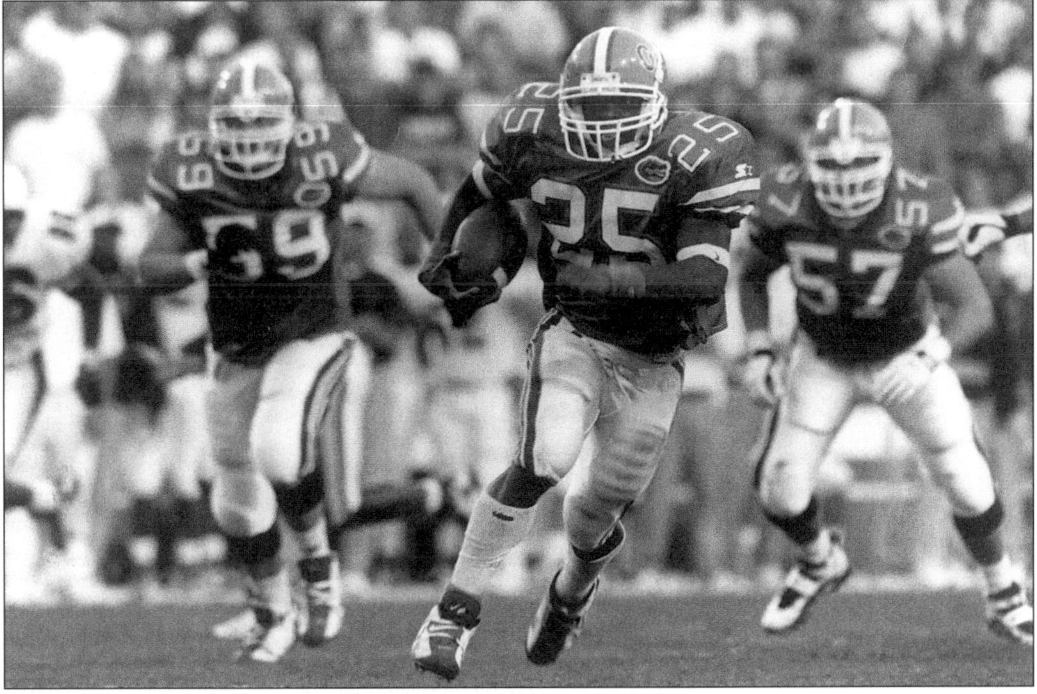

Elijah Williams (#25), with blocking from center Wyley Ritch (#59) and tackle Scott Bryan (#57), was a strong runner in 1997. Williams went on to play for the Atlanta Falcons in the NFL. (Courtesy UF News & Public Affairs: Jeff Gage.)

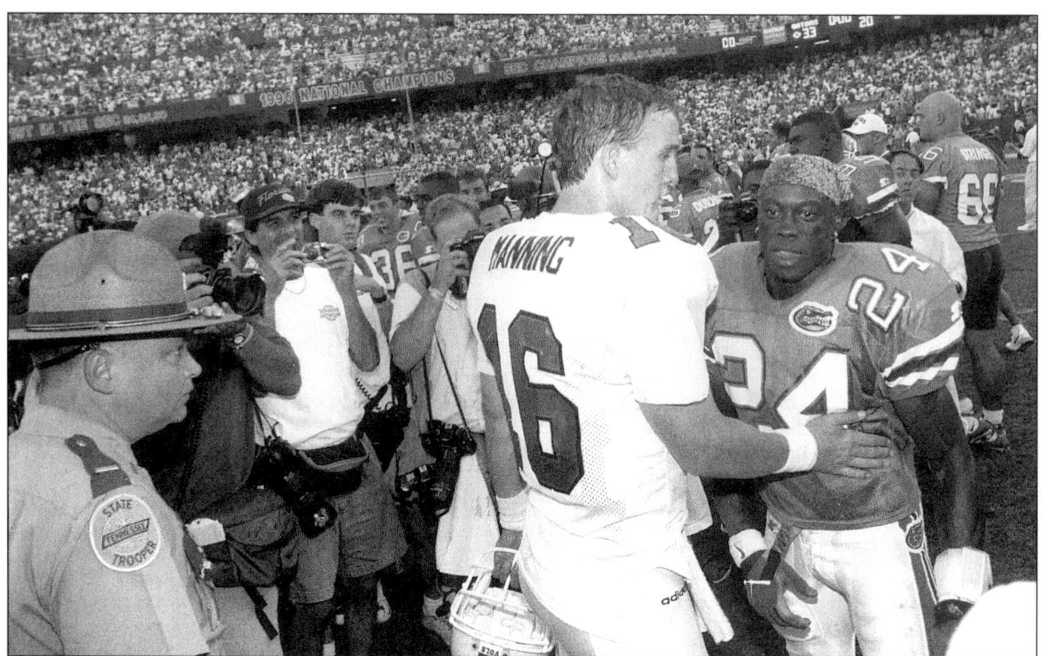

Peyton Manning, star Tennessee quarterback and later quarterback of the NFL Colts, mingled with the other players and fans after the game in Gainesville in 1997. In his four years at UT, Manning never beat the Gators. UF cornerback Fred Weary (#24) held the UF career-interception record (15) during his four years as a Gator (1994–1997). (Courtesy UF News & Public Affairs: Jeff Gage.)

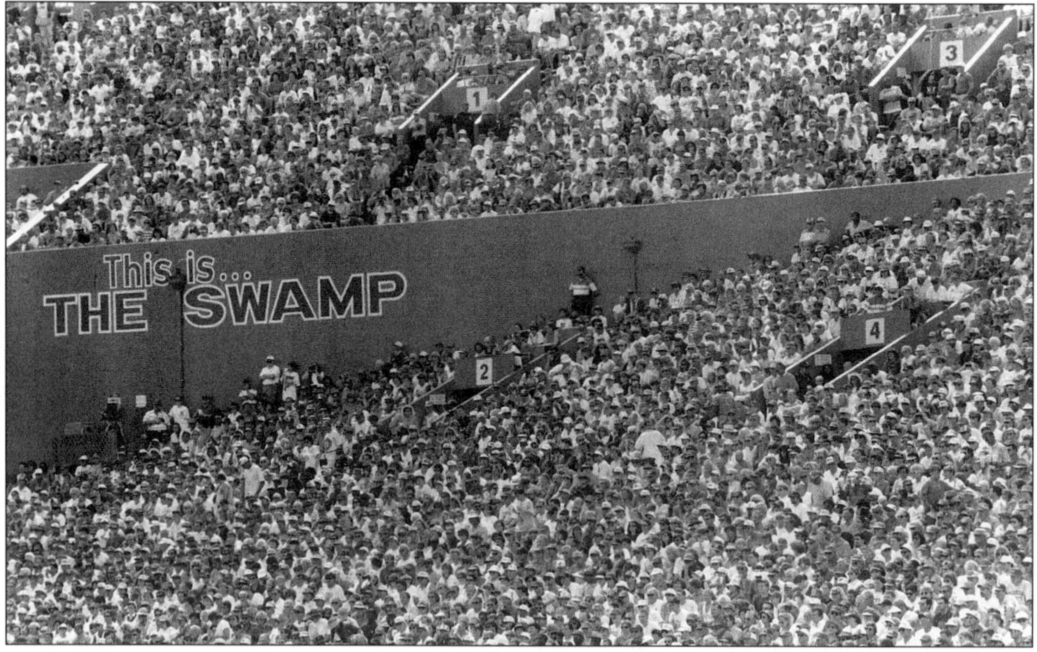

The Swamp was consistently named the noisiest college football stadium in the country, especially for visiting teams from Tallahassee and Knoxville. (Courtesy UF News & Public Affairs: Ray Carson.)

Erron Kinney (#89), the 6-foot-6-inch tight end from Ashland, Virginia, who was named to the SEC Academic Honor Roll, also played forward for the 1997 Gator basketball team. His touchdown reception in the 1999 SEC championship game against Alabama was a fitting climax to a strong career at UF, one in which the tight end became an increasingly important part of the team's offense. (Courtesy UF News & Public Affairs: Marty Morrow.)

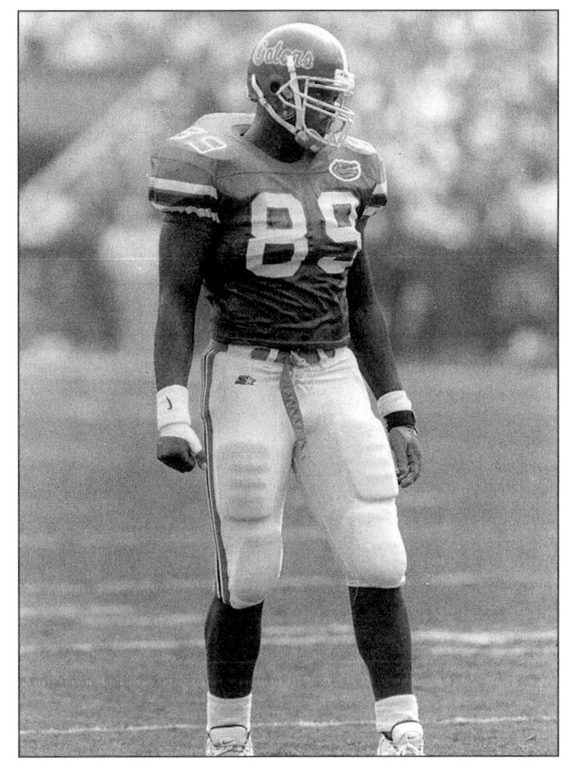

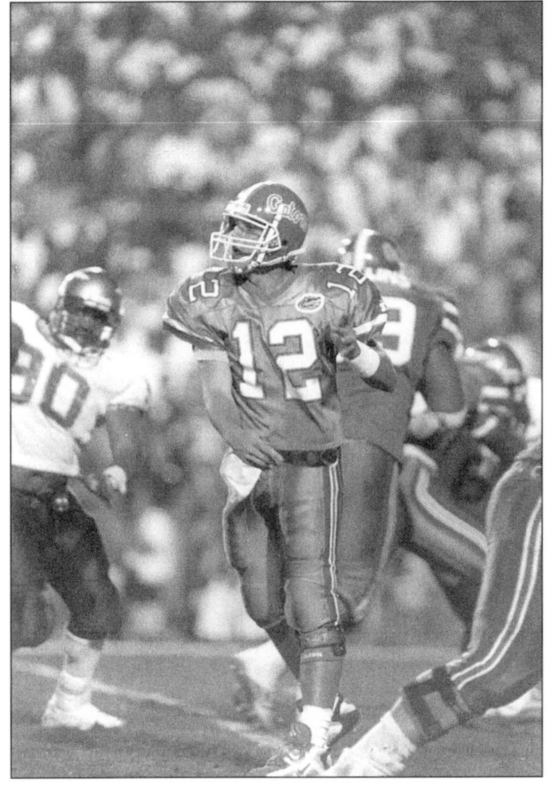

Doug Johnson, who played professional baseball for the Tampa Bay Devil Rays organization, helped quarterback the Gators to records of 41-8 from 1996 through 1999. (Courtesy UF News & Public Affairs: Jeff Gage.)

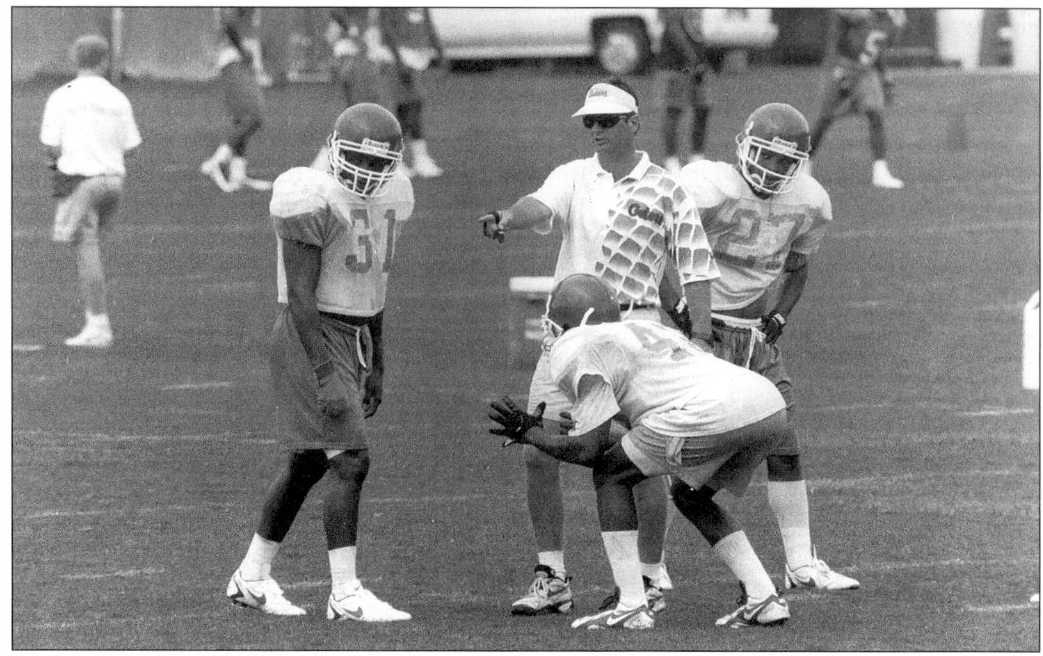

Coach Bobby Stoops was UF's defensive coordinator for three years (1996–1998) before becoming head coach of the Oklahoma Sooners in 1999. He would be replaced in 1999 by Jon Hoke, who had 17 years of collegiate coaching experience and who would continue the strong defensive strategy that marked the Gator teams of the 1990s. (Courtesy UF News & Public Affairs: Jeff Gage.)

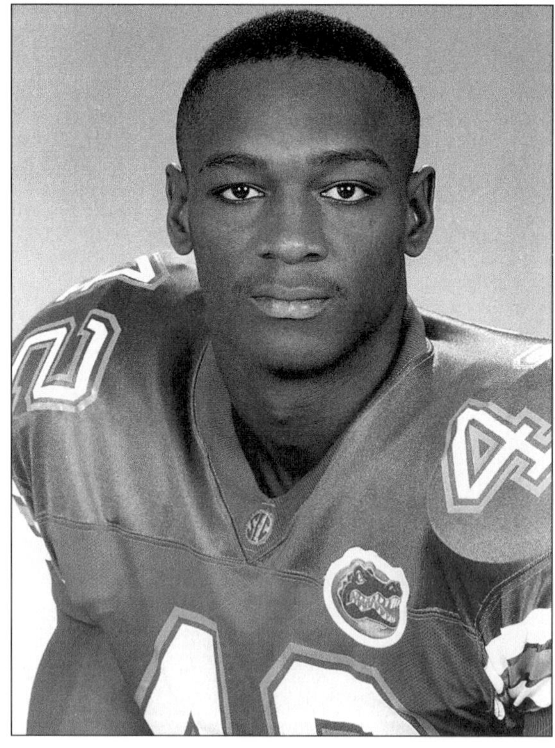

Linebacker Jevon Kearse, who lettered at UF for three years (1996–1998) before playing in the NFL for the Tennessee Titans, joined defensive tackle Reggie McGrew as first-round picks in the 1999 NFL draft. That raised the total UF number of 1st-round picks to 21 since 1983, which tied it for the best total for a school over the past 17 years. (Courtesy UF News & Public Affairs.)

For the 1997 season, after winning the 1996 National Championship, the Gators could remember that fact in their game tickets. The Gators consistently sell out the Swamp for home games. (Courtesy UF News & Public Affairs: Jeff Gage.)

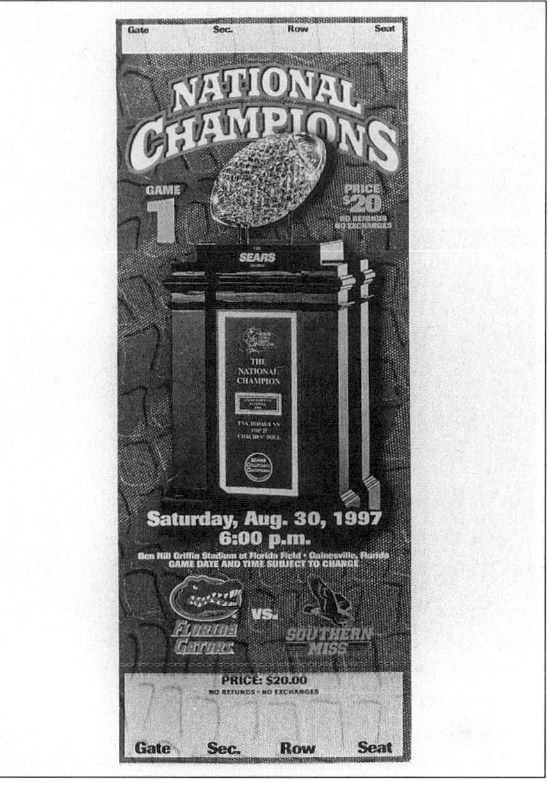

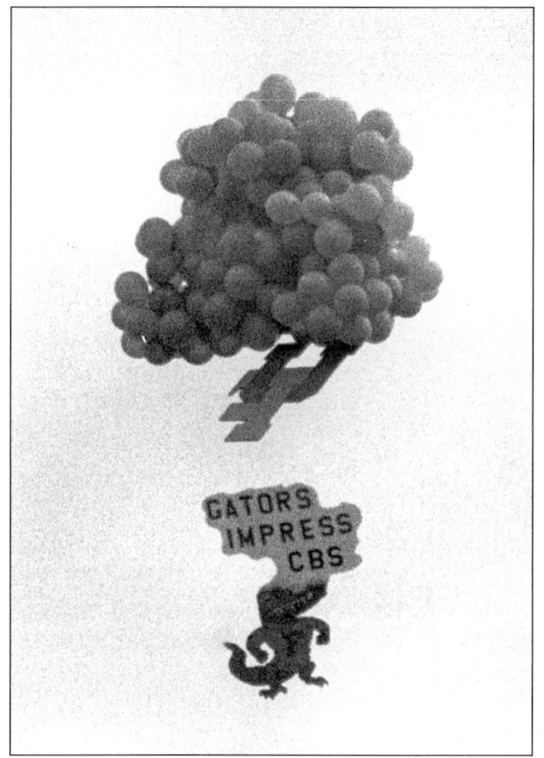

An aerial display during a nationally televised game joined one of the many planes flying over Florida Field, advertising different products. (Courtesy UF News & Public Affairs: Chris Runk.)

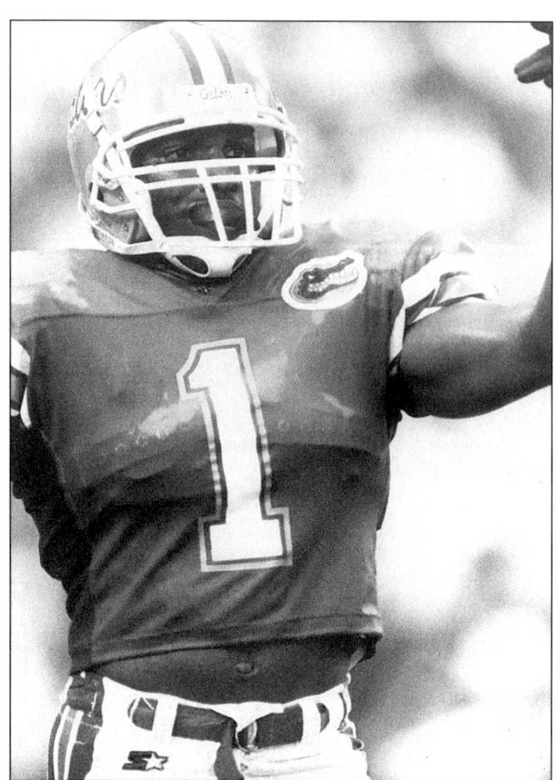

Cornerback Tony George, who lettered for four years (1995–1998), is third on the list for longest Gator returns for his 89-yard interception in a 1997 game against Tennessee. (Courtesy UF News & Public Affairs: Jason.)

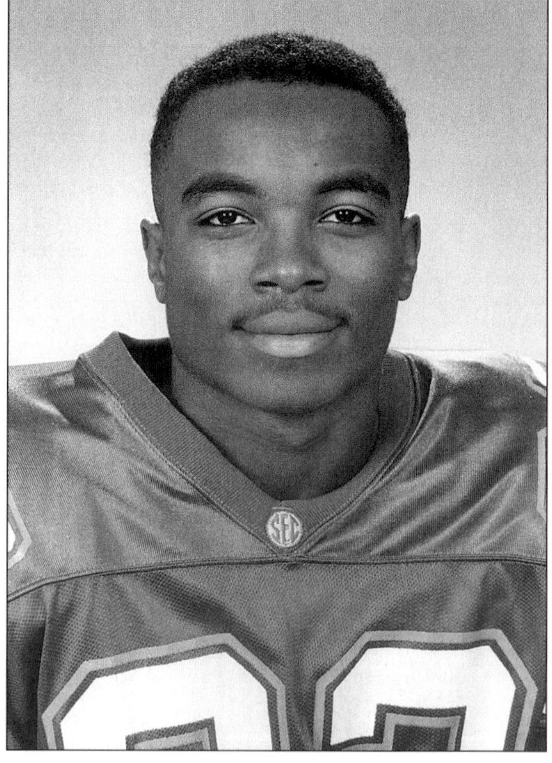

Jacquez Green, who lettered for three years at UF (1995–1997) before going on to play in the NFL for the Buccaneers, is sixth in school history with 23 career touchdowns. As a kick returner, he holds school records for a single season (392 yards on 27 returns in 1997) and for a career (766 yards). (Courtesy UF News & Public Affairs: Herb Press.)

While Doug Johnson and other Gator quarterbacks were better known for their passing, their occasional running surprised opponents and led to some important gains, especially during the times when the team went for it on fourth down. (Courtesy UF News & Public Affairs: Jeff Gage.)

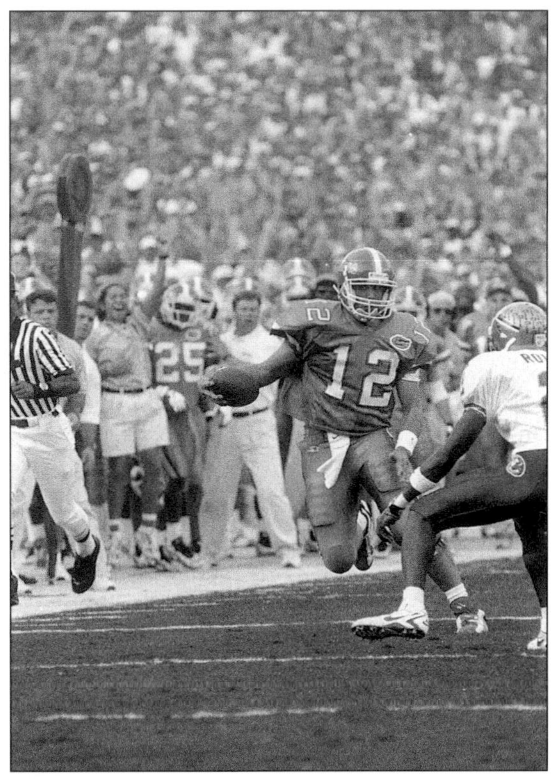

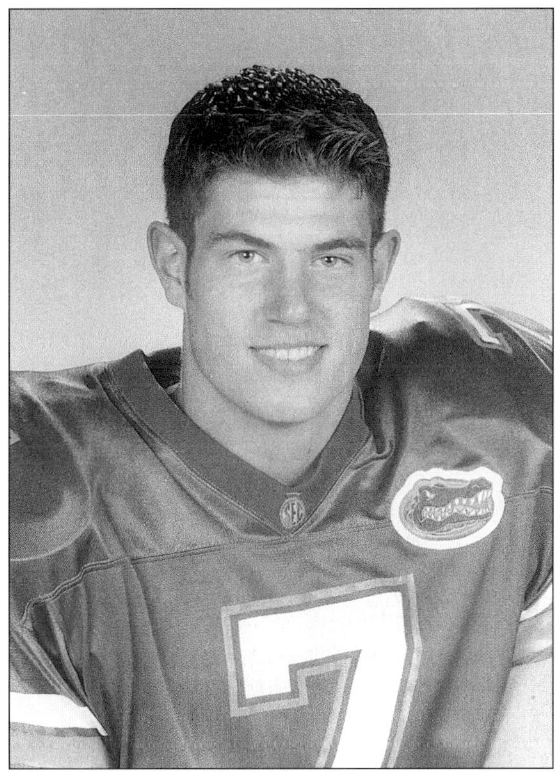

Jessie Palmer, who hailed from Canada, was one of the growing number of skilled passers who came to UF to learn from what many consider the best offensive strategist at the college level: Mr. Spurrier. (Courtesy UF News & Public Affairs: Jeff Gage.)

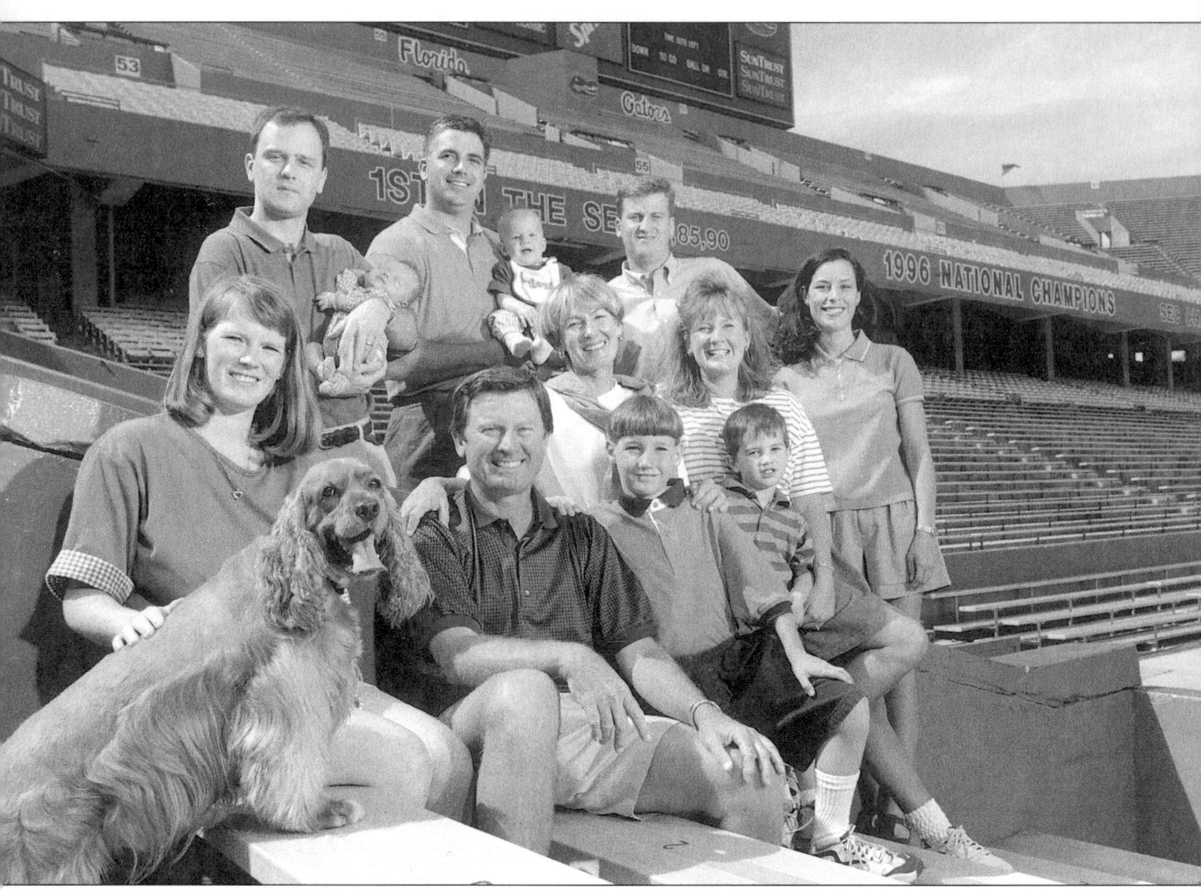

Steve Spurrier, shown here with his extended family, lent his voice and support to many charities in the area, charities that raised money through such activities as golf tournaments and auctions. His son, Steve Spurrier Jr. (far right in back row), joined Bob Stoops as a football coach at the University of Oklahoma. (Courtesy UF News & Public Affairs: Ray Carson.)

Index of People